D1271891

THE TESTIMONY OF LIVES

The break-up of the Soviet Union from 1989 made anthropological work in Latvia possible, and the attendant euphoria fired Latvian memories. *The Testimony of Lives* is based on more than a hundred interviews carried out between 1992 and 1993 in the wake of the declaration of independence. Narrative accounts focus on a past which could not be talked about under Soviet rule. Informants were keen to set the record straight and to challenge the version of history found in Soviet textbooks.

The heart of this book lies in the narratives themselves, in which the narrators provide an oral history of the past fifty years of Soviet occupation: the appropriation of land and houses, deportation and imprisonment, the violence and the chaos of the post-war years, the brutal process of collectivization, the problems of the return from exile. The narratives open a window on the past, and in the course of so doing they construct a new social reality in which the past is shaped by the present and by aspirations for the future. Memories of deportation and exile have come to have central importance for the definition of Latvian identity.

Latvian narratives represent both the personal past and a shared cultural and literary history, and illustrate the difficulty of prising apart personal and textual memory. In particular, recollections of violence incorporate cultural symbols and are framed by cultural plots. Individual accounts of the past, which in most cases have not been shared earlier, demonstrate the specific ways in which the social permeates the personal. This book draws on narrative theory which has been a feature of recent anthropological discussion and shows how oral testimonies may provide both a social and a cultural history of Latvia and at the same time offer theoretical insights about the nature of memory, identity and narrative.

Vieda Skultans is Senior Lecturer in the Department of Psychiatry at the University of Bristol.

THE TESTIMONY OF LIVES

narrative and memory in post-Soviet Latvia

VIEDA SKULTANS

LONDON AND NEW YORK

First published 1998
by Routledge
11 New Fetter Lane, London EC4P 4EE

Simultaneously published in the USA and Canada
by Routledge
29 West 35th Street, New York, NY 10001

© 1998 Vieda Skultans

Typeset in Baskerville and Frutiger by Solidus (Bristol) Ltd
Printed and bound in Great Britain by
Redwood Books, Trowbridge, Wiltshire

British Library Cataloguing in Publication Data
A catalogue record for this book is available from the British Library

Library of Congress Cataloging in Publication Data
Skultans, Vieda.
The testimony of lives : narrative and memory in post-Soviet Latvia /
Vieda Skultans.
p.   cm.
Includes bibliographical references and index.
1. Latvia—History—1940–1991—Biography. 2. Latvia—Biography.
3. Skultans, Vieda. I. Title.
DK505.78.S57   1998   97–12949
947.96 ' 085—dc21   CIP

ISBN 0–415–16289–0 (hbk)
ISBN 0–415–16290–4 (pbk)

*For the three cousins Velta, Jānis and Andrejs and for those whose
stories cannot be heard*

Going to war
I locked my heart in a stone
The light comes the sun rises
The stone splits open singing.
                    (Latvian folk song)

CONTENTS

ILLUSTRATIONS

ACKNOWLEDGEMENTS

Many people read parts of or the whole manuscript and helped me to revise this book. I would like to especially thank Richard Jenkins, Nigel Rapport and Ronnie Frankenberg. Without their encouragement this book would not have been completed. At Bristol, Rowena Fowler, Theresa Bridgeman, Tony Antonovics, Cathy Merridale and Steve Fenton were particularly helpful and generous with their time. Ian Hamnett read and re-read successive versions of translations and chapters. Roger Bartlett read Chapter 10. The anthropologists at the University of Sussex and University College Swansea helped me to impose some structure on material which at the time threatened to overwhelm me. In Riga, Aivita Putniṇa gave much needed help with the footnotes. My long telephone conversations with Roberts Ķīlis enabled me to share some of my obsessions about memory and Latvia. However, none of these people would have written this book the way I have done: I could not see a way to implement all their suggestions and the responsibility for its shape must rest with me. Finally, I would like to thank the British Academy for financing my fieldwork in 1992 and the ESRC for financing it in 1993.

INTRODUCTION

I have been asked how I came to write a book about Latvian narrative. My answer, in the spirit of all true narratives, links necessity with coincidence. I am Latvian by birth. This and my being an anthropologist made Latvia a natural fieldwork destination.

The unfreezing of the Soviet Union from 1989 made anthropological work there a real possibility. Although the Baltic states do not form part of the traditional heartland of the anthropologist, they have about them an air of remoteness and the unknown. (They were the last in Europe to be Christianized.) The relative inaccessibility of Soviet Latvia for some forty-five years imbued its opening up with great feeling and romance. I first visited Latvia in 1990. It was a time when many other exiled Latvians were returning, trying to find a link between memories and perceived realities. At each of my visits the tiny airport in Riga was full of people clutching bunches of red carnations or roses and crying. Old people met who had last seen each other as children or adolescents. Some touched each other's faces enquiringly as though sight alone could not give them the evidence they were seeking. The airport officials had already become inured to such emotional outbursts: loudspeakers announced five more minutes of crying time.

The nature of my re-encounter with Latvia was no less emotional than theirs but of a different kind. As an infant in arms I had no personal memories of Latvia. More potent perhaps were my childhood readings of Latvian folk songs and literature. These evoked for me a timeless and pantheistic world, far removed from the reality of life in north London. My image of Latvia was literary, built of books and readings. In so far as I was brought up on school books published in the 1920s and 1930s I belonged to a textual community who were a generation older than me. Indeed, many of my closest contacts were with older women.

My research project began as an anthropological study of neurasthenia. The professional isolation of Latvian psychiatrists had meant that their diagnostic practice was closer to the nineteenth century than to contemporary western practices. Neurasthenia or nervous exhaustion was and remains a much used diagnosis in Latvia. I planned my project in terms of the conventional academic concerns of medical anthropology. I wanted to investigate the meanings of neurasthenia for doctors and their patients; to look at how the diagnosis might be used to deflect personal and social disaffection and to explore its symbolism in everyday speech. In the event I did investigate neurasthenia in this way, but also found myself pulled ineludibly by people's memories of the past. The past could not be laid to rest and left people little motivation to talk about the present. The brutal and chaotic events following the Second World War did not release their hold on memory. Arbitrary arrests, deportation to Siberian labour camps, the appropriation of farms, forced labour and famine were remembered over and over again. I found that my modest and circumscribed piece of research was prised open and forced to accommodate more of life and of death than I felt it could bear. Eventually I let myself be carried by the narrative flow. In this way I found myself listening to accounts of events central to Latvian and, indeed, Soviet history.

Latvia lost one-fifth of its population as a direct result of the Soviet occupation of 1940. On one night of June 15th 15,000 people were arrested and either killed outright or deported. On March 25th 1949 one-tenth of the rural population was arrested and deported thus facilitating the process of collectivization. These events are the focus of present-day commemorative practices and shape social memory through their re-enactment. They have come to play a central role in defining national identity. However, such practices do not provide an absolute contrast against narratives of the personal past, which also incorporate elements of collective memory.

I had moved out of my familiar area of academic work and entered a remembered landscape of unpredictability and violence. I felt stunned by the force and fluency with which people spoke. Many spoke in long monologues for hours at a time, which translated into nearly 200 hours of tape recordings. These narratives presented not only a fearful and strange subject matter but also a challenge for theoretical analysis. As a result this book can be read in a number of ways. It is above all a record of the experiences of individual men and women under Soviet rule. Their voices have more power than any academic commentary. They speak of the experiences which underlie statistics of population change and agricultural productivity.

However, once taped, transcribed and translated, the narratives seemed to take on lives of their own. The transformation of memory into narrative loosens the ties with the original experience and opens the way for the substitution of schematized images. Like literary texts breaking free of their authors' intentions, Latvian narratives possess commonalities of structure and theme which override individual experience. In order to make sense of these narratives I had to draw upon theoretical writing from several disciplines. These Latvian narratives inhabit an uneasy and shifting theoretical terrain. Treated as anthropological fact, their literary quality stands out. Yet treated as literature, vast areas of social and historical experience remain unaccounted for. In the end I sought help without regard to disciplinary boundaries and drew upon whatever ideas illuminated the narratives.

Anthropology directed me towards recurring social representations and images within narratives. Although memories are in one sense the most personal of possessions, they also necessarily embody the ways in which people connect or fail to connect with society and history. I grouped narratives into chapters according to the dominant social representations which underpin their structure.

Shared devices for structuring narrative appeared. As memories are cast into a narrative mould so they must of necessity conform to the conventions of story telling. In recounting the past, narrators choose the literary strategies which best convey their experience. Thus meaning is conveyed almost as much by form as it is by content.

If conventions of story telling influence the way we remember our lives then we can expect the destruction of those conventions to have an effect on the narrative coherence of remembered lives. Indeed, this is what has happened. Narratives of people growing up in the 1950s and 1960s are not built upon literary paradigms in the same way as those of an earlier generation. In the narratives of older people values are affirmed through the development of a plot or the unfolding of a life. By contrast, in the narratives of younger people values are affirmed only to be undermined by the course which their lives take. Values fail to find a plot. This applies particularly to illness narratives.

There is in all the narratives an exchange between the purely personal and shared social, literary and linguistic worlds. Social metaphors and literary structures are brought in to support people in extreme situations and to preserve their humanity. Conversely, metaphors and literary paradigms take on new meaning when seen working in such adverse circumstances. Although my theoretical approach has structuralist elements I do not see the narratives as mere instantiations of a paradigm. There is a stock of social and literary commonalities known to all, but not everyone draws upon them or does so in the same way. Although membership of a textual community is important, people's use of paradigms also has a personal dimension which arises from their experience and intentions. Many people with eventful lives have little to say about them. There is no perfect match between lives lived and lives remembered.

The quality of narrative experience stems from the tension between author and agent. The narrative I is ambiguous – referring as it does to both the teller of the tale and the earlier self – victim or hero of the story. The precise nature of this narrative I varies: author and hero coexist more happily than author and victim. After all, western literary conventions stipulate that plots should have heroes. Thus certain kinds of personal narrative are more difficult to articulate and to anchor within shared meta-narratives. These narratives share problems experienced by all victims of state perpetrated violence: their subject matter lacks a temporal and moral framework and for this reason they do not lend themselves readily to story telling. However, many people with a terrible past do manage to author lives which give a sense of satisfaction and completeness. Those who fail in this enterprise complain not only of the painfulness of past experience but also of the incoherence of their life stories. They have failed twice over, both as agents and as authors.

The elusive concept of coherence is central to an exegesis of narrative. If the truth claims of narrative depend upon their correspondence with past reality, then its powers to convince and move the listener depend upon coherence. Jerome Bruner makes greater claims for narrative coherence: he has suggested that we attend carefully to narrative structure because it mirrors the structure of experience (Bruner and Feldman 1996, p. 291). I am not sure that we can accept this except in the tautological and unhelpful sense that narrative form mirrors narrative experience. Although the raw data of past experience may create the need for narrativization, its allegiances are not towards the past but towards other narratives. It seeks for connections and where it succeeds in making these we as listeners and readers recognize coherence. Coherence is thus about belonging. European literary traditions shore up Latvian narratives and enable us to recognize and respond to them.

Latvian narratives have a marked literary quality: lives are heavily theorized before ever they reach anthropologists such as myself. This is true of all life stories but particularly true of Latvian and other east European lives where the development of a national literature has been particularly associated with the shaping of a national identity. Whereas the ordinary Englishman or woman is unlikely to call upon a character from say Dickens when remembering times of personal crisis, this is not true for Latvians who make explicit and implicit comparisons between their lives and literature.

This book can, therefore, also be read as an attempt to combine literary and anthropological theory for the understanding of narrative. However, the theory is only present to serve the narrative text. The general criticism of the literary turn in anthropology is that its discussions of form and theory have failed to generate new fieldwork material. My movement, by contrast, was from field material to theory. The unstoppable thrust of Latvian narratives forced me into the complex world of narrative theory.

At yet another level the unfolding of my research is also the recapitulation of my autobiography. In a sense, given my history, it was perhaps inevitable although not consciously willed. Indeed, the coming together of narrative themes with my own imagery of Latvia and its past filled me with alarm. To what extent were the narrators conforming to my ideas? I see now, of course, that both they and I had access to the same pool of cultural conceptions. Although my schooling was entirely English I found I shared with my older informants ideas about Latvian destiny, about the farmstead as a pastoral idyll and about the joy of being a shepherd.

As the narratives unfolded I found that I too had become part of the story. Many of the recorded narratives culminated in a homecoming from the war, from Siberian exile or from prison labour camps. However, during the period of my research the most obvious and talked about homecoming was that of exiles. If, as many anthropologists have argued, the shape and selection of memories is largely dependent upon the present, then it was my homecoming as much as theirs which they were celebrating. Homecomings are, of course, related to the idea of a home and the homeland, and formed a trinity of emotive meanings which were central to the independence movement. Exiles were described as coming 'home' although many found that 'home' was no longer home.

* * *

Chapter 1 is about my family history. It is based on what I learnt as a child about my family and relatives and about Latvia. I can identify in these family memories the selfsame elements that structure my informants' narratives.

Chapter 2 is a brief account of the history and methodology of the research.

Chapter 3 describes the theoretical writing which I found most useful for understanding the narratives. It looks in particular at the way in which narrators use literary and textual memories to structure personal memories. I seek to show how metaphors function as a way into the society, 'but also as a way out, as ways people come to "understand" and then act' (Crocker 1977, p. 50).

Chapter 4 looks at the fifty letters which I received from Latvia. It explores the dominant concerns of these letters and shows how the unaccountability of the past is linked in people's minds with ill-health.

Chapters 5, 6, 7 and 8 are structured around the accounts of narrators themselves.

Chapter 5 is about destiny and its multiple meanings in structuring memories of deportation and imprisonment. Destiny is used in contradictory ways and yet despite, or perhaps because of, its linguistic ambiguity, it has become a national emblem. In this chapter destiny is used to give narrators a sense of agency and control: to wrest victories, however small, from history.

Chapter 6 looks at the specific meaning of 'having a biography' in the context of Soviet Latvia. A biography is a euphemism for a politically undesirable biography, similar to 'having a past' in English. The political attribution of 'a biography' inhibits people's ability to construct an autobiographical account of their lives built around themselves as the principal actor. People give accounts of their lives as a series of disconnected happenings.

Chapter 7 gives narratives of partisans who lived in hiding in the forests during the post-war years. The harsh realities of the actual experience, namely famine, cold and terror, are structured in terms of a literary and pastoral vision of the forest.

Chapter 8 returns to my original medical investigation to look at the meaning of neurasthenia. Narratives describe the erosion of health. Illness is attributed to the breakdown of values, most often linked to ethnicity. For example, narrators assert the importance of the homeland or of self-control to Latvians and then in the course of the narrative proceed to deconstruct such values.

Chapter 9 takes up some of the theoretical themes of Chapter 4, and sets out the differences between illness narratives and other more optimistic narratives. It looks at the way in which the quest paradigm has been adapted within Latvian literature to provide a political allegory, and the way in which this localized version of the quest is used by Latvian narrators.

Chapter 10 deals with the national awakening of the second half of the nineteenth century and the agenda which it set for Latvian literature. Many of the literary themes which were enlisted to construct a habitable Latvian identity reappear in present day narratives.

Appendix I gives a historical background essential for understanding the oral narratives. Appendix II lists the principal narrators whose words appear in this book. They appear in two groups. There are those who wrote me letters and whom I subsequently sought out in Latvia and there are others whom I met in the course of my fieldwork. Their basic characteristics are given in this second appendix.

Map 1 Latvia 1997

Plate 1 1952. A formal portrait of Antra with her mother, grandmother and brothers. Her father was imprisoned in Vorkuta during this period

Plate 2 1946. Antra's father standing in the ruins of his church

Plate 3 1960. Antra's mother. Even after her husband's return in 1956 life was not easy

Plate 4 c. 1960. Antra's father's congregations were small. Services were frequently held in side rooms which were easier to heat

Plate 5 1947. Peasant woman handing over her calf. Heavy taxes were imposed upon peasants, paving the way for collectivization of farms

Plate 6 1947 or 1948. Working out the taxes

Plate 7 1945. In the post-war years there was a deficit of men, and women were left to sort out the problems

Plate 8 1946. The state imposed obligatory felling work on all peasants, women included

Plate 9 1946. Women were expected to do heavy manual work of a kind they were not accustomed to

Plate 10 1949. Andrejs with his class in Koknese a few years before being forced to resign

1

A FAMILY HISTORY

My own life history is relevant to fieldwork and its subsequent representation. My autobiography overlaps in several ways with the cultural reality which I have documented. As a result this book is multi-vocal and the result of a dialogue.

Although I was, of course, aware of the personal implications of my fieldwork, I did not fully comprehend their extent. I did not foresee the resonances which would arise between the memory structures of my family history and those of the narrators.

Autobiographies are to some extent constructed in response to the expectations of others. Vincent Crapanzano describes the life history as 'doubly edited: during the encounter itself and during the literary (re)-encounter' (1980, p. 8). During the initial encounter the questions of the fieldworker shape the way in which the life history is told. Narrators draw selectively upon the past in order to secure the attention of the listener. In my case, the attribution of a shared past must have influenced the way in which narrators selected from past experience. Although, of course, our lives were recognized as taking quite different shapes the assumption of a common destiny was nearly always there. The fact that I was born in Riga and fled following the Communist invasion meant that narrators were able to endow me with a past which was familiar to them. My life history like theirs was radically altered by political events. Johannes Fabian's description of the preconditions for communication – 'Somehow we must be able to share each other's past in order to be knowingly in each other's present' (1983, p. 92) – identified for me one of the reasons why people were so willing and eager to talk about the past.

During the course of fieldwork I was not aware of shaping the narrative to any significant extent and a reading of the transcripts confirms my impression that my verbal interventions were slight. However, many of the concepts which structure Latvian narratives also played an important role in my world view as a child. These shared concepts play a particularly important role in editing and interpreting texts. It is on the representation of the final text that the anthropologist's professional and personal constructs have the most profound influence. In the course of my fieldwork many people expressed interest and curiosity in my family and life history. If asked I always responded as fully as I could. As a result, an exchange of stories took place. Since I do not wish this to be 'a vicarious or closet biography' (Olney 1980, p. 26) my own life may reveal its links with other lives. I have long been familiar with ideas of loss and destiny from my grandmother. Although I grew up in north London, I learnt a great deal about the Latvian farmstead and about the importance of shepherd boys and girls; about the importance of work and stoicism. Perhaps, I should come clean and admit that I share the pastoral idyll with my narrators. I knew too about the ambivalent relationship between wild forests and people. My knowledge and memories were in part based on inherited family narratives and in part textual. My very early reading was all in Latvian. That haunting sense of familiarity which I experienced on my first visit to Latvia derives, I think, from this coupling of textual familiarity and memory with experiential strangeness. The Latvian film-maker Juris Podnieks in his film *Homeland* captured the emotionally charged encounters of relatives separated for some forty-five years. For me the reality was different. I was six months old at the time of leaving Latvia and have no personal memories of the country. In my case, the encounter was one between my textual memory and reality. It was also, given the nature of my research, an encounter between my memory and the memories, both textual and personal, of my narrators.

My image of the Latvian countryside belongs to fairy tales. It is of a sparsely populated, undulating and magical landscape. There is a perfect balance of wild forest and cultivated fields and lonely farmsteads; between wild animals, such as wolves and wild-boars, and much loved farm animals. It is never boring because it has the right mixture of ingredients, the right proportion of land to water. There are many streams, rivers and lakes but none so large as to overwhelm.[1] Its horizons are near. In short, it is an intimate country of perfect scale and proportion. The country shares sufficient ingredients with the literary representation for the mnemonic image to survive encounter: in other words, I found it beautiful. I was thus attuned to pastoral visions of the past in the narratives of others.

My knowledge of family history is, I now see, governed by certain thematic principles. This knowledge is episodic and my analysis, editing and representation of others' narratives has helped me to recognize the selection mechanisms in my own family's narratives. The pastoral vision is of supreme importance in selecting and securing memories in a number of areas. For example, the most salient image I have of Jānis, my great-grandfather, is of his death in his orchard. His life story moves from great poverty and hardship to considerable material success. In family memory that success is associated with his library and his orchard. Although he had only one winter of schooling, he acquired by local country standards a considerable library and subscribed to all the current newspapers and periodicals. He cultivated an orchard in which he grew every variety of known apple as well as melons and peaches in his greenhouse. As he lay dying in the autumn of 1913 from a chest disease attributed to an earlier fall from his roof, he asked that his bed be carried into the orchard. On my first visit to Latvia I found the site of his house and some gnarled remnants of the orchard. The house itself had been burned down in 1915 when it was on the front line of battle. All that was left was a substantial door leading to the cellars where I imagined him to have kept his apples. The house which had been so opportunely sited for trade was disastrously sited in war. Historical maps show the eastern front as a line slicing through the Gulf of Riga and continuing south. (See, e.g., Kinder 1978, p. 124.) There is a blank either side of the line but I know that my great-grandfather's house was wiped out by that line.

The image of the lost orchard continued to exert a powerful influence. My maternal grandparents were townspeople. But long summers were spent initially in Jūrmala (the seaside) and later in the country. It seems that it was the pull of the orchard which brought about this change of practice. My grandfather apparently decided that his children needed a more natural peasant style existence than the sophisticated resorts of Jūrmala could offer. He bought a plot of land in Ogre south of Riga at the confluence of the rivers Pērse and Daugava. Here he built a house and planted an orchard. My mother remembers taking several hours on late summer mornings to taste the fruit of each tree. Her memory is of its vastness. Taking into account the fact that she was small and, therefore, scaling down the remembered orchard, she was recently surprised to find that it was, after all, big. There are now two multi-storey apartment blocks on the old site, but a few trees still survive. My grandfather's acquisition of a farm in Vidzeme also formed part of the pursuit of the pastoral.

The themes of independence, work and stoicism are intertwined in family history. These themes come together in a family memory concerning Reinis, my great-great-grandfather and Jānis' father. He was born in 1835 in Selpils, in what was then Kurzeme and worked as a farm labourer. Although in this part of Latvia serfdom was abolished in 1817, he still owed the baron statute labour in return for the lease of land. The baron controlled many aspects of his life and had the right to beat him if he defaulted in his work. Family memory claims that when Reinis, along with several others was in line for a beating, he asked to be beaten first as he had furthest to walk home. With this incident enshrined in ancestral memory, he overcomes the powerlessness imposed upon him by the baronial system. Reinis asserts control, even if it is at the cost of physical humiliation. Another legacy which he bequeathed was his name Vecainis. The importance of that name and its associations were articulated in family memory: whereas many Latvian surnames were chosen by the German barons, the meaning of Vecainis suggested that it was unlikely to have been assigned in this somewhat arbitrary way. In folklore *vecainis* refers to an ancestral spirit or the spirit of the house. Thus the name suggests embeddedness in a locality and continuity with the past. Awareness of these meanings has always given me particular pleasure.

Reinis died at the young age of thirty, leaving his wife with four young children and a cow. The cow was sold and the eldest child, my great-grandfather Jānis, was sent away at the age of five to work as a shepherd. Family memory has twinned his early experiences of physical and emotional hardship with his great energy, revolutionary spirit and fiery temper. Early deprivation turned him into something of a revolutionary. Much to my grandmother's embarrassment he forbade her and her sister to kiss the priest's hand in the way that all children were required to do. I had supposed this practice to belong to the nineteenth century. However, I encountered it in the descriptions of several older narrators together with their reluctance and sometimes refusal to conform. Jānis agitated for land reform and for the rights of peasants and as a result spent several spells in prison. Perhaps his revolutionary ideas had earned him enemies, for the first house which he built as a young married man was burnt down in 1905. He rebuilt and reroofed the house himself, but in the course of doing so fell from the roof. His chest injury was, according to his family, the cause of his later ill-health and untimely death in the orchard. His life story moves from poverty to material success. His prescience in acquiring a house near the newly built railway line running from St Petersburg to Jelgava ensured that the inn and shop which he opened had a brisk trade. It enabled him to purchase land and branch out into the manufacture of wooden roof tiles. He died in the confidence that he was leaving his family well provided for. My grandmother's ironic memory is of his urging them not to cry, saying that although they might miss him they would not want for anything. His confidence was, of course, misplaced in that the war reversed fortunes.

Jānis' life story embodies a cataclysmic clash of individual talent and endeavour against the obstacle of world events, and this theme reappears in a later generation. House, orchard and books were all destroyed. Jānis died leaving his wife Madele and two daughters. The younger was my grandmother aged fourteen and her elder sister Mīle was aged nineteen. I have a letter from Madele written in July 1910 to her elder daughter Mīle at boarding school in Jēkabpils. The letter is written in Latvian, but the orthography is German. It is full of homely details about weddings, funerals and illness matters. It embodies for me that mixture of textual familiarity and physical strangeness which characterize my Latvian encounters. The German spelling lies like a veil between the present and the past. The image of relentless hard work and self-denial is preserved in memory. Madele trained and worked as a midwife. Perhaps her choice of career was influenced by the death of her first and second born infant sons. (My grandmother experienced an identical bereavement through the death of her two elder sons.) My grandmother and her sister always recalled how excessively their mother had worked: she was called out at all hours and travelled long distances on rough country roads to remote farmsteads. Her death too is memorable: hard work and self-denial join together in the account of her death. In August 1914 her eldest daughter married a university graduate. The following summer her newly acquired son-in-law's family arrived fleeing from the German army which was advancing through Kurzeme and bringing typhoid with it. Her son-in-law's mother Grosīte was ill with typhoid. The rest of the family fled further eastward, but Madele stayed behind to nurse her new in-law. As it turned out Grosīte recovered but Madele fell ill and died. Her sacrificial death in the face of the advancing German army is again a variation of the theme of the individual sided against history.

The themes which structure the memories about the earlier two generations, namely stoicism, work, reparation and loss, continue to structure the memories of the next generation. My grandmother's childhood came to an end with the burning down of the house and her mother's death, both of which took place in 1915. Edīte had already met my grandfather Alfrēdis in the summer of 1914. She was still a schoolgirl, he had been posted to Sēlpils to work as an agricultural inspector. She was not particularly taken with him and perhaps her bereavement, loss of home and general uncertainty contributed to her eventual capitulation to his persistent wooing. Alfrēdis fled to escape the battle front.[2] In the event he found a job as an estate manager in Barkanova near Moscow. Edīte travelled alone to Moscow where Alfrēdis was waiting for her. She was seventeen and already pregnant when she married at the Lutheran church in July 1916. Materially life was good, but marauding revolutionaries made it dangerous. In the winter of 1917 a party of Bolsheviks broke into their house, smashed the furniture and killed their dog. Neither Alfrēdis, Edīte nor their baby son were hurt, but they were very shaken. They moved eastwards into Siberia to Tomsk in search of greater security. Here there were no signs of revolution yet and Alfrēdis again landed a job as manager of an estate. At a time when her sister in St Petersburg was fighting hunger, Edīte wanted for nothing. She had a coach and four horses, a bevy of servants and a nanny for her baby son Vilnis. The nanny was young and in the throes of a romantic involvement. She had arranged an assignment with her lover, lost track of time and forgot that in the Siberian winter her one-year-old charge was freezing to death in his pram. As a result Vilnis fell ill with meningitis, died and is buried in Tomsk. Their second son Uldis was born shortly after and my mother Velta in 1921. My grandparents saw their sojourn in Siberia as a temporary measure and planned to return to Latvia once the fighting there was finished. Their return journey was delayed by Edīte's pregnancy. They set off in the autumn of 1921 when my mother was four months old. Alfrēdis, with his opportune knack of getting things done, had reserved an entire coach which was fitted out with furs and furniture. The journey from Tomsk to Riga took six months. On the way two-year-old Uldis caught dysentery and died. Alfrēdis buried him in a makeshift coffin in an unmarked patch of land by the railway line. My mother escaped dysentery probably because she was still breast fed. Alfrēdis caught up with the slow moving train a few days later. Their grief at the baby's loss must have been accentuated by the isolation and anonymity of their transitory circumstances. They arrived back in Riga in the spring of 1922 and stayed with Edīte's sister Mīle. Edīte recalled that they brought with them six months' worth of dirty linen. The account emphasizes arrival preceded by loss – the dirty linen but not the surviving baby.

Another image which has been handed on to me is of Edīte and Mīle returning to their childhood home in Sēlpils. The event belongs to some point in the 1920s when both would have been elegant Riga ladies. They motored down to Sēlpils with my mother in attendance. She recalls how both women fell to their knees on the mound which used to be their home and wept. I wonder whether in searching out that same mound some seventy years later, I was not matching my behaviour to that powerful image of women weeping.

Despite the losses and upheavals my grandparents' life in Riga was one of rapid material success. My grandmother used building metaphors when describing life in Riga. Foundations, structure, elements and, of course, the desire to build figured in her memories. Her personal memories of the family's fortunes form part of the master narrative of the independence period which put so much emphasis on working to rebuild life. Indeed, Riga in the 1920s offered plenty of scope for Alfrēdis' entrepreneurial spirit. Within a year of opening a market stall, he had bought a shop and by the mid-1920s he owned a string of shops and a food-processing factory. His business success permitted a comfortable, even lavish life-style. My grandparents showed an undisguised enthusiasm for the pleasures which their newly acquired wealth brought them, with none of the stuffiness which sometimes appears to be a feature of the more established middle classes. Alfrēdis' purchases were flamboyant. His first car in 1928 was a convertible Buick. He hired a chauffeur to teach him to drive whilst my mother had to sit in the boot. Alfrēdis' newly acquired wealth allowed Edīte to lead the life of a lady of leisure and my mother recalls a succession of pointless activities: visits by a masseuse, visits to shops, hairdressers, cosmeticians and endless rounds of coffee afternoons and dinners. For my mother the memories of such activities are selected in contrast to her own grindingly hard work in England. My grandparents' marriage seems in many ways stereotypical of the period, even down to the partial invalidism to which Edīte succumbed. At the time her vague and shifting symptoms were attributed to a weak and sensitive constitution. How much of her unhappiness was due to her early losses and how much to the dramatic changes of social situation is impossible to establish. My mother's description of her, as her husband's much loved and treasured possession, conforms to the stereotypes of the period.

Alfrēdis had aspirations for a liberal and above all non-provincial education for his children. My mother and her younger brother Guntis were sent to the French Lycée considered at the time to be the best and certainly the smartest school in Riga. Whatever the limitations which they attributed to their parents' world, it seems to have enveloped them with a sense of security and stability which ill prepared them for the Soviet invasion in 1940.[3] Family accounts of that year emphasize arbitrariness and bad luck. The property in Riga was confiscated and grandfather moved his family to their farm in Vidzeme. He was pleased, so he told my mother, that at least the farm enabled them to be self-sufficient. During the summer of 1941 with deportations threatening, my grandfather took to the forests. On the night of 15th June he decided he wanted to sleep in his own bed. At two in the morning the house was surrounded and he and Guntis, then fourteen, were arrested by the secret police and taken to prison in Valmiera.[4] Grandfather managed to bribe one of the guards: in exchange for his gold watch Guntis was released. His parting words were, 'You must take care of the women now'. My grandfather was killed on 7th July. Guntis was not able to fulfil his last instruction. Early pampering – my mother remembers him dressed in white velvet suits – the arrest and witnessing his father's torture proved an impossible combination and he killed himself at the age of thirty-eight. The account of the arrest and death always emphasized the 'if only' element: if only grandfather had heeded my grandmother's warning and stayed in the forest, if only he had not come home that one night. His death left my grandmother distraught and helpless and effectively made my mother head of the household and in charge of the running of the farm. Here she met Andrejs, my father and the son of a neighbouring farmer. I know relatively little about him but two associations stand out: that he had a passion for jam and liked the smell of dried apples. They married within a year and he was killed three years later fighting in the 19th division of the Latvian legion in what has come to be called 'Kurzeme's cauldron' – the province that held out longest against Soviet invasion hoping for reinforcements from the Allies. It has a mild air about it and an unsurpassed quiet beauty which like jam and the smell of apples is so difficult to reconcile with despair and violent death.

That same sense of arbitrariness and chance imbues accounts of the flight from Latvia in October 1944. Riga had been overrun on 13th October and it was clear that Kurzeme would fall to the Soviet army at any moment. My mother who was twenty-three at the time decided to try to escape to Sweden with her mother and me, a six-month old baby. The only possibility was an overloaded fishing boat. Apparently we boarded it in the conviction that it was taking us to Sweden. When the boat arrived in some German port whose name no one can remember, my mother insisted on going back to Liepāja. However, having managed to return it became obvious that Liepāja was about to be taken as well. The choice was between boarding a boat for Danzig or not going at all. The account of how we eventually fetched up in Germany is, to put it paradoxically, structured around chance, chaos or a lack of structure. After four years in refugee camps my mother eventually succeeded in getting to England, recently widowed, suffering the grief of her father's death and leaving her mother behind in Germany. As in so much of our family history, there are structural similarities with the events of an earlier generation. There is multiple bereavement, arrival in another country and the presence of a young child.

The process of putting intergenerational memories on paper creates a necessary distance. In this case it enabled me to identify certain recurring narrative themes and identities. Much of my family's past is filtered through a pastoral lens: in this vision the orphaned young shepherd boy and the orchard are given a prominent place. It forms both the sustaining background and the reward for relentless hard work, stoical acceptance of pain and the building up of one's life. And finally there is the engulfment of individual narratives by the collective narrative of history. Each attempt to re-establish control of individual destiny is perceived as thwarted by the brute force of historical events. In narratives this collision between family history and collective history is linked to competing notions of destiny. In my family there were three uses of destiny: it was used as synonymous with collective history – the interlinking of collective history with individual lives; its destructive consequences offer a second meaning of destiny; and finally there is the notion of individual destiny as good or bad luck. For example, what dreadful things might have happened 'If we hadn't' caught that last boat, or, what less terrible turn life might have taken 'if only' my grandfather had stayed one more night in the forest. This last version of destiny, whether used in the context of good or bad happenings, attempts to re-establish control over individual lives and narratives in the wake of violence and destruction. Although a meaningful past has been shattered, it lays claim once again to a personal destiny.

I was familiar with destiny from childhood. Destiny had brought my grandmother to England. It had robbed her of a husband and ruined her health. Destiny was hard at work in our family, but it had a particular affinity for me. I was born on 23rd April which is St George's day.[5] According to Latvian custom, servants and labourers change masters and move from one farm to another on that day. St George's day is associated with movement and change and any child born on that day is destined not to remain long in one place. My early and perhaps my later life were perceived as the working out of this early destiny. And yet there is a contradiction of the kind found in many other narratives. Inscribed in the stone foundations of my grandfather's house in Riga is a verse extolling the virtues of work and effort:

> Dear God, let me climb the hill
> Not go down from the hill.
> Dear God let me give to others
> Not ask sweetly from others.

That same verse was written by my grandmother on a scrap of paper and together with a piece of black bread and salt they were wrapped in a small piece of linen and given to me at my Christening. In our family destiny did not preclude effort: it was reserved for the inexplicable aspects of life.

As a child of destiny I might be expected to be attuned to the workings of destiny in the lives of others. In the course of my work in Latvia it became clear to me that many, though not all, of the narrative themes and identities of my narrators were familiar to me from my own past and family. However, I identified them first in the Latvian narratives and only later did I recognize their importance for my own family memories. I suspect that the process of analysing narrative themes in Latvia enabled me to step back and categorize my own memories. Achieving a measure of detachment was a difficult process. George Steiner has written:

> I am not sure whether anyone, however scrupulous, who spends time and imaginative resources on these dark places, can, or indeed, ought to, leave them personally intact. Yet the dark places are at the centre. Pass them by and there can be no serious discussion of the human potential.
>
> (1971, p. 32)

I did not feel intact after my fieldwork in Latvia. I had not anticipated the rawness of people's pain nor the force and urgency of their drive to narrate the past. Their effect on me was an uncomfortable combination of exhaustion and a determination to do justice to the narratives entrusted to me.

The personal framework which I brought to bear upon the fieldwork included my accumulated textual knowledge about Latvia. It was so heavily textual that as a very young child I had doubts about the real existence of Latvia. My mother recounts how on the arrival of a letter from Latvia I pronounced, 'Ah, so Latvia really does exist'. I don't myself remember saying this, but I do remember doubting its existence. At times I thought it was an imaginary land, a fictional device used by my family to legitimate their difference from those around us in north London. Its complete separation from experience heightened its mythical status. Like many exiled Latvians of my generation, I was groomed for a return to the homeland. I went to Latvian school on Sundays and learnt about Latvian literature, history and geography. However, it was through literary narratives and images that I built up my conception of Latvia.

2

A CHRONICLE OF RESEARCH

My fieldwork in Latvia was carried out in the wake of the political disintegration of the Soviet Union and the re-emergence of the Baltic countries as independent nation states. Throughout 1990 and 1991 their pivotal role in the break-up of the Soviet Union made headline news.[1] As an emigre Latvian born in Riga a few months before its capitulation to the Soviet forces, I found these events deeply moving.

My first visit to Latvia was in January 1990 when Soviet rule was still much in evidence. Foreigners needed special permission to travel outside Riga to any but designated tourist sites. By the summer of 1991 dramatic changes had occurred: no one seemed to care a hoot for such rules and regulations. I spent three months in Latvia that summer feeding my insatiable appetite to see and hear everything. I was in Latvia during the time of the putsch, fearing for the country and for myself: that I would lose what I had so recently found.[2]

In the context of establishing academic links with the university and medical school I got to know doctors and psychiatrists and learnt something of the way in which medicine and especially psychiatry were practised. I learnt too of the frequency of the diagnosis of neurasthenia.[3] Alongside these academic contacts I got to know my relatives and made friends, stayed with them and travelled extensively throughout Latvia taking advantage of what to me was very cheap petrol. My activities were very much those of any other returning emigré. We were called foreigners (Latvian *ārzemnieki* – literally someone from abroad), a term which has recently come to be used exclusively for emigres in contrast to, for example, Scandinavian tourists. We were endowed with glamour and made to feel special. Although I looked upon myself as bilingual my voice betrayed the fact that I had grown up and lived abroad. The fact that towards the end of my fieldwork period country people thought I came from Riga was, therefore, a source of personal satisfaction to me.

My first summer in Latvia was an unsettling experience. It was coloured by a disturbing blend of the familiar and the strange. I felt I already knew Riga and the countryside. Reason insisted that this familiarity must derive from salvaged family albums and my reading, and yet my feelings were that I had been here before, that I remembered. Although photographs had introduced me to the landscape and architecture, I was unprepared for their beauty. The old city of Riga founded in 1201 is intersected by narrow cobbled streets and irregular architecture. St Peter's church boasts the tallest wooden spire, now reconstructed, in Europe. A most shocking photograph inside the church captures it at an angle of 45 degrees as it comes crashing to the ground during a Soviet air raid in 1944. During the summer of 1992 the old city was full of traditional Latvian music. Economic hardship had forced many highly talented musicians to sing in the streets and squares of old Riga. Riga is, however, renowned for its exuberant Jugendstil architecture, built at the turn of the century.[4] There are mile upon mile of houses adorned with extravagant sinnous detail. It is as though escape from centuries of repression had left the new house owners with unspent energy: every door knob, every staircase is marked out with some leaf or curving stem. Riga is a large city with a population of about one and a half million. Soviet industrial development encircles Riga and required housing for the workers brought in from the towns of Russia and the Ukraine. Vast tracts of land are covered by anonymous configurations of apartment blocks.[5]

My early visits provided the seed bed for ideas for the subsequent research. Being a medical anthropologist the mention of neurasthenia aroused my interest. I was familiar with Kleinman's writing on neurasthenia and somatization in Taiwan and China. I was also familiar with the writing of medical historians on women and neurasthenia in nineteenth-century America and Europe. I knew that it was a diagnosis which perhaps more than most was linked to social issues of power and control and which as a concept was impregnated with social and biographical meanings. It seemed, therefore, an appropriate and interesting area to research.

In February 1992 I placed an advertisement in two national papers: *Diena* and *Neatkarīgā Cīņa*. The advertisements were headed 'Neurasthenia' and invited neurasthenia sufferers to write to me about their experiences of the illness in as much detail as possible.[6] I specified the areas people might write about in order to facilitate their letter writing. I wanted to avoid creating any feelings of embarrassment or implications of blame, and I therefore took care to present neurasthenia as connected in an intelligible way to people's earlier experience. I purposefully omitted a definition of neurasthenia, thus putting at risk my reputation as a bona fide researcher among some Latvian psychiatrists.

Over the next few months I received sixty-two letters. Rightly or wrongly I decided to exclude twelve of them. Eight of these were mothers writing about their child's disability. The others were about some other family member and one was about a pet dog's skin disorder. I replied to these twelve letters saying that sadly their problem fell outside my research remit. The remaining fifty letters provided me, I felt, with sufficient food for thought and challenge.

Older women proved to be more prolific letter-writers. Forty-one of the fifty letters were written by women. Only ten of the letter-writers were born after the war. The letters came from all parts of Latvia: twenty letter-writers lived in provincial towns, seventeen in the countryside and thirteen in Riga. The geographical location of the letter-writers thus reflects fairly accurately the distribution of the Latvian population, with Latvians having difficulty in finding accommodation in Riga and living in the smaller provincial towns. Letters came from people in all occupations from professionals to agricultural workers. (Details are to be found in Appendix II.) Because the advertisements were placed in Latvian language papers the respondents were all Latvians and Latvian speaking.[7] In giving my university address, I identified myself as an exile and thus to a certain extent discouraged those Latvians who had done particularly well under the Communist system from writing. I wrote suggesting that I would visit the remaining forty-nine letter-writers in the summer of 1992.

My field was defined by the letters and dispersed throughout Latvia and my fieldwork, therefore, entailed much travelling. This affected the research outcome both practically and theoretically. On a mundane practical level long distances were tiring and often frustrating: after a journey of many hours I might find that the person I was looking for had gone to stay with relatives. Although Latvia is a small country roads are bad and it takes a long time to get anywhere. In fact, I managed to clock up some 15,000 miles in the course of the research. At a more fundamental level this scattered distribution of respondents restricted the kind of information I was able to glean: at times I felt like a parachute anthropologist. I am surprised that people were as open and welcoming as they were, taking me on trust and confiding past lives and sorrows to a stranger. Looking back I feel I was a stranger they had been waiting for. I was thrown back to an earlier era where truth was linked to listening and yet I knew that my role was one of mediator and that to gain an audience these voices had to be translated into texts.

The rapid political transformations helped. The mood in 1992 was euphoric; it was slightly less so in 1993 as the harsh economic realities began to bite. The general euphoria gave people the confidence to speak about things they had not spoken about before. On the crest of this euphoric movement towards independence emigres and local Latvians were spiritually united. I can only speculate how the narratives would have differed if I had carried out the research at another time. The anthropological writing on memory which claims that memories or the narrated past are really about the present has some bearing here. I do not believe I would have gained access to memories to the extent that I did at an earlier or, indeed, at a later period. In particular, narratives of spiritual victory, recognition and homecoming were, I feel, influenced by recent political developments.

In the event I managed to meet thirty-five of the letter-writers. All meetings were tape-recorded and subsequently transcribed. Five of the respondents befriended me and contributed to the research on a continuous basis as well as helping me in many other ways. One of these friendly informants lived in the parish of Drusti in north western Vidzeme. Throughout my stay I visited and stayed in Drusti regularly thus getting to know one locality more intensively.

In the course of tracking down the letter-writers I was getting to know the country, meeting relatives and consolidating friendships. Everyone naturally wanted to know what my research was about. When I told them that

I was interested in neurasthenia and that informants were in fact recounting those aspects of their lives which they felt had made them ill, I was
directed to others who, it was suggested, could provide a key to the past and
its pathogenic powers. Alongside the pursuit of the original letters, I found
myself talking to people about their lives: neighbours and friends of letter-
writers, relatives, friends and friends of friends. Initially, I felt uneasy about
being what I thought was side-tracked in this way. However, I found the life
stories so compelling that my guilt was soon dispelled. More than that, I
sensed that these narratives possessed a structure radically different from
the illness narratives which might, therefore, enable me to see and describe
the distinctiveness of illness narratives. Although this extension was
unplanned I came to see these less formal narratives as having as much
importance to my research as did the core neurasthenia sample. I spoke to
some eighty people in this way. Most of the conversations were recorded.
People were not only willing to speak and be tape recorded, they wanted a
permanent record of what they were saying. This was despite the fact that
the small portable tape recorder of the kind that I was using had been the
trademark of the KGB representative found in every work place. Narrators
identified by way of the newspaper advertisements were anxious to remain
anonymous. By contrast, the other narrators encountered in the course of
my stay were more often anxious that they should not be anonymized.
Narrators gave their stories in the spirit of testimonies, frequently prefacing
these with a formal introduction of themselves, their parentage and their
place of origin, particularly if they came from the country.

In one sense, then, this research project was hijacked by the narrators
and pointed in a direction whose importance overrode any academic plans
I might have had. In another sense, this redirection was inevitable and I can
only illustrate its inevitability by describing events from my childhood. In
the early years after our arrival in England our family attended church
services regularly. My memory of these services is that the first few notes of
familiar hymns set the congregation sobbing. The sense of sadness and loss
was profound and my feeling was that nothing could make it better. I too
felt sad and was reduced to tears. I particularly remember my grandmother's face which remained blotchy for a long while after the service. My
research is, therefore, an attempt to find an answer to my grandmother's
anguish. The narratives explain my grandmother's tears and blotchy face.

I distributed all the tape recordings among several typists for transcription. Some were transcribed with great precision, others in a somewhat
cursory fashion and yet others were systematically censored as I later found
out.[8] For example, references to God and fate were systematically excised
from some texts. Despite the excisions and abbreviations of some typists I
ended up with somewhere near 2,000 pages of transcripts. I felt over-
whelmed and menaced by the huge volume of material I had collected. In
the event I began the analysis gradually with the lives of people I knew best.
Not everyone I interviewed is represented verbatim in this book, although
all have contributed to the development of my thought and the final shape
of the book.

In the course of these interviews I got to know some people well and this knowledge is encapsulated in some twenty or thirty hours of recordings. In other cases I gained a mere glimpse of what their life had been like, represented perhaps in some forty minutes of recording. I have set out details of the narrators in Appendix II. I found the transition from voices to the written Latvian text and then the translated English text hard. The better I had got to know the person, the harder I found it. I have read somewhere that the problem with life histories is knowing what to do with them. My problem was not not knowing what to do, but a psychological barrier to doing anything at all. Lives are already edited by those to whom they belong and conform to certain shared understandings of what constitutes an autobiography. Re-editing felt like unauthorized tampering. I spent a long time listening to the tapes. The typed transcripts, even where they were exact, seemed to belong to another person and another world. It took me a long while to achieve a state of mind sufficiently detached from the lived encounters to approach the narratives in an analytical way. I was reminded of the paradox of oral history that although historians may pay lip service to orality, they immediately feel compelled to translate spoken into written words. Of course, I knew that this had to be done: that the narrators themselves expected and wanted a public and written outcome. Indeed, their willingness to participate in the research was because they understood it to contribute to the dissemination of the 'truth' about Latvia. The process of analysis and writing has proceeded as the immediacy of the fieldwork experience has faded.

Looking back on my post-fieldwork period, I think I returned saturated with borrowed pain. I found it particularly difficult to work on the illness narratives. Vincent Crapanzano writes of the nature of the ties between the ethnographer and the persons whose lives are reproduced: 'The life-history is often a memorial to an informant-become-(distant-)friend, a commemoration of a field experience, and an expiation for abstraction and depersonalization – for ruthless departure' (1984, p. 954). For me the narratives were a memorial to lives lived and the problem of working on them was that they resisted abstraction or depersonalization. I started my analysis with those narratives which embodied a strong sense of personal destiny and whose life stories achieved a purposiveness. Only after I had dealt with these did I feel able to deal with the illness narratives. During the actual period of fieldwork, friends worried about this aspect of the work. Although not openly talked about, everyone born in the post-war period or before knew the nature of the memories I was being told.

I was, as I said, drawn initially to the more purposive and literary narratives. The reason for this lies not only in the discomfort generated by failure of meaning but also through common membership of a textual community. As a Latvian exile I was brought up on school books that had been used by children in the 1920s and 1930s a full generation older than me. My grandmother played a large part in my upbringing and for these reasons I think I linked more readily with people a generation older than me. We had learnt to read with the same books and this formed a common bond.

Alongside the collection of narratives I was reading the work of earlier historians, autobiographers and novelists. It was this reading, as well as faint recollections from my childhood and adolescent reading which suggested to me the influence that such reading might have on the way in which people remember the past and recount their lives. I was struck by important similarities between Latvian literary themes and structures and autobiographical frames. At times such similarities appeared fortuitous – produced by a certain cyclicity in historical circumstances rather than the reproduction of shared literary frames. For example, the complaints about the devastating consequences of collectivization uncannily echo the writing of the eighteenth-century humanist Garlieb Merkel. Here is Merkel writing in 1796:

> Zum Heumahen, zur Erndte zu jeder grossern Arbeit stellt ein Bauergut drey, vier, funf Menschen oder so viel der Hof verlangt, so dass alle Arbeitsfahige zur Frohn versammelt sind. Die eigene Wirtschaft des Bauern steht indessen still; ein Feld liegt unbesaet, sein Heu verdirbt, seine Saat riesst aus. Aber was tut das? Der Hof hat das gute Wetter benutzt un keinen verlust mehr zu befurchten.
>
> (1797, p. 88)

> (At haymaking, at harvest, at every big task the peasant farm had to supply three, four or five people or however many the manor demanded, so that all those capable of working were collected together early in the morning. Meanwhile the peasant's farm was motionless; one field was not sown, his hay was rotting, his seed was sprouting. But what did that matter? The manor had taken advantage of the good weather and was not worried about any more losses.)

And here is a country woman from north-west Vidzeme recalling in her first letter to me the early years of the kolhoz:

> The hay could only be mown when the feed for the kolhoz was ensured, that was in late autumn. If someone had mown some hay from rough pasture around the bushes earlier, that was taken away to the communal barn. It was no use saying my family is big, my children are small.

And here she is describing the same problems when I met her in her farmhouse:

> The government wanted to restrict people so that they wouldn't rely on their own work, but work for free for the kolhoz. One's own small piece of land, one's own hay could only be mown by stealth so to speak – secretly one had to mow. One couldn't mow hay in good weather, one had to do it for the kolhoz first, and for oneself only late in the autumn. The fodder was so bad that it was difficult to keep cows, only one could be kept and even that one was thin. Once I had mown the hay in good weather, then they came and took the hay away.

These kinds of resonances across time occurred repeatedly. It was, thus, the very nature of the material which was given to me which directed me towards narrative analysis and close attention to language. Although individuals may forget language does not.

I have been asked what the research meant to me personally and to answer I have to borrow a frequently recurring phrase from the narratives. Asked what deportation was like many people said that it was beyond words or beyond description. My first reaction was that I could not communicate what my first visits to Latvia were like nor my first encounters with narratives of the past. However, having asserted its impossibility, narrators do succeed in verbally capturing the past. For my part, I was able to match imagined fragments of a literary landscape with the physical reality to which they had been addressed. My own beginnings belonged to a world to which I had had no access. My research enabled me to fit my private narrative into a larger shared meta-narrative. People gave me accounts of their past, but also wanted to know about my family's past. The result was an exchange of life stories. For me many of these stories represented an imaginative rehearsal of alternative lives. In my mind was the possibility that I too might have had an alternative life history. Had we not escaped from Latvia in October 1944, how would we have fared in exile in Siberia or perhaps in an arctic labour camp? Not all my memories are strictly speaking my own, nor were those of the tellers' theirs. But then this book is about memories of memories and stories of stories. In the process of this exchange I made some very good friends.

3

ORDER IN NARRATIVE

EXPERIENCE

This chapter addresses the mismatch found between experience, language and narrative framework. Many of my informants claimed that there were 'no words to describe' what they had gone through. Despite such claims and despite the absence of an appropriate ready-made language, many narrators do, nevertheless, succeed in finding a strong personal voice. How they do this, which languages they choose to discard and which to adopt form the subject of my analysis.

This book has grown from a fusion of interests: my own and those of the people I encountered in Latvia. What started out as an anthropological study of neurasthenia moved on to confront narratives of violence and upheaval in Latvia during the life time of the narrators. The force of their narrative drive took me aback. I had planned to investigate popular and psychiatric conceptions of neurasthenia. In the event, this was not what people wanted to talk about and neurasthenia turned out to be a door, both for them and for myself, through which we passed to painful and urgent areas of past experience. Had I not recorded this narrative experience I would, I believe, have been guilty of silencing their voices and imposing my own, to them, irrelevant agenda. I would also have lost the opportunity of recording an elusive history, the experience of individual men and women. There was also an additional reason for attending to narrative experience which relates to the state monopoly of historical truth in the Baltic States. Michael Taussig's statement about the colonial history of the Amazon applies with equal force to Soviet Latvia. 'The history that showed things as "they really were" ... was the strongest narcotic of our century' (1984, p. xiv). My readiness to be drawn into narrative experience was thus influenced by the nature of Soviet history: its rigid and monopolistic view of history which was at odds with individual experience.

Neurasthenia does play an opening part in this account. My initial sample of narrators wrote letters in response to an advertisement inviting neurasthenia sufferers to write to me about their experiences of illness. In this one sense, they were all self-identified sufferers from neurasthenia. In another sense, this most commonly used diagnosis was totally irrelevant to what my narrators felt had gone wrong with their lives and to the way in which this was remembered. Illness narratives focused on the intersection between individual lives and historical facts. These critical meeting points – collisions might a better word – between narrative experience and meta-narratives of history are perceived as the ground in which later illnesses have their roots. The repercussion of world events on individual lives played a large part in personal narratives. Some other studies such as Zonabend's historical study of French rural village life found that world events played little part in people's memories of the past (1984). The war was 'remembered' by most narrators, even those who were too young to have personal memories of it. Memories of this nature bring home the fact that they are not private property. One example will serve to illuminate a corner of what Mary Steedly calls this 'overinhabited terrain . . . possessed of other people's experiences' (1993, p. 22). Lidija recounted her life history to me punctuated by the deaths of her close male relatives: her brothers during the First World War, her first husband arrested and killed in June 1941 and her only son dying prematurely of a heart attack ten years ago. This litany of deaths produced a kind of numbness in me until I awoke to the horror of one particular account and incidentally the only death whose retelling made Lidija cry:

> When the big battles took place with the Germans they laid him out on a white cloth because he was bleeding. He died and when they carried him away they found that the cloth was stained red, white and red with his blood.

Who was he? I asked, guiltily aware that my attention had lapsed. It turned out that Lidija was describing the death of Namejs, the thirteenth-century Latvian chieftain who resisted the invasion of the German crusaders and whose death she links with the colours of the Latvian flag.[1] Lidija's narrative draws no temporal distinctions between the deaths of husband, brother and son, and the medieval chieftain. Personal loss is shaped by and is located alongside textual memories adapted from school history and literature lessons. Lidija's narrative of Namejs' death is probably influenced by the medieval rhyming chronicle which is retrospectively read as documenting the first appearance of what was subsequently adopted as the Latvian flag. Personal memories are inscribed on a palimpsest which still bears the imprint of other earlier memories.

There is, however, a problem of mismatch between experience and theoretical framework (both anthropological and local) which has been found in other studies of terror and violence. John Davis has commented on the fact that medical anthroplogy has had conceptual difficulties in giving an account of mass suffering (1992). Michael Taussig's historical and anthropological studies of cultures of terror make the important point that terror, rather than being the breakdown of culture, is the systematic expression of a culture:

> Torture and institutionalized terror is like a ritual art form, and [that] far from being spontaneous, sui generis, and an abandonment of what are called the 'values of civilization,' such rites have a deep history deriving power and meaning from those values.
>
> (1984, p. 495)

However, responses to terror have been given relatively little attention by anthropologists. Marcelo Suarez-Orozco is an exception to this generalization and has worked with political refugees from Central America. He emphasizes that there is a grammar underlying systems of collective terror (1990, p. 353). His analysis:

> relates state-mandated terror to universal human psychological coping mechanisms. How do human beings respond to extreme situations of political terror? What are the psychological mechanisms involved in such responses to terror? What are the psychological substrata of encounters with a culture of terror?
>
> (ibid., p. 354)

In this analysis the cultural grammar is perceived as part of the collective system of terror, as belonging to the perpetration of terror and not to the responses to it. These last are presented as a matter of individual coping mechanisms, even where they possess a shared structure. For example, Judith Zur in her study of Guatemalan war widows refers to the 'thinning' of culture in extreme situations: 'The webs of significance that inform a cultural system collapse or at least become severely shaken' (1993, p. 23). For this reason Zur, like others researching extreme situations, draws upon a psychological perspective to understand the response to terror and the ensuing suffering. The experience of torture and pain have been described as language destroying (see, e.g., Scarry 1985). Their recollection, however, makes use of all available linguistic and literary resources. In contrast, during my own work in Latvia I encountered a cultural grammar of the responses to terror and it is this grammar which I seek to identify and describe.

RESISTING MEDICAL TRANSLATION

There are, it seems, major obstacles to carrying out an anthropological study of the victims of cultures of terror. They are similar to the moral and practical obstacles encountered in studies of famine. Paul Richards has pointed to the impossibility of a well-fed anthropologist carrying out a participant observation study of famine (1992, p. 4). One of the few exceptions to such generalizations is Nancy Scheper-Hughes' magisterial study of the poor of Brazil (1992). She originally went to Brazil as a health worker and not an anthropologist and thus perhaps avoided some of the moral dilemmas. The focus of her own study is on infant deaths and maternal responses, but I am more interested in her discussion of the medicalization of social and political oppression. There is an important difference between Brazilians and Latvians. In Brazil, poverty, famine and oppression are medicalized both by the medical profession and by the poor and hungry. In Latvia the use of psychiatry to suppress political dissent served to distance ordinary people from psychiatrists and to sensitize them to attempts to medicalize discontent. Scheper-Hughes' fundamental theoretical question is:

> How have these people come to see themselves primarily as nervous and only secondarily as hungry? How is it that the mortally tired cane

cutters and washerwomen define themselves as weak rather than exploited? Worse, when overwork and exploitation are recognized, how in the world do these get reinterpreted as an illness, *nervos de trabalhar muito,* for which the appropriate cure is a tonic, vitamin A, or a sugar injection? Finally, how does it happen that chronically hungry people 'eat' medicines while going without food?

(ibid., p. 177)

This process of semantic translation from politics to medicine is not found to operate in a systematic way among lay people in Latvia. The overtly political uses of medicine and psychiatry created a resistance to the ideological appropriation of lay ideas of illness. Latvian respondents saw themselves during the Soviet period as primarily oppressed and only secondarily as suffering from damaged nerves. This crucial difference is illuminated by the concept of hegemony. Scheper-Hughes writes:

In general, medicine does not act on people coercively but rather through the subtle transformation of everyday knowledge concerning the body – body praxis. By the time people start lining up in clinics and waiting long hours for three minute consultations and a prescription, it is not because they have been forced to do so; and once inside those clinics they do not have the doctor's social and medical views thrust on them. They do so because they have already come to share those views.

(ibid., pp. 199–200)

In this way the dominant ideology and contradictions of a society come to be both accepted and yet not explicitly acknowledged by their reinterpretation as illness. Jean Comaroff has focused attention on the way in which social interests are 'seamlessly incorporated' into medical ideas (1982, p. 50), and how such incorporation 'deflects the responsibility for illness from contradictions in the socio-cultural domain to conflicts within the person as a social being.... Therapeutic forms impress upon us the opposition between man and nature, and they eclipse the conflict between man and man' (ibid., p. 63). In Latvia medical categories are constructed in such a way as to deflect attention away from the social sources of dissatisfaction, but the dissatisfaction was not contained, and it breached those categories.

The process of medicalization – this reinterpretation of historical and social discontents – has been fragmented and incomplete in Latvia. It relates, I suggest, to forms of personal resistance, even if muted, throughout the Communist period. This is not to say that no connections are made between political and social events, and health and illness. On the contrary, most illness narratives are overtly political. However, oppression and violence are not reinterpreted as illness, but rather are held directly responsible for illness. The development of two distinct languages of illness relates to this small but vital difference. This explicit political attribution of responsibility for personal health hinders the transformation of 'active protest into passive forms of breakdown' (ibid., p. 215). In terms of the narratives themselves it means that greater narrative significance and time are given to events causing illness than to actual illnesses. There is also a lesser need for concepts of illness to carry symbolic and metaphorical meanings. This is not to say that they are stripped of all symbols and metaphors. It is impossible to remove all the metaphorical associations of illness. Some illness categories, such as osteochondrosis, continue to bear heavy metaphorical loads. Nevertheless overt political criticism removes the urgency of a symbolic metamorphosis from politics to medicine. This explicit political attribution of responsibility for illness results in a major rift between medical and lay conceptualizations of illness.

Māra's account encapsulates the experience of estrangement between doctors and patients:

> Everyone, men and women, had to work. The women, even if they had small children. One was only let off work with a doctor's certificate. But the doctors were hesitant: everyone feared deportation. Even the sick couldn't get a certificate and often they died working. In hospitals they used the word malingerer [Latvian – *simulants*] or rogue. Here's an anecdote. In the morning the doctor asks the duty nurse, What's new? She answers, Nothing much, only the malingerer has died.

In Latvia such accounts point to the close interrelationship between medical and political oppression. They point to a society riven with conflict and a past about which individuals have been unable to speak. Resistance to medical categories can be seen as an index of political resistance to the regime.

AN ANTHROPOLOGY OF TERROR

Narratives of the past circumvent some of the moral and practical problems of doing fieldwork in extreme situations. Narrative stands as an intermediary between the narrator's past experience of terror and the anthropologist. However, the problem of finding an appropriate language to encompass experiences of violence and terror confronts each narrator. Narrative is often presented as a 'natural' medium of discourse, whose construction is independent of social and historical context, and one which therefore presents no problems of cross-cultural understanding and requires no translation. Hayden White writes:

> To raise the question of the nature of narrative is to invite reflection on the very nature of culture and, possibly, even on the nature of humanity itself.... Far from being a problem, then, narrative might well be considered a solution to a problem of general human concern, namely the problem of translating knowing into telling, the problem of fashioning human experience into a form assimilable to structures of meaning that are generally human rather than culture specific.
>
> (1980, p. 1)

This claim to a universal human status is underlined in the accounts themselves: narratives of terror are founded upon the act of witnessing in which there is a fusion between the witness and the act witnessed, between experience and representation. Many people said they could not describe their experiences to those who had not experienced something similar. In these circumstances narrative description is felt to possess a kind of organic fusion with the events described. However, those experiences which do find their way into narratives are no longer merely a direct expression of the past. Thus narrative operates at two levels. At one level it insists upon immediacy and the fusion of the past with the present. At another level structural devices are used which distance the experience from the present. For example, different temporal frameworks are introduced.

Latvian narratives belie Adorno's claim, 'After Auschwitz, no poetry.'[2] Although narratives constantly revert to the act of witnessing, their form and construction undermine claims to immediacy. Narrative form reveals the cultural resources upon which people draw in order to restore meaning to lives. The process of restoring meaning has a metaphorical and poetic dimension. In this context the traditional sociological relationship of cultural resources to individuals is reversed. Instead of individuals being enlisted by ideology or of society reproducing itself by disseminating its core concepts and values amongst its members, narrative grants a more radical role to individuals in the shaping of their ideas. Like the autobiographer, the narrator imposes a design on her life and this offers scope for creativity. The victims of history may reverse their status and devise strategies for wresting personal victories, however small, from history.[3]

NATURAL AND LITERARY NARRATIVES

Narrative creativity raises questions about the distinction between literature and so-called 'ordinary' language.[4] Mary Louise Pratt has pointed out how little we know about ordinary language and develops a theoretically sophisticated argument that 'ordinary language' was invented in order to support a particular exclusionist view of aesthetics:

> Throughout the exhaustive literature this century has produced on metrics, syllabification, metaphor, rhyme, parallelism of every kind, the role these devices do play in real utterances outside literature was never seriously examined or recognized. Likewise, throughout the brilliant body of Formalist scholarship on prose fiction, nary a scholar seriously poses the question of whether or to what extent devices like palpableness of form, estrangement, foregrounding, and laying bare of devices do exist outside literature.
>
> (1977, p. 5)

Pratt argues that the distinction does not sustain serious scrutiny, and introduces William Labov's work on narratives of personal experience to further her argument. Narratives, Labov claimed, share an underlying structure:

A complete narrative begins with an orientation, proceeds to a complicating action, is suspended at the focus of evaluation before the resolution, concludes with the resolution, and returns the reader to the present time with the coda.

(1972, p. 369)

Pratt also identifies the structure of natural narratives within literary prose. However, she cautions against supposing that similarities in the structure of natural narratives derive from literary narratives:

> Unless we are foolish enough to claim that people organize their oral anecdotes around patterns they learn from reading literature, we are obliged to draw the more obvious conclusion that the formal similarities between natural narrative and literary narrative derive from the fact that at some level of analysis they are utterances of the same type.
>
> (1977, p. 69)

For Pratt the point of uncovering these structural similarities is not to claim natural discourse for literature but to ask, 'What is the speaker trying to do in forming this discourse?'

My own interest lies rather in conceptual analysis and the way in which narrators structure thematic concerns. My thematic analysis refers to literary texts to account for the narrative transformation of experience. In doing this I am not claiming that the structure and poetry of individual narratives are simply borrowed from texts which they then passively reflect. Narrators actively construct accounts and they do so using all the means at their disposal, both organizational and thematic. It would be strange if reading material were excluded from this endeavour. In one sense Pratt is right, in that the structure of natural narratives is not a simple mirror image of literary templates, which robs the narrator of any claim to creativity. However, in another sense, she is surely wrong in that people do organize their accounts around patterns and themes they have read, although not in a rigidly predictable way. In order to make sense of past confrontations with terror and violence narrators draw upon both their individual creativity and any cultural or literary resources which they can bring to bear upon the narrative reconstruction.

For this reason individual experience and its retelling are sensitive to changes in attitudes and evaluations of literature. For the older generation born and growing up during the independence period both the ability to read and write and much of the content of Latvian literature were linked to national identity. These meanings were destroyed by the Soviet occupation, in the literal destruction or concealment of whole libraries. As a result these books lost their original meanings and were never to regain them. The gradual reappearance of Latvian authors after the death of Stalin still lacked their earlier authority as arbiters of national life and identity. Editorial prefaces gave instructions on how the books should be read and curtailed the influence of these books. Such events have had consequences for individual narrative. If literary traditions shape the way in which we remember the past, then the breakdown of those traditions means that individuals are less able to recall their lives in a meaningful way. With the physical destruction of books went the destruction of a textual community.

My theoretical concern with narrative is thus the outcome of actual encounters I had in Latvia, but in the process I have come to recognize the theoretical power and relevance of narrative analysis for social anthropology. Narratives taught me to reconsider the nature of language. Although language reaches out to its referents, including the past, it is, even less than I had supposed, a transparent medium offering unproblematic access. Rather, it is a dense medium which holds in suspension the residues of personal and social histories. To use a metaphor with Baltic connections, language is the amber which preserves relics of past feelings and ideas. Mikhail Bakhtin has written that, 'Each word tastes of the context and contexts in which it has lived its socially charged life; all words and forms are populated by intentions' (1981, p. 293). However, beyond the intentions of past individuals, language absorbs and reflects history and social structure. Individual narrators draw in varying degrees upon conceptual structures derived from history and literature in order to rearrange disrupted lives into a meaningful pattern. The narrator retrieves events and relocates them in 'a realm of order where events bear to one another a relationship of significance other than chronology' (Olney 1980b, p. 247), and in this process the original event is endowed with a meaning which it may not have possessed at the time. Georges Gusdorf develops a similar argument:

> The act of reflecting that is essential to conscious awareness is transferred, by a kind of optical illusion, back to the stage of the event itself. ... The narrative confers a meaning on the event which, when it actually occurred, no doubt had several meanings or perhaps none.
>
> (1980, pp. 41–42)

In this creative reordering of events the new order which is achieved does not derive from temporal, contiguous or syntagmatic sequencing but from paradigmatic or metaphorical order. The narrator seeks to bestow a unity of experience upon the narrated life. In the interests of unity all narrative histories are to a greater or lesser extent revisionist.

It is in this process that textual memory combines with personal memory. It is a commonplace of modern literary theory that all texts can be situated in relation to other texts. Oral narratives also bear a relationship to texts, and in the Latvian context these are principally literary and historical texts drawn from primary school books. Since schools during the independence period used a fairly small number of textbooks the task of identifying the formative role of textual memory is not impossible. Personal narratives often contain or are shaped by well known (in the Latvian context) literary themes. For example, Vija Lapiņa, describing her childhood home, is quite explicit about the interconnections between her memories and literature:

> It was a beautiful house. It was real country. Now whenever I read a book I imagine that it might be set in that house.

I am not suggesting that personal narratives are later versions of some archetypal folk narrative nor am I advocating a dualistic approach to narrative. Rather, I am suggesting that individuals confronted by extreme situations bring all their past experience, both textual and personal, to bear upon these events. Roland Barthes' description of the experience of reading applies equally to the experience of terror: 'Ce "moi" qui s'approche du texte est déjà lui-même une pluralité d'autres textes, de codes infinis, ou plus exactement: perdus (dont l'origine se perd)' (1970, pp. 16–17. ('This "I" which approaches the text is already a plurality of other texts, of infinite codes, or more exactly of lost codes, codes whose origin has been lost.')

However, although personal narratives of experience are not paler versions of a literary meta-narrative, literary theory can help elucidate them. The claim by the Baltic German K. Ullmann that Latvians have no epics because they have never done anything worth recording is one under which Latvians have smarted since it was first uttered in 1877. Ullmann wrote for the *Baltische Monatschrift*:

> A people who do not possess an epic, why is it they have none? Quite simply, it is because they have never done anything in their past that would be worth singing about, they have no history worth the mention. They have lived only in contact with nature, but they have not reached a level of equality in their contact with other nations.
>
> (quoted in Vike-Freiberga 1985, p. 524)

Perhaps such views play a small part in contributing to the intensity of narrative drive. Although driven by such personal intensity, narratives possess a structure which can be analysed. One example will illustrate this. Time is both a frequent, direct referent in Latvian narrative and an important component of identity and society. In some narratives there is little sense of historical time. Rather the action oscillates between a contingent world of happenings, both terrible and lucky, and a world of unchanging repetitions in which archetypal selves are set in mythical time.

BIOGRAPHICAL DISRUPTION AND NARRATIVE UNITY

Several writers have commented on the importance of narrative in situations where there is a mismatch between individual expectation and outcome. 'Respondents narrativize particular experiences in their lives, often where there has been a breach between ideal and real, self and society' (Riessman 1993, p. 3). Personal narrative also has a special importance in societies which fail to secure the moral allegiance of their members. Where social values and meanings are not accepted, individuals may engage in a personal search for meaning within a narrative past. This has, of course, a special relevance for the countries of eastern Europe and the former Soviet Union. In Latvia severance from the Soviet Union and the breaking up of old structures has released a deluge of personal memoirs, life histories and diaries. Similar literary developments have taken place in Poland and other eastern European countries (see, e.g., Paul

Thompson 1982).[5] This autobiographical writing marks an end to the retreat into privacy observed throughout the Soviet Union and eastern Europe and represents an attempt to reconnect private with public life.

Most importantly, narrators attempt to compensate for biographical disruption by restoring unity and coherence to narrated lives. The breakdown of the everyday structures of living creates a need to reconstitute meaning in story telling. Analyses of narratives of chronic illness (Williams 1984), of life crises such as divorce (Riessman 1990b) and of adoption show processes of meaning reconstitution at work. These recent studies concentrate on the narrative itself in order to extract the social categories underpinning discourse. They contrast with earlier studies whose focus was not the narrative itself but rather its usefulness in opening windows on unknown, often deviant, realities. In presenting Latvian narratives I am seeking to reconcile these two approaches. Clearly, narrators select and organize memories. But equally the substance of those memories is rooted in past experience, as population statistics, dismembered families and disfigured landscapes testify.[6] Historical narratives are born in the re-encounter between past events and the individual's unifying vision. I want to reconcile these two approaches and find a means of acknowledging both past events and present narrative form.

Georges Gusdorf's important essay on the development of autobiography links it to a particular awareness of the perils of historical change and 'the breakdown of forms and of beings' (1980, p. 30). The urgent need to give an account of one's life makes sense when set against the background of perceived social breakdown. However, Gusdorf explains the autobiographical enterprise with reference to the development of a particular kind of individualism which is incompatible with mythical and traditional thought. Although oral narratives do have a similar motivation to autobiographical writing, Latvian narrative experience does not embody the same links with individualism and a perception of history as constant change which Gusdorf postulates as necessary features of the autobiographical enterprise. For example, Latvian narratives of childhood construct a timeless world of archetypal images. Individual memories are subsumed under a general vision: 'My childhood was happy like all childhoods'. This, or some similar phrase, was repeated by many. Sometimes there is little attempt to recall personal memories because the past is perceived as being like everyone else's. Descriptions of the past refer explicitly to Latvian children or country children as a group and particular accounts derive their authenticity as instantiations of an archetype. This is not to say that such archetypes have a transhistorical and immutable reality; there is a constant interaction between past experience and cultural and literary representations. Thus, Roberts Ķīlis shows how in the context of exile, famine and threat of death, stereotypes of ethnic rather than individual identity are used to construct narrative accounts (1994, p. 14). For example, narratives describe the ambivalent ethnic attributes which can promote either survival or early death. Hard work in the context of the Siberian taiga or forests enabled Latvians to build houses and survive the winter. In the context of Arctic labour camps it speeded their death.

SOCIAL MEMORY

In listening to Latvian narratives I was, as I said, presented with a paradox. It was the problem of reconciling the intentions of narrators to bear witness to past events with my perception that recurring themes, concepts and strategies organized the narrative itself. For narrators the recurrence of narrative patterns points to a shared past. My approach does not challenge the truth of the past as witnessed, but rather investigates the cultural resources used to make sense of the past and incorporate it into a personal history. In relation to 'the lives of obscure and ordinary individuals' Luisa Passerini has written of the importance of knowing about:

> the ideas feeding into their everyday experience. It is true that these ideas (self-images, myths, stories and jokes) are for the most part belied by reality. And yet, all these mental representations are the other face of reality, which includes and is shaped by them. A parallel can perhaps be drawn with the way dreams during sleep are indispensable to life during waking hours. Out of this arises the curious life led by mental representations – their power to form diverse associations in a dynamic of continuity and change, being both functional to and distinct from the social division of labour.
>
> (1987, p. 1)

Passerini rightly highlights the ambivalent relationship of cultural representations to social reality. The shared representations may be either a distillation or an inversion of reality. Although this ambivalence means that cultural representations do not offer simple access to the past, neither are they unrelated to the past. However, their significance lies primarily in the power which they give to individuals to organize their experience rather than in any direct access to the past. Yet just as there is an ambivalence in the relationship between cultural representations and the reality of the past, so there is no straightforward relationship between individuals and the way they draw upon these collective ideas. Latvian narrators enlist cultural resources according to their personal needs. Whilst all narrators draw upon shared cultural representations they do not, of course, do so in identical ways. Nevertheless, there is a continuity and commonality of narratives. Like Mary Steedly, 'I want to propose a history that is not about change and conversely an anthropology that is not about continuity' (1993, p. 40).

With the emergence of characteristic patterns and themes, narratives, like texts, take on lives of their own. Lévi-Strauss' claim: 'Les mythes se pensent dans les hommes, et à leur insu' (1964, p. 20) applies to Latvian narratives. However, the narrator, unlike the author, cannot be magicked out of existence so easily. Barthes' famous claim that the author's presence in the text is merely as an invited guest, is more difficult to sustain. Narrative is undoubtedly a vehicle for shared cultural representations, but it also offers scope for imaginative truth and creativity. So whilst a corollary to the textual self can be found in the transcriptions, yet the voice of narrators cannot be erased in quite the same way from an audible recording. The qualities of the recorded voice – uneven delivery, pain, anger, irony and humour – serve as a reminder of the person narrating and her present re-encounter with the past. The intention of narrators to bear witness to past events demands the right to an individual voice. I have felt torn between the demands of anthropology and those of my narrators. In the end the narrators won. This book, therefore, contains much larger segments of direct speech than is customary in an anthropological monograph.

Geoffrey Hosking's retelling of an Armenian anecdote is relevant. The Armenian radio is asked whether it is possible to foretell the future: 'Yes, that is no problem: we know exactly what the future will be like. Our problem is with the past. That keeps changing' (quoted in Butler 1989, p. 115). The custodianship of history by the state puts a special onus on personal testimony. Here, the anthropological debate about representation is relevant. The inseparability of form and content and of both from issues of power and powerlessness compel me to respect the narrative form in which memories were recounted. Social anthropologists have commented on the decline of memory as a source of truth coupled with the ascendancy of the textual paradigm of knowledge in western society (Fentress and Wickham 1992). Literacy has led to a gradual but systematic erosion of the value put upon memory (Carrithers 1990). The situation in Soviet Latvia was somewhat different: the spoken not the written word was the bearer of truth. The textual paradigm did not have undisputed dominance and the printed word was mistrusted and sometimes seen as deliberately mislead-ing. If history books lie, memory acquires a central importance for the preservation of authenticity and truth as well as a peculiar poignancy. The role of memory has certain similarities in all totalitarian societies where the state has claimed a monopoly of truth (Passerini 1987). Under such conditions, individual lives bear witness against the state. Paradoxically, the collective and mythical components of memory are emphasized (Samuel and Thompson 1990). However, because Latvian memories conflicted with official versions of history, their commonality could not be explicitly acknowledged. Instead they reinforced feelings of loneliness and ultimately made people ill. The consequences of remembering in Latvia bear out Luria's claim that it is far more debilitating always to remember than never to forget.

The literature on social memory has emphasized the selective nature of memory and the way in which present social categories mould memory. This may provoke concern among narrators that memory is equated with imagination, and that the past is therefore treated as no more than fiction. This is not my intention. In identifying shared commonalities of Latvian memories I am not questioning their authenticity. Although narrative experience necessarily draws upon shared cultural values and representa-tions it retains a historical value as a 'window on the past'. In seeking to reconcile an anthropological with a historical approach, I am not arguing that a special case should be made for narrative experience. Much interesting work has recently been published which shows the way in which the writing of macro-history has been shaped by factors extrinsic to the events themselves. The titles indicate the shift of interest towards memory and the writing of history. For example, Paul Fussell's *The Great War and Modern Memory* (1976) documents the mismatch between the events of the First World War and the language and concepts available to describe them. As a result contemporary accounts of the war were couched in the language of medieval chivalry and heroism. George Mosse's *Fallen Soldiers. Reshaping the Memory of the World Wars* (1990) examines the role of mythologies in writing about the world wars. Historians no less than ordinary people are constrained by the cultural spectacles of the societies to which they belong.

The importance attached in Latvia to oral testimony bears close resemblance to Ong's characterization of the difference between oral and literate cultures:

> A present-day literate usually assumes that written records have more force than spoken words as evidence of long-past state of affairs, especially in court. Earlier cultures that knew literacy but had not so fully interiorized it, have often assumed quite the opposite.... Witnesses were prima facie more credible than texts because they could be challenged and made to defend their statements.
>
> (1982, p. 96)

Even Goody's association of writing with secret power and magic (1987) finds an echo in Latvian ideas concerning the belief, very largely true, of inaccessible records kept about everyone. Solveig's reply to the KGB officer who, on arresting her, asks for her documents, is 'You know much more about me than I do myself' (see p. 64). Against this background it is not surprising that it is the private and evanescent spoken word rather than the potentially incriminating written word which is trusted. My conversations with people were nearly always in private and would not have been possible otherwise. Ong wrote 'Sight isolates, sound incorporates' (1982, p. 72). In listening to narratives I felt I was incorporated into hitherto sealed-off worlds.

LOCAL TRUTH AND TRANSLATION

My admission to this world rested on the attribution of a shared past. Johannes Fabian has written about the importance of shared temporality for shared knowledge: 'Somehow we must be able to share each other's past in order to be knowingly in each other's present' (1983, p. 92). My past, the fact of my being born in Latvia, of being caught up in the meta-narrative of history, of having family killed during the Communist invasion, of escaping at the eleventh hour – all this conferred the privilege of sharing the past with others. This same need for shared temporality provoked anxiety as to how narratives would be perceived by English speakers. Surely they would not be interested, and if they were would they be able to understand? An almost formulaic response was 'Only those who have experienced it, can understand it'. Latvian fears about meaning lost or betrayed in the course of translation reflects the anxieties of a small country being swallowed up and annihilated. Asad writes about 'the problem of reproducing an alien discourse' (1986, p. 156), and the fact that the rhythms and idiosyncracies of one discourse are suppressed and give way to a dominant discourse. This was certainly an issue for me: my first translations were governed by an intense sense of allegiance to the narrators. This resulted in transcriptions which attempted to follow the exact interlocutions and speech rhythms of narrators. I ended up, of course, with English narratives that were unreadable and had none of the fluency and power of the Latvian originals. In the end, I opted for fluency, but in the course of so doing I am aware of having ignored Asad's caution against adapting the structures of a minority language to those of a dominant language, rather than letting the dominant be altered by the minority language. Rather I have followed Paul Ricoeur's model of translation: 'To translate is to invent an identical constellation, in which each word is influenced by all the others and, bit by bit, profits from its relation to the whole language' (1978, p. 79). This problem of translation is one with which Johann Herder, who was an eighteenth-century citizen of Riga, was familiar. His views about the undesirability and travesties of translation and the importance of understanding a culture from within are well known. His views on the language and poetry of Latvians are less well known:

> Die Dichtkunst und Musik der Letten ist besonders und zeugt von der Natur, die ihr Lehrmeister gewesen und noch ist. Ihre Poesie hat Reime, aber nur mannliche. Einerlei Wort zweimal hinter einander gesetzt, heisst bei ihnen schon ein Reim.

(n.d., p. 84)

> (The art of poetry and music of the Latvians is special and is drawn from nature, which was and is their teacher. Their poetry has rhymes but only masculine ones (i.e. stressed). With them, the same word repeated twice already counts as a rhyme.)

Herder's views are a mixture of fascination and ill-concealed contempt, which is reflected in his inability to judge the language on its own terms.

TIME, PLACE AND METAPHOR

It is by now a commonplace that narratives bestow unity and meaning on the past. But the interesting questions relate to the precise conceptual techniques used to create that unity. Classical Greek ideas suggest a pointer. Aristotle defined three dramatic unities: time, place and action.[7] For Latvian narrators these unifying principles are not available. War, imprisonment and exile fragmented accepted notions of time and space. Terror and oppression undermined conventional notions of a free agent and free action. However, many Latvian narratives do possess a unity and this is achieved through metaphor which draws together what would otherwise be disjointed narrative sequences. Roman Jakobson distinguished metaphor and metonymy and used that distinction to define two ways in which language operates. Metaphor is based on relations of similarity and metonymy on contiguity. By definition narratives contain sequences of contiguous events. However, pure contiguity does not produce meaning. In the case of Latvian narratives it produces sequences of arbitrary events which in fact break down customary structures of meaning. The interweaving of metaphor contributes a meaning beyond chance juxtaposition to what would otherwise be perceived as arbitrary sequences of events. The more purely metonymic the account – history as one damned thing after another – the more it stands in need of metaphor. Metaphor reaches into the fractured and irreconciled corners of people's lives. Its centripetal force brings to life similarities and patterns which would otherwise not be perceived. Metaphor enables some people to reconcile themselves to the past; its absence prevents others from coming to terms with it. Metaphor attributes an underlying unity to life and in doing so binds together past and present. Narratives without metaphor fail to reconcile past and present and the past is perceived as interfering with the present, as a continued source of grievance. Metaphor endows narratives and lives with a significance which transcends historical time.

The dominant metaphors in Latvian narratives relate to ruptures in customary structures of time and space. For example, a personal significance is retrieved from the breakdown of habitual patterns of life by attributing the workings of destiny to seemingly random coincidences. Exile and the removal of large segments of the population from accustomed localities puts a special onus on memories of place. The farmstead comes to be seen as an embodiment of happiness and virtue, a pastoral metaphor for the good life. Thus the geography and physical attributes of the farmstead are infused with moral and emotive attributes.[8] Metaphors of destiny and pastoral permeate many narratives which succeed in constructing a meaningful past. However, the point of such metaphors is also the achievement of intimacy (see, e.g., Ted Cohen 1979). Their use rests on an assumption of shared experience and shared understanding. Destiny was always prefaced by the possessive adjective 'our', thus drawing narrator and listener together. Shared country roots were established by questioning me on my ancestors and their place of origin. 'Metaphor gestures towards what transcends language' (Harries 1979, p. 82). Metaphors of destiny rest on shared experiences which are felt to be beyond language.

Narrative and time are closely interrelated. Indeed, Paul Ricoeur refers to 'the structural reciprocity of temporality and narrativity' and takes 'temporality to be that structure of existence that reaches language in narrativity and narrativity to be the language structure that has temporality as its ultimate referent' (1980, p. 165). I take this to mean that narration takes place in time and that the narratives themselves deal with the unfolding of events in time. The point of intersection between past and present time lies in the plot or form of the narrative. However, this shaping of the past experience moves beyond temporal ordering and interleaves the temporal sequence with atemporal metaphorical meanings. Narratives are constructed around a dialectic between the accidents of time and timeless truths.

However, despite the importance of time within narrative, it fails to provide unity, because narratives encompass different 'times'. Time is splintered. In addition to providing temporal frameworks for narratives, time frequently appears as a direct referent. There are references to happy times, to lost, smashed, destroyed and stolen times. There is time survived. There are times eked out and endured. There are lucky times and times of destiny. There are shared times and times which set one apart and isolate. There is frequently a sense of life and time being mocked. In such examples, time, as the object of narrative experience, is a referent. However, time also provides a framework or marker for different social and moral universes, sometimes signalling the narrator's passage between these worlds. Temporal frameworks provide a closure which the real world lacks. For example, terror and violence and the disruption of social forms are marked by an asocial, private temporality which is unpredictable and chancey. Memories of childhood, youth and often the entire pre-Communist period are associated with a shared, repetitive temporality intimately linked with locality and landscape. This cyclical temporality bears a close ressemblance to pastoral temporality. Thus narratives move between different 'times', but without a sense of chronological progression.[9]

The construction of alternating temporalities is a way of indicating changes in society, in identity and in the relationship between the two. The construction of a private and unpredictable temporality is one attempt to find a suitable language for the experience of violence and terror. The representation of the terror of past experience within a distinct temporality is one way of framing those experiences and thereby creating a sense of distance. The shared, repetitive past provides a necessary contrast or ballast for the lonely narratives of terror. This repetitive past time has certain affinities with ritual time. In the process clock time, the temporality of discipline and work which must have been the experience of at least those narrators living in towns, is elided. A recurring memory and a formulaic component of many narratives are the first words which Latvian soldiers heard after capitulation: 'Atdavai chasi' – the Russian for 'give me your watch'. As well as losing accustomed structures of time, they also literally lost their watches.

Many narratives are constructed around peregrinations, some voluntary, many forced. The encounter with foreign landscapes and the emotionally heightened reconstruction of the landscape of home provide frameworks for narrative experience as well as being direct referents within narratives. I gained entry to ahistorical, empty landscapes of terror and inhabited, historically inscribed landscapes of magic and beauty. Anne Salmond describes western discourse about knowledge as riddled with spatial metaphors (1982, pp. 65–87). Spatial metaphors play an important role in the creation of autobiographies. Latvian narrators embed personal memories in landscape and landscape is used to construct time and identity. People exiled to Siberia or imprisoned in labour camps emphasized the vastness and absence of human habitation:

> We were in the swamps, jungles, with insects biting. . . .Where we lived the

Russians recounted that hunters would go hunting, there is a great emptiness, there was only one *gerevna* (Russian for village) where the hunters lived, and beyond that no one else lived there. Emptiness. Taiga. Hunters would disappear for weeks.

(Maiga Puķīte)

This contrasts with memories of Latvian landscapes:

Our family owned a so-called one horse piece of land. My father didn't have farm labourers, we managed ourselves. Well, my childhood like all childhoods was happy.

(Ernests Kļaviņš)

The notion of a one-horse plot, a piece of land small enough to be worked by one horse, conveys the intimacy between land, animals and people. In Siberia the landscape swallows time and people. It is also described as inverting the natural order:

We were allowed out of the barracks to look around. There was a terrible extreme transformation. With us trees and grass grow gradually, but there it happens under your very eyes. But despite all that we longed for Latvia, even though we don't have the excesses of nature . . . even so. Our tones are quieter, softer, there isn't the rapid change. With us spring comes gradually, then summer and autumn. There it happens all at once. The last snow falls in May, sometimes in June – June is spring, July is summer, August autumn, by September the snow is back. And then those terrible nights start when day and night join together . . .

(Elza Glaudāne)

Elza's account of a disordered landscape match her experience of social and moral disorder in Siberia. By contrast, memories of Latvian landscapes are linked to ordered activity and ordered lives.

Finally, there is the agent within the narrative account and the relationship between agent and narrator to consider. The narrative use of a single word 'I' conceals the fluidity of the person to whom it refers. James Olney refers to this aspect of narrative identity as 'this double-referent "I"' (1980b, p. 247), which links the 'I' of the narrative present with the 'I' of the remembered past. In Latvian narratives there is a problem not only of double, but of multiple referents for the 'I'. Narrators recount widely different experiences of themselves and their autonomy and yet draw these diverse experiences together. The narrative self is located in many different settings – some happy, some terrifying. Hence, narrative selves do not readily fit dualistic models of self and society. The humanistic notion of the individual self, opposed and distinct from society, has been attacked. The dualistic model of the individual and society fails to give an account of the 'distinctly human aspects of persons' (Henriques et al. 1984, p. 13). However, the opposing view that 'the individual is not a fixed or given entity, but rather a particular product of historically specific practices of social regulation' (ibid., p. 12) does not fully encompass Latvian narrative experience. It fails to take account of the narrative 'I' which judges those same historical practices which regulate selves and which scours memory to produce meaningful patterns from the most ill-assorted and unpromising contexts.

Metaphorical processes are important in this meaning-creation enterprise. However, narrators make their own selection and in doing so resist available medical metaphors. Lakoff and Johnson (1980), have shown the way in which everyday thought is permeated by implicit, for the most part unrecognized metaphors. They provide important clues to understanding our taken for granted structures of thought. Terence Hawkes describes all languages as containing 'deeply embedded metaphorical structures which covertly influence overt "meaning"' (1989, p. 60). In this view, rather than being the exception to literal truth, metaphor forms part of the very nature of language and cannot be removed. The classical view to which this is opposed is represented by Aristotle. It has been described as the 'detachable' view of metaphor (ibid., p. 92), and it is one which Susan Sontag follows in urging us to resist the metaphorical meanings which have become attached to certain diseases (1989). I am aware of the role attributed to language and metaphor in constituting reality, however, ordinary people no less than anthropologists can develop an awareness of the force and direction of metaphors. This awareness gives choice and produces narratives in which cultural representations blend with personal imagination.

In summary then, I was drawn into narrative at the insistence of my narrators. At the margins of society where conventional relationships have broken down, the truly cultural as well as the truly bestial becomes evident. The experiential content of many of the narratives was held to be so bestial as to resist telling. However, although the actual narration was emotionally fraught both for the narrator and for me, the retelling of experience had a literary structure and tone. Such narratives make the distinction between natural and literary language difficult to uphold: they empower individuals to take up centre stage as the imaginative recreators of their world.

4

READING LETTERS

Although oral testimony forms the heart of this book, it began and ended with written records. Thus the temporal framework for the reliving of memories and for their narration was constituted by letters and later by transcribed narratives. I moved from the written to the spoken and back to the written. At the beginning of 1992 I solicited and received a large number of letters. They were my first introduction to the lives I was later to hear recounted. The movement from the written to the oral was difficult; the movement back from the oral to the written even more so. Why this should have been so needs some exploration.

I approached the letters much like any other academic text which I was using to advance my research. Some were more fluent and interesting than others. None moved me in the way that the spoken narratives were to do later on when meaning lay as much in the narrator's face, gestures and physical surroundings as in the words used. Although some of the interviews were emotionally fraught I was caught up in the feelings they generated. However, the process of translating the tapes into written transcripts and then into an academic text was far more difficult. Why did I encounter such psychological barriers to doing this? I knew that my informants wanted their lives to be made public and yet in the process of doing this I felt I was betraying them. Looking back I can only explain this in terms of the distinction between experience and narrative. Although experience can only be communicated to others through narrative accounts they are not synonymous. Narrative representations of grief move beyond the witnessing and embodiment of narration. In representing lives as narrative texts I felt I was betraying the embodied grief which I had witnessed. Familiarity with representations of suffering may not only move to pity but may also distance and harden the heart. All of this made it difficult to write. However, since writing was both my original aim and that of my informants, I returned to the letters.

How did the letters compare with the spoken narratives? Unsurprisingly, letters were more restrained and oblique than the narratives. What was most important to the structure of the letter was frequently an implied interconnecting thread. Although spoken narratives also conveyed meanings implicitly and by silences, implication did not underpin and draw together spoken narratives as it did letters. When what was implied surfaced later in speech it brought with it suppressed grief and anger. Some examples will illustrate what I have in mind.

Letters were respectful and confiding in tone and were structured around the person's life history. Letter-writers were explicit about the need to understand illness in the context of their lives. For example, phrases such as 'I shall begin my tale with the year 1951' act as narrative markers. Or, 'Perhaps, my narrative will be chaotic, but I hope you will be able to extract from it what is useful to you' or, 'After consideration I decided to write. The writing will be long because it will contain not only a description of illnesses, but also of life'. Or, simply 'I shall write about myself'. Although all the letters abide by a rigid code for letter writing and address me in honorific terms as 'honoured doctor', the opening sentences draw me into the confidence of the writer as someone who is familiar with 'Latvia's fate'. My relationship with one letter-writer can best be conveyed by the opening fragment of her second letter to me, written shortly after the first meeting. She writes:

> I still haven't recovered from the happy surprise connected with your visit. I didn't collect myself sufficiently to thank you more sincerely for your visit and to send greetings to your mother. I was reflecting on the difficulties which a young woman like her with a little infant would find in moving to a foreign country. To settling there, to acquiring means and there would be the business of helping you to gain such a high education, I am therefore without delay putting it in writing.

Writers start by situating the self morally and socially. This textualization of the self may be carried out with reference to a past social structure or to an unchanging set of moral values. For example, Antra introduces herself thus:

> I was born in 1944 into a pastor's family in Riga.[1] My father, a theologian, a doctor of philosophy, a professor, died recently.

Her account then changes course to a narrative of terrible events remembered. Another writer situates herself thus:

> I am a country woman, 67 years old, the mother of three grown sons.

Or:

> I was born in 1932 in Riga. My father was a Latvian Army Officer, my mother did not work.

Some others concentrate on defining themselves within an emotional and moral context: 'Neurasthenia develops particularly among emotional and reactive people' writes one woman.

Or:

> I love solitude, books, but sometimes I long for gay, sensible, honest, open company.

Or:

I am an optimist, even in difficult circumstances of life. I did not know sleeplessness excitability or lack of control.

These extracts illustrate the way in which writers derive their identity from the moral values and social structures of the past.

Country life is depicted as hard, but predictable and rewarding.

I started my working life at the age of five and a half, because my parents at the time were building on inherited land. They started on a bare hillside. During the first summer starting from 23rd April [St George's Day][2] we lived in a newly built shed without heating. Food for the family, craftsmen and house builders was prepared in a little timber hut. My duty was to herd 3 or 4 cows and small animals.

Despite the description of the hardships of her childhood she invites us to infer that life was regulated and meaningful. The apparent jump in the text from her own herding activities to her parents' house building points us towards the underlying theme or concept around which the text is organised, the implicit ideas which guide the letter but are not spelt out are that everyone was committed to hard work and willing to put up with physical hardships and deprivation for long-term gain. That reward was a beautiful house built from scratch on a bare hillside. This commitment bound family members together and ideally introduced quasi-familial relations between employer and labourer as illustrated by, for example, eating together.

Thus deprivation and hard work are seen to have a visible reward and are made meaningful. This initial depiction of a structured meaningful existence is followed by a narrative of events which break that structure. Anthropology has typically concerned itself with structure rather than events. Narrators emphasized the importance of events for their lives and contrasted this with remembered structure:

During the war (the German period) at the age of eighteen and a half I got married. With that various anxieties entered my life which have recurred to this day. First, that my husband could be called into the army. Second, that as the army retreated we wouldn't be able to stay in our house, that we would have to become refugees and that our house would be burnt[3] (that was the rule but in the end it was repealed because the refugees were obstructing the roads too much). During and after the war there were large levies on agricultural produce, and revenue taxes.[4] There was much obligatory forestry felling and clearing which was often a long way from home: we had to live in strange houses for two or three weeks.[5] My children were born during the impoverished post-war years. In 1949 there were the deportations which affected my close relatives and neighbours. There was nervousness, that the same might happen to us. There were even explicit threats: if you don't join the kolhoz, you'll find yourself travelling towards the white bears. Well cultivated land, farm animals, an inventory of farming equipment all had to be given to the kolhoz. The heavy and badly paid work during the first few years – working virtually for free in the kolhoz. The family had to survive from the small piece of land around the house and the one cow.

Irrespective of how large one's family was one wasn't allowed to keep more.[6] One could only work on one's own land on Sundays. The Khruschev period was critical, particularly for those who owned a private house. The specified area of land included the land under the house and the courtyard, but every Latvian country house has trees, lilacs and flower beds planted around. The garden land fell beyond this boundary and there wasn't anywhere to plant potatoes and root vegetables for the family's needs. As far as farm animals were concerned there could only be one cow and one pig. Apart from these no goat or sheep was allowed. Although in more remote places (our house was like that) a lot remained unmown under the snow. The number of farm animals was checked regularly, they checked whether one wasn't using more land, whether one didn't mow hay from one's little plot before the permitted date. The hay could only be mown when the feed for the collective herd was gathered, that was in late autumn. If someone had mown some hay in the bushes earlier it was taken away to the communal barn. If some little animal was found above the regulation number then a heavy tax was imposed. It was no use saying my children are little, my family is big. One cold winter heavy with snow I was awaiting the birth of my baby and I did not go to do the required forestry work. The supervisors arrived in my house to force me out. I said my husband was always a first class worker and had done much forestry work in remote places. The horse farm where I could get transport is two and a half kilometres away, at home I have a two and a half year old boy. I don't have any neighbours nearby, how will I get to the hospital to give birth? Then the supervisors became preoccupied and left without saying anything definite. The fact that children are going to be the next workers didn't interest the supervisors. It was difficult to obtain a house, to get to school or to get a doctor. Larger families didn't have enough produce from the little bit of land which was around the buildings. Those who didn't have a privately owned house had land measured out in a field and were better off. The areas of garden which were taken away grew over with weeds because they were too small for the kolhoz to cultivate. So as to avoid the big taxes weak sheep that had been suckled dry by the lambs were killed. Round about in the bushes there was no shortage of grass, and it just stayed there and grew. But one had to provide potatoes, vegetables and meat for the children's lunch at school. Meat was needed too for the midday sandwiches of the labourers doing their farm work, but there were no potatoes to give the piglet. During Khruschev's time one couldn't keep two pigs. With the heavy wet work, no gloves, clothes get worn out but there are no sheep and little money. In the winter I was working with a hand saw and sawing, chopping and carrying wood to the edge of the forest, so that the lorry could reach. I managed 1–2 'stopi'[7] a day and earned 40 rubles a day.[8] When I was thirty years old and working in the forest I fell ill with pneumonia.

The letter then goes on to deal specifically with health issues. Māra's narrative begins abruptly with the war and marriage. It is a chronological, highly condensed narrative of unreasonable acts and cruelty documented in meticulous detail. At first reading, the letter appears somewhat disconnected. Closer reading, however, reveals a systematically constructed narrative in which the connecting theme is developed through an interplay between what is stated and what is implied, for example, 'if some little animal was found, a heavy duty was imposed'.

Māra uses the Latvian diminutive for a farm animal, '*lopiņs*', which conveys the care which she feels for farming and animals. The implicit statement is, however, that the animal is necessary for the family's upkeep. Her statement emphasizes the absurdity of a system which imposes fines for such an innocent practice. It was taken away. She writes that individuals were only allowed to mow hay in the late autumn. The implicit statement is that Latvian winters came early and that hay in late autumn has been rain-soaked and is mouldy. Thus the kolhoz, which ostensibly provides communal and private hay, in fact deprives the individual of fodder for his few farm animals. The only alternative was to mow grass secretly at night, but this would also be confiscated. However, the kolhoz itself did not bother with the grass around bushes, it simply didn't want private individuals to have it. Because of this the sheep and farm animals had to be killed. Māra writes of inadequate farm clothing for heavy forestry work, but then moves on to 'no sheep and little money'. If she had a sheep she could knit a replacement for her torn gloves or if she had money she could buy another pair. As it is she has neither and the historical narrative culminates in her falling ill with pneumonia. The narrative is not simply a record of hardships sustained. The connecting link between the hardships is that of senselessness and needlessness. She presents us with an interlinked chain of irrationality, where each discrete hardship is linked through an irrational practice or regulation to the generation of further hardships. Even apparent benefits are transformed through such irrationality to disadvantage. For example, those who own private houses are deprived of land since the area occupied by the buildings is subtracted from the permitted half hectare of land, thus apparent advantage is turned to disadvantage through a dialectic of irrationality.

Iser has written of the way in which blanks and abrupt changes of subject in literary texts 'provide the unseen joints of the text' (in Suleiman 1980, p. 112). Attention to these features also provides an interpretative strategy for the reading of letters. The circumstances of post-war Latvian existence are chronicled. The linkages are provided by the barely concealed irrationality underlying the chronicle. The abrupt change from childhood to early adulthood and war is also linked to the irrationality theme. Childhood hardships are linked to a meaningful way of life. They stand in contrast to later meaningless hardships which serve no purpose for the individual but rather deprive life of meaning. These submerged semantic linkages substitute for the complete lack of connective prepositions: the narrative strings together events with no connective or inferential particles.

Antra was born in 1944 and therefore has no memories of the war or pre-war period. She situates herself as her father's daughter:

My father, a theologian, doctor of philosophy, a professor, died recently, but I shall begin my tale in 1951 when a group of armed chekists arrived in our house, carried out a search but arrested my father and later sent him to Siberia to build Communist youth buildings. It is difficult to describe the feelings which were evoked in my childish soul during the time of the search and later when I saw that make of car in which the chekists had taken my father away. I would run and hide in the meadow [diminutive]. I would often cry. That year I started to go to school and there I was openly laughed at about my arrested father and his profession – a pastor – both by my teacher and school companions. I grew up as prickly as a hedgehog, I often talked back, was disobedient, at moments I myself thought that I am not quite normal. The years passed, I finished school, I couldn't find a job, because although my father was released as unjustly punished, he didn't give up his faith in God and he didn't change his priestly vocation up to his death. During the whole period of Communist power I had to suffer for that. How? One could only write all that in a novel. I started to live independently. There was nowhere to live, I have spent the night in strange stairwells, but in the morning sat smiling and working at work (I have worked eighteen years in this work place). Despite everything things gradually started sorting themselves out. I got a flat, I married, my real feelings, neuroses I strove to hide from everyone as far as possible. More and more often I felt tense, almost without reason, tired at times I felt a pain in the region of the heart, I felt dizzy, I felt unwell.

Like Māra in the earlier narrative, Antra gives a dense account of events, so much so that several major events share the same sentence. For example, moving away from parents, not having anywhere to live, sleeping rough and hiding this from work colleagues are all packaged into one sentence. Antra's narrative develops through a series of contrasts between outer events and personal attributes. The first contrast is between her learned father and the armed chekists, the crying child in the meadow and the chekists' cars. Crying, the implication being that this took place secretly, is contrasted with open laughter and derision at school. The secret fearful night spent in the stairwells of apartment houses is set against the smiling composure at work. The theme of inner and outer, of secret and open is encapsulated in Antra's apt simile likening herself to a hedgehog – an animal whose soft centre is surrounded by a threatening exterior. Antra's account is more self-conscious than Māra's and she spells out the contrasts herself. Her account includes characterization of herself as a dual being and the development of her illness is linked explicitly to the duality. Her hidden real feelings are equated with neurosis, and her string of symptoms are summed up in the simple statement 'I felt unwell'. Māra uses no inferential particles such as, 'because', 'for', 'and so'. Her letters contain one 'then', otherwise even such connective links are dispensed with. Antra's letter also lacks inferential particles and, indeed, avoids using them where they might be expected. She writes of being made fun of at school about her father's arrest, not because of his arrest. Such a backward-looking inferential particle would suggest that events were logically connected, that the present events bear a meaningful relationship to past events. The narratives contain no such semantic connections.

Forward-looking inferential particles do not figure in the narratives either. Their use would imply that future events or actions were related to present decisions and would therefore not be a true reflection of the writer's experience. The complete absence of a common device for strengthening written narrative reinforces the quality of arbitrariness which all the narratives convey.

Both letter-writers link the onset of their illness to the narrative sequence of earlier events. Māra does so by implication, Antra quite explicitly. For Māra, pneumonia is a consequence of the unreasonable expectations that she work in the forest inadequately dressed:

Working in the forest I fell ill with acute pneumonia and afterwards with bronchial asthma. The illness got worse in winter, I couldn't do anything outside, I couldn't accompany the children to their school seven kilometres away. I didn't dare get hot preparing food, washing clothes, because after that there would be acute attacks. It was very difficult to breathe, with every movement it got worse – I was suffocating, my lungs creaked, I could not draw the air in. Shortage of breath, a tormenting cough often started in the night towards morning and at times continued for several days. At such times I couldn't get to the doctor because, as I said, at every movement it became intolerable. As I said, one lived a solitary life because the nearest neighbours had been deported, other houses were far away and in the winter there were no roads around our house. Husband to work, schoolboy to school, trudging on foot or on skis. It was a problem to bring the doctor home, because the supervisor was unwilling to release my husband from work. In that fashion I was ill for eighteen years. In between attacks I went to several doctors in the regional polyclinic to the doctors in the neighbouring village clinic. But such journeys often ended sadly. Buses were a long way away [7 km] the better doctors twenty kilometres away. The journey, the long wait in the overfilled waiting rooms would trigger off a new attack, but not of course straight away. It turned out like this: as I already said, I would go after an attack when I felt stronger, when movement didn't precipitate a shortage of breath, the doctor couldn't establish anything, because there was no noise in the lungs, and so they say that everything is fine, but arriving home at night I start getting short of breath again and neither the prescribed medicine nor anything works. The simpler injections in the muscle my husband injected or I myself. I treated myself with bees' venom – getting the bees to sting me. I started with a smaller number and increased the number every day. All according to the doctor's instructions. I use herbal teas a lot. During these eighteen years I was often treated in hospital, but I ended up there when I was not in the most acute stage. However, lying in hospital I kept well, but on arriving back home the journey by horse, starting some work, everything was the same again. Besides, in that hospital where our village had to be treated, the doctors viewed people of working age as simulants [malingerers] who did not want to work and expected to be fed in hospital and they said so openly – 'I don't know what you want from hospital' and so on. . . . I very much wanted to be cured but came up against suspicion, all the family members suffered, because they were always reminded of my not working in a waged capacity. With great effort, even writing to the Ministry of Health I succeeded in being issued with a temporary medical certificate that I was not able to work in damp and cold weather and that I was not able to do heavy work. The doctor's attitude towards the patient is also characterized by the following incident. For a long time I felt a lump in my breast – a largish one. We took the journal *Veselība* [*Health*] which encouraged women to show anything like that to the doctor. I showed it – laughter: 'a painless lump and she's upset' – I became ashamed. It happened that due to an enlarged thyroid gland I was sent to Stradiņu hospital in Riga. Before the doctor's examination I wasn't told to get undressed (although I offered). Quickly pushing a hand under my clothes they examined my breasts – 'healthy'. I said, 'there's a lump' – another shove – 'there's nothing – it's fine', but I just got undressed and said that there is a lump. 'Well that's nothing', if I want to stay another day in Riga then I can show it to an oncologist. For certain it was unpleasant for the examiner and she would have wanted me to go back home. I myself was quite satisfied, pleased that there was nothing, but as I had to stay a second day on account of the thyroid gland, I determined to go also to the oncology consulting room. I got a proper telling off that I had waited so long, was it cancer – straight off to operate. I had an operation, now I'm well, it wasn't malignant. With the thyroid gland too they didn't find anything bad, although it is enlarged. During my school years, my tonsils were taken out, otherwise I haven't had anything operated. During these eighteen years of illness I was ill with a kidney infection, probably also with jaundice with which I was ill at home. I also went to a good doctor in the neighbouring village because my eyes were yellow, but it just so happened that on that day the other doctor was on duty, the same one who had laughed at the lump in my breast, and on that occasion too she laughed – 'eyes like eyes, nothing wrong'. I got home, the next day the whites of my eyes were really yellow, but should my husband ask for a horse and a free day from the field brigade for the twenty-kilometre long journey? And so I had to endure the illness at home. At that time many people in our village were ill with Botkins disease and no doubt I had it too. School children were ill, my children too had already been taken to hospital. As far as I remember my children (three) were able to return home after six weeks. I tried to feed them the way the doctor said so that they would get better. They were forbidden any physical exertion. But the school required apprentice work in the school fields and work in the sugar beet fields in the summer.[9] Even today I remember the conversation in the headmaster's office about the fact that they couldn't do physical work on account of their health. She said, 'Many have been ill, if all were to be excused who would be left to work'. If the required days weren't worked they wouldn't go on to the next class, although their marks were not insufficient. They had to work during their school days, although it was harmful to their health, and that's so to this day with excessive hours [*pārslodze*].

Nineteen years ago we were forced to leave our house.[10] It was recently built, on a dry hill, round about were fir, elder and other forest trees, the air was fresh, without dust. Although there was a marsh nearby. We bought [a house] right by the main road, in the summer there is dust. It is in a low-lying damp place. The living quarters are in an old stone-walled building, over a hundred years old. It's damp and cold. In this house the asthma attacks have not appeared in a heavy form. In the previous house there was no electricity because it wasn't allowed. We were supposed to move to the village, clothes had to be washed by hand. After washing the clothes for six people I was often ill. Here clothes were immediately washed by machine, food was prepared on a gas cooker [in preparing food on a wood-burning stove there is a greater amount of heat]. My family also shrank in size, my sons had military service and their own life. Maybe that or the change of dwelling place but the asthma got very much better. Of course, I myself take care not to get overheated, and not to catch cold. One of the children suffered from shortage of breath until they were of school age. One of his little daughters [diminutive] has shortage of breath. He resembles me in eye colour, the other two are like their father. Apparently my great-grandfather had such a complaint, that when he fell asleep he couldn't wake up, he had to be woken. And so he died in the prime of life when no one was nearby. There are times, although few, when both I and my two sons feel unwell in the heart, when we would like to wake up, when we can, so to speak, hear everything and so to speak understand, but are unable to move. If we manage somehow or other to move an arm or leg then it's possible to wake up. Recently I've been ill with enlarged veins. My left leg has been X-rayed, and something can be seen there. It's very difficult to walk. In the autumn I fell ill with pneumonia, after that I hardly do any work. I've been ill with pneumonia four times.

Māra's long chronicle of a lifetime of ill-health has an internal coherence of structure which contrasts so markedly with her earlier history of life events. It has a transparency and logic which frees the reader from the hermeneutic enterprise. In contrast to the felt arbitrariness and unreasonableness of her life events, Māra's health is always perceived as flowing from some antecedent physical or social conditions. In other words, whereas her life does not make sense, her health, whether good or bad, does.

The transition from life history narrative to illness narrative occurs in the context of forestry work which Māra perceives as the acme of injustice. She graphically details both the symptoms of the condition and the ways in which it restricts her life. Disjuncture reappears with the description of treatment and contact with doctors. The search for treatment emphasizes those aspects of society, namely irrationality and unfairness which underpin the narrative of her life history. Doctors, kolhoz supervisors and headmasters are all perceived as implementing this irrational system. In order to see the doctor Māra had to be reasonably well and the doctor would not accept her retrospective account of her symptoms and suffering. As a result she was accused of being work shy and a malingerer. By contrast her illness history is rooted in the social and physical conditions of her life. She mentions the possible genetic element in her susceptibility to asthma and describes the physical characteristics of her house, the nature of her domestic work, forced labour and the pointless destruction of their garden by kolhoz tractors. Finally a sentence about the many years of work for the kolhoz and valueless savings is followed by a statement of her susceptibility to tiredness. Her account of ill-health leaves no untidy gaps, symptoms are accounted for in terms of antecedent conditions to which they bear a meaningful relationship.

Antra's account of ill-health resembles Māra's narrative in certain important respects. She too perceives her illness as being related to life history and encounters the same lack of understanding on the part of doctors. She writes:

> I tried to hide my real feelings, neuroses, from everyone as far as possible. However, ever more frequently I felt tense almost without a reason, tired, at times I felt a pain in the region of the heart, I was dizzy, I felt unwell. Turning for medical help, I was diagnosed as healthy. Later my blood pressure became de-stabilized, both down and up. Yes, by the way, I have learnt to control my blood pressure by autosuggestion. True, not always, particularly if the tension is too great I don't succeed. After a time the menopause started but even about that the doctors weren't concerned, for there was a healthy son growing up in the family, now a scientist in the making, a philologist, who finished our university. Sleep disturbances began. At night my arms were paralysed at times, my legs were caught by cramp, the doctors explained it by osteochondrosis, which by the way I tried to treat by holding my head correctly during the day and whilst sleeping at night. I have to admit that the results are surprisingly good and I started doing it long before the medical diagnoses, knowing that osteochondrosis would certainly develop because of my sedentary work, I work as a technical drawer and draw very detailed plans for eight hours a day. So, during the day I was nervous and ordered my son and husband about, I especially attacked my husband, but at work I was calm and respected by everybody. All these changes started about 1972. Menstruation ceased completely, with alarm I acknowledged that I had interferences of vision, that I had double vision, but I linked everything to my detailed and complicated work. At the end of 1981 I turned to an eye doctor who found almost complete narrowing of the field of vision and impaired colour vision. The neuropatholo- gist after carrying out a head X-ray, diagnosed an adenoma. I should add that during this time my weight increased. I had an operation opening up the skull, the results of which I feel are good, nevertheless I was assigned to the second invalid's category for life. For the first few years after the operation I felt well, I didn't work, foreign travel had a big impact on me, I visited Canada. There also I consulted a doctor, but the consultation was without any benefit to me. During the last few years I have started to feel nervous again without reason, everyday trivia upset me, the high cost of living, the queues. I understand that is the nature of our life, but nevertheless I can't reconcile myself to it. It becomes even more difficult to struggle with myself. After the operation, my field of vision improved greatly. I am convinced that neurasthenia is my illness even from that unhappy year 1951, but everything else has developed on its foundation.

Antra's illness is perceived as stemming less from her immediate circum- stances, which she acknowledges have improved, but from the arrest of her father in 1951 and its aftermath. Her varied symptoms including the dramatic discovery of a brain tumour are attributed to this occurrence. Like Māra, Antra recalls being described as a *simulant* and because of the ineffectiveness of medical treatment proceeds to develop techniques of self treatment. Antra's diagnosis of osteochondrosis precedes the doctor's diagnosis and lays the blame squarely on her unhealthy occupation. In contrast with the arbitrary events of her childhood and early adulthood, the history of her illness is presented as a logical sequence of interconnected events. In both letters the onset of illness concludes the historical narrative and provides a bridging concept and the semantic transformation to the inner world of the individual. Thus the narrative trajectory moves from perfect to impaired structure. The past is perceived as timeless and idealized. This perfect structure is dismantled by historical events and results in eventual disease.

The letters conclude by drawing together the social and historical circumstances of the writers' life and linking these firmly to a statement of ill-health. Thus Māra writes:

> various upsets often occur, for example, the land round the house is rutted by the kolhoz tractors, making it almost unusable, an electric transformer is forcibly built on our cultivated vegetable garden, the shares which are due to us for many years work in the kolhoz are not paid, the money which has been carefully saved for one's old age making miserly economies has no value. As regards illnesses I have always tired easily and have little strength. At times I have high blood pressure.

The letter moves between political events and circumstances and their implication for the health of the writer. The conclusion is an overtly political statement: unstable and impaired health is presented as the logical consequence of an arbitrary and irrational social system.

Antra too concludes her letter by returning to the social circumstances of her life:

> I can tell you some more about myself, that I work more or less at the same difficult and detailed work because I can earn well there, but the doctors have forbidden it. I like to be in company, because at home I am alone all day. My son is married and lives independently, but my husband is at work the whole day. My family and all my relatives are Latvian. The social standing of my family is quite high. My husband is the director of a surveyor's office. My brother is a government minister, about my son I've written already but despite all this all the problems whether material or political do not exclude our family. I have various X-rays and diagrams of my field of vision to show you.

Thus Antra too gathers together the main themes of her letter and concludes by attributing her damaged health to material and political problems.

Not all letters were of comparable length and thoroughness. However, nearly all introduced a social and political theme which they linked to an individual medical theme. Most letters offered a conclusion which aimed to integrate these themes. For example, Dzintra wrote:

> I like everything that is light and the colour of the sun, but I am oppressed by the fate of Latvia. In waking in the night I dare not think about it, for fear of falling into despair and thus suffering sleeplessness.

Accounts of ill-health leave no untidy gaps; symptoms are accounted for in terms of antecedent conditions to which they bear a meaningful relationship. However, whereas letters were about illness, albeit embedded in life histories, informants used the face-to-face encounters in order to discuss what was of most concern to them. In this process they were able to elaborate the implicit connecting threads of the letters – in particular the charge of irrationality and meaninglessness.

5

DESTINY AND THE SHAPING OF AUTOBIOGRAPHY

'Singing (Curing) Latvian Dziedāšana (Dziedināšana)'

You just sing. Don't think of anything,
For the song will think bright thoughts through you.
You just sing. And nothing else.
And forget your thousand roles.

You just sing. Don't do anything,
For now the song will carry out its tasks through you.
It will clean out stables, clear refuse
And also scrub lime tables white.

You just sing. And nothing else.
For the song itself knows all, knows everything.
Just sing, entrust yourself and let
The song cure you again.

(Māra Zālīte)

Memories of individual suffering derive meaning from their positioning within national history. They do this by using the concept of destiny. This chapter looks at how destiny structures narratives and at the kinds of bridges it builds between individual and cultural resources. It looks at the contradictory meanings of destiny and the usefulness of these contra-dictions for coming to terms with the breakdown of purposive action and meaningful structures.

Latvian narrators employ various strategies in order to endow the past with meaning. This preoccupation with questions of meaning is shared by many trauma victims. It is 'The need to make habitable meanings from uninhabitable truths' (Colin Davis 1991, p. 302). The search for meaning is a powerful force in the narratives of Latvian lives. Some narratives seek but fail to find meaning. Others succeed by drawing upon cultural symbols learnt in early childhood. Thus the traumas of a personal past may be redeemed by joining personal with collective memories. Narratives are, therefore, constructed of an interweaving of personal lived experience and textual recollections.

Liktenis (destiny) provides a good illustration of the two-tiered and polysemous nature of certain core concepts. In part, *liktenis* is used as an admission of explanatory failure. For example, some narrators use the concept as a final summing up of their narrative, a kind of verbal marker indicating that they have nothing more to say. This form of narrative closure may indicate a failure to find meaning. *Liktenis* in such cases is used interchangeably with life events and circumstances which have broken down structure and expected meanings. I have in mind phrases such as 'That's been my destiny' or 'That's what our destiny has been like'. Such phrases are interchanged or are sometimes interlinked with phrases like 'That's what my life has been' or 'Now my life is over'. As a stylistic strategy *liktenis* works well in this context, gathering into itself the tone of the earlier narrative and acting as a verbal full stop. As an explanatory device it is less successful, since it is used to indicate failure to retrieve meaning from the past. In Latvian narratives the use of *liktenis* sometimes signals a failure to achieve explanation and is a kind of sad summing up of a life. It is a shared conceptual strategy which has its roots in the violent events which have dislocated lives.

There is a problem for all narratives of violence and terror of finding an appropriate language. In the context of the Holocaust this has been referred to as 'thinking the unthinkable', but it has been a problem for all experiences of mass or social suffering. Whereas individual suffering may be acknowledged and encompassed within existing conceptual structures, mass suffering always challenges and exceeds available explanatory resources. I found interesting parallels between my analysis of Latvian narratives and Paul Fussell's account of the language used to describe the battles of the First World War. He wrote of 'the collision between events and the language available or thought appropriate to describe them. To put it more accurately, the collision was one between events and the public language used for over a century to celebrate the idea of progress' (1976, p. 169). Latvian narrators repeatedly emphasize that what they have seen and experienced is beyond description. However, they do describe their experiences and one way of doing this is to borrow from literature. Narratives contain a repeated interweaving between what has been lived and what has been read, heard or sung. In such narratives *liktenis* provides a bridge and a meeting point between the personal and the cultural.

Liktenis is, to borrow I.A. Richards' description, a 'resourceful' word (1943). Like 'freedom' it is an emotive term which lends itself to many different usages. For example, it has an established academic usage where it is a synonym for national history. The emigre Latvian historian Švābe, subtitled his classical work on Latvian history '*The Destiny of the Latvian Nation*' (1952). Švābe's contribution to the eleven-volume collected folk songs or *dainas* is entitled '*The Destiny of the Latvian Dainas*'. Kundziņš' social and architectural history of the Latvian farmstead ends with a reference to national destiny (1974, p. 380). Within the growing body of autobiographies and memoirs of survivors, there is frequent reference to *liktenis* (see, e.g., Līce's *Via Dolorosa*, 1990). The term *likteņa stāsti* – literally translated as tales of destiny – is used interchangeably with life histories of the politically repressed. Thus references to the fate of the nation or to companions in destiny, *likteņa biedri*, are following an established literary and academic tradition.

Liktenis has also penetrated perceptions of landscape. For example, certain rocks, lakes and rivers are linked to ideas of national destiny. The rock 'Staburags' on the river Daugava has become part of national mythology through the work of the poet Rainis. It is the site of a struggle over national survival represented as a struggle between the forces of good and evil. For this reason alone the building of a power station which raised the water level and flooded Staburags was an important political move. The river Daugava herself is portrayed in folk songs as the bearer of the fate of the nation:

> Daugava [diminutive] – black eyes
> Flows black in the evening
> How should she not flow black
> Being full of precious souls?

Such uses of destiny challenge the mutual exclusivity of the distinction between 'natural' and 'fictive' discourse. A reading of the narratives suggests the notion of prefabricated discourse. This consists of 'verbal formulas – conventional phrases, idiomatic expressions, even whole sentences – that we have heard and used many times before, preassembled sections, like an automobile or prefabricated building' (Smith 1979, pp. 60–61). These ready-made verbal parts 'are freely donated to us for our immediate use by the linguistic community' (ibid., p. 62). References to destiny are made using these preassembled segments and in so doing they help bind together a narrative whose meaning or lack of it may otherwise threaten to destroy the individual narrator. They are, as Smith suggests, devices shared by the linguistic community but they also draw heavily upon literary texts.

The use of literature in the context of political oppression is not new. During the period of national awakening – *atmodas laikmets* – in the second half of the nineteenth century, literature played an important role in evoking and shaping a specifically national consciousness. A new language of heroism drew upon epics of the classical world and a few scattered medieval legends from Latvia. In particular, the work of two poets, Pumpurs and Auseklis, played a key role in the awakening. In reconstructing the legendary figure of Lāčausis or Lāčplēsis, bear-ears or bear-slayer, Pumpurs emphasizes his heroic courage. By describing a legendary and heroic past these poets focused on the characteristics required to carry that alleged tradition of fearless heroism into the future (see, e.g., Plakans 1979, p. 244). By the late nineteenth century Latvian literacy rates were already high, reading was much valued and books could, therefore, shape individual experience. However, whereas this early literature emphasized superhuman courage and strength, during the late Soviet period the literary term used most is *liktenis*, which links individual suffering with national history. Its frequent recurrence testifies to its importance and gives a unique insight into social structure. John Davis has described the way in which reactions to suffering are concerned with the preservation of threatened social relations. In disastrous circumstances people strive 'to maintain those characteristic forms of life which define what it is to be human' (1992, p. 157). Similarly, when a Latvian narrator uses the term *liktenis* to sum up the devastation of her life, she is calling into being resonances which link her to national history and cultural institutions. For example, Anna says:

> I don't for one moment consider that I am the only one who hasn't succeeded or something like that. I have always told myself that I am not the only one like that. The whole Latvian nation is like that. I think that every other family has all sorts of problems. You could call it destiny, or the situation or this Communist epoch. I don't know how to put it more precisely: there is nowhere where this mystical epoch hasn't interfered and hasn't transformed life. My destiny isn't anything special. There are many more tragic destinies than mine.

References to a shared destiny contrast with narrators' claims to testify and document the past. The propelling force of many narratives derives from a need to tell the truth, to bear witness or testify. Phrases such as 'I was there', or 'I saw it with my own eyes' or 'I lived through it myself' recur, and suggest an indissoluble fusion of narrative with the events narrated. For example, Andrejs begins his narrative thus: 'And this is how it really was'. As a scout Andrejs was sent ahead of his division to search out the amenities of a village. On one occasion he found the village high street piled high with corpses. 'I have seen such sights many times in my life. I have been an eye witness'. Another way of emphasizing the indissolubility of witness and event, of narrator and events narrated is by switching to the present tense. The recurrence of passages narrated in the first tense signals the centrality of those events to the act of witnessing. Under these cicumstances to try to prise open the link between the narrative and the past narrated may appear to threaten the authenticity of the narrator's experience, indeed, it may seem to question the very reality of that past. James Young has described the sources of resistance to the hermeneutic approach to Holocaust literature. He describes:

> The fear that too much attention to the critical method or to the literary construction of texts threatens to supplant not only the literature but the horrible events at the heart of our enquiry.... To concentrate on the poetics of a witness' testimony, for example, over the substance of testimony seems to risk displacing the events under discussion altogether.... The aim here is to explore both the plurality of meanings in the Holocaust these texts generate and the actions that issue from these meanings outside of the texts.
>
> (1988, pp. 3–4)

My own purpose is not unlimited deconstruction for its own sake, but rather an understanding of the narrative devices which enable people to find meaning in the past, and therefore to continue to find meaning in the present. If the past has no meaning then the future will be bleak.

A prerequisite of this search for meaning is the act of witnessing. Felman's discussion of testimony as a dominant literary and cultural genre sets it in the context of a crisis of truth. Starting with its 'routine use in the legal context' she links it to situations where 'historical accuracy is in doubt and when both the truth and its supporting elements are called into question. The legal model of the trial dramatizes, in this way, a contained, and culturally channeled, institutionalized, crisis of truth' (Felman and Laub 1992, p. 6).

In the context of Soviet Latvia there has been a crisis of historical truth. Official history books were never wholly trusted and were revoked for a period at the time of re-establishing independence.[1] Pitted against official versions of the past are the steadily growing numbers of testimonies of witnesses. The constraints of large-scale historical events necessarily produce a certain measure of similarity and repetition. However, testimony resists generalization. It emphasizes the separateness and solitude of each narrator. Its impact is cumulative rather than abstractly generalizeable. Feelings of solitude and responsibility are characteristic of the Latvian narratives. For example, the theme of loneliness is characteristic of Anna's narrative but is particularly noticeable upon her return to Latvia from Siberia. The phrase 'we were left alone' recurs. Anna describes her mother's death as follows:

> Then suddenly in 1978 – it was 8th January, my birthday, and also the day of my father's death – a neighbour phoned me from home that my mother was taken ill. When I got home my mother died in my arms. She had a stroke, it was the third. . . . I was 23 years old and I was left alone in that little room.

In many cases loneliness stems from not wanting to burden others, particularly children, with memories of the past because this may make it more difficult for them to live in the present. In other cases the desire is not to burden others who already have sorrows of their own. Māra Zālīte's poem 'Latvia's Stones' captures just that situation (see p. 102). Zālīte writes how she wanted to put her sorrow under a stone following the advice of the folk song, but found all the stones occupied with other people's sorrows.[2]

Testimonies of horror, violence and destruction arise directly from remembering or bearing witness to the past. Indeed, many narrators said that I was the first person to whom they had recounted the events of their earlier lives. To my question as to whether she had ever shared her experiences with anyone Anna replied:

> I've never spoken to anyone about my personal destiny, I've never recounted it to any one as I have to you. And why haven't I told it to anyone, not even the family? Well firstly, perhaps because it's painful for the Latvian nation, because every family has experienced it and pointlessly to bring attention to the pain, I think is simply tactless and cruel to torture a person and tell them one's problem when they have their own version. And then all these years of Communism. In childhood one was told 'You mustn't speak about it'. And that was so ingrained that I haven't particularly spoken about it. Nor in the circle where I move or at work. At work they only learnt in the last year that I'm counted . . . that I have been politically repressed, that I have been exiled. And so I didn't bother to tell anyone . . . It seemed to me that there wasn't anything to boast about. And I'm telling you now how I experience it, because I haven't talked about it anywhere.

And I'm telling you the way I feel it. A lot is wrong, because all those people who've suffered have either been in exile or been forced to flee abroad. Every person feels it in themselves, some express it in writing, but the majority of people keep it to themselves.

In this sense the narration could be said to constitute as opposed to reconstitute the past. My role in this situation has similarities with the recording and listening to Holocaust testimonies described by Dori Laub: 'The listener, therefore, is a party to the creation of knowledge de novo' (1992, p. 57). And yet in the process of such acts of witnessing the narrator is telling a story which threatens, in the course of the narration, to destroy her identity. One way of protecting against this deconstruction of the self is to embed the testimony of personal history more firmly within a literary structure or plot and to endow it with literary meanings.

These necessary points of literary anchoring are derived primarily from folk songs and folk tales which offer a limited but highly adaptable repertoire of themes. This folk tradition supplies individual narratives with certain recurring ideas. In part, the notion of destiny is a direct response to the feelings of powerlessness and loss of control experienced by narrators. However, the concept also has deep roots within Latvian oral culture. In using the term, narrators are not only responding to their own perceptions of past experience, but also drawing upon widely disseminated literary formulations and meanings. Many *dainas* (Latvian oral poems) are about the workings of destiny and the goddesses of destiny Mára and Laima. They are particularly apposite because like contemporary narrators, they simultaneously exemplify two seemingly contradictory views of destiny. The inevitability and power of destiny is both affirmed and denied. On the one hand, destiny sets a predetermined course to which the successes and failures of an individual's life are attributed. On the other hand, the authors of the *dainas* show a complete disregard and even disdain for their destiny.

For example, the power of destiny is illustrated by the following:

> Although I fled day and night
> I could not escape Laima's will
> I had to live
> As Laima had decided.

> Laima has decided for me
> She hasn't chosen a good life
> Running I wipe the sweat
> Standing the tears.

> Laima chose my life
> While she was standing in a valley
> So that I should drown in tears
> Like a valley under water.

However, other accounts of the role of Laima in individual lives subvert the standard meaning. The songs also issue a strong challenge to fate:

> Sit by the roadside little Laima
> Not in my sledge.
> You have allotted a hard life
> And yet you want an easy ride.

Or:

> Go on foot Laima
> Why do you pile yourself on my cart?
> Let those girls give you a ride
> For whom you have decided an easy life.

> Can I cry away
> A hard life by crying?
> Let Laima herself cry
> Who gave it to me.

Perhaps, the best known verse is the following:

> I sat down and cried
> By the grey stone.
> Let the bad day stay
> By the grey stone.

Thus traditional conceptions of destiny are paradoxical, affirming contradictory meanings. Destiny sets the course of life and yet can be challenged or simply ignored. The author of the last song simply walks away from her evil destiny. These contradictory voices can be heard in the paradoxical construction of contemporary life stories which simultaneously acknowledge the power of history over individual lives and individual luck and ingenuity. These paradoxical meanings facilitate the narrative appropriation of history by individuals. Such conflicting meanings are not of course unique to the Latvian use of destiny. For example, John Gould has shown the way in which destiny has several meanings for Herodotus (1989, p. 74).There is in Herodotus' writing a similar tension between the inevitablity of events and scope for individual action.

The simultaneous use of *liktenis* in two contradictory senses is characteristic of Andrejs' narrative. Andrejs pays lip service to what might be termed the orthodox meaning of *liktenis*: 'We Latvians have had a hard fate', but he then goes on to endow the term with a subversive personal meaning. Andrejs' account is underpinned by a sense of being protected by a good destiny which manifests itself in serendipitous coincidences. In 1943 at the age of 19 Andrejs was conscripted into the Latvian legion of the German army in Jelgava. He was sent to the front near Ostrov. Andrejs was allocated to the fourth division. He, together with a veterinary doctor, were given a horse and sledge and told to find the division:

And I remember, that we both drove in search of the division, but as he'd arrived at the same time as me neither one of us had much idea. I also remember that we had a little sledge ... and as a soldier I took the reins from the veterinary doctor and set off. But after all I'm a townsman and I've only driven a horse during school years as part of the obligatory farmwork[3] and I'm not much of a driver and after the first kilometre he said 'You know what son, give me the reins, I've had more to do with horses.' And this is how it really was. We drove so quickly. It was a dark night. It grew dark quickly. It was January and it got dark quickly. And night came and we were lost in Russia. I also remember that we entered a wood and were driving through the wood. And then I remember, as though it were today, that someone started shouting in Russian '*Stoi, kto, tam*'[4] . . . but they didn't shoot yet. It seems we had crossed over the front and had driven among the Russians. The Russian army was there. But as we had a horse and no engine, there was no noise. There were no weapons and no shooting. I think that the Russian [diminutive] couldn't make out who was driving in the dark and what was being pulled along. And in some way or other the horse had managed to turn itself around and we were back out of the wood, but there was no shooting. We had just driven into the wood and somehow or other we had managed to turn around.

And then something else has stayed in my mind, that we drove into a village and there were these little cardboard cartons of burning fat or oil with a wick like candles. I went inside and it turns out that the infantry of the Latvian legion is stationed there. And I hear someone shouting from a top bunk. 'Andrej! How come you're here?' And I'm perplexed but I see that it is Commander Lobe's son [with whom he had served in Jelgava] and he says: 'Look where we meet! In some little house . . .'

Throughout the narrative there is a sense of looming dangers miraculously circumvented and fortuitous encounters in remote and unlikely places. It bears parallels with Paul Fussell's comparison of the narratives of First World War soldiers with typical narratives of medieval romance and quest:

> The protagonist, first of all, moves forward through successive stages involving 'miracles and dangers' towards a crucial test.... The landscape is 'enchanted', full of 'secret murmurings and whispers'. The setting in which 'perilous encounters' and testing take place is 'fixed and isolated', distinct from the settings of the normal world.
>
> (1976, p. 135)

Andrejs' description of the forest episode bears the hallmarks of medieval romance.

His description of his return to Riga after the bombardment of Rēzekne conveys a similar feeling of surfacing from supernatural terror. In April 1944 Rēzekne in Latgale, the eastern province of Latvia, was bombarded.[5] Andrejs remembers it was Good Friday. He had arrived in Rēzekne with eight or nine soldiers travelling by lorry from Abrene:

On the way we got vodka and chocolate . . . well, all those good things which soldiers at the front were given. And all of us eight or nine boys who were there were in great spirits. And we drank all the way from Abrene to Rēzekne. And when we got out in Rēzekne then we were all staggering. But one was so drunk that he had to be carried. And as we walk along the platform an officer is coming towards us and he asks us 'Is he injured?' And he wants to call the red cross. But we say 'No, no he is drunk.' And then he waved us on, laughed and went on. And then I remember we went into the waiting room of Rēzekne station and we laid out the ones who were more heavily drunk. And this is how it was, the evening train was due to leave for Krustpils at 8.05. And I still had a bit of sense and understanding and was on my feet and after about fifteen minutes I went to look to see if the train was coming or not, because of course I was longing for Riga and my parents and all the others. And I went out to look ... but I couldn't see anything. On the next siding there was an eschelon with petrol barrels. And then I went back into the waiting room and the time was five minutes to eight and then the first explosion was heard. And then all the tipsy boys who had been stretched out, they were all on their feet and they grabbed their rifles and ran out. We couldn't understand what was happening. There weren't any partisans or any others, but it was the bombardment of Rēzekne. And according to my reckoning that was between Maundy Thursday and Good Friday, the huge bombing of Rēzekne in which practically the whole town was burnt. All the little houses were burnt down, many were burning, many had their walls peeled away by the bombs. You could see the room, what was inside. One young couple lay with their arms around each other, they were dead, so that ... it was a terrible sight at that time.... One more thing I remember is the barrels burning. And those barrels they were either pushed or dragged burning and those that had not yet caught fire were unhooked, those railway cisterns, the railway workers worked there ... I don't know, perhaps I hadn't drunk as much, but I remember it very well, it is all in my mind ... And then all those who were drunk, they were all sober as the day. I suppose I drank less because I thought I would get to Riga by the evening. And that's why the drinking interested me less ... I was thinking more of home.

Andrejs, like many other narrators, remembers his youthful past as a time of fearlessness:

Well, actually we became frightened only with the first bombs. We couldn't understand whether it was some organization of partisans that was attacking us or whether there were some explosives.... It was one such moment. And those planes were bombing to their hearts' content. And then we wandered around Rezekne, actually we were warming ourselves by the burning houses. Easter nights are still cold. And that was Latgale of course, so that it was quite far east. And that's where I saw those terrible things, where those people were dead and wounded and so on. And then only the next morning did we have a train to Riga. And then we arrived in Krustpils and I remember a very beautiful journey from Krustpils to Riga. That was the route which I had taken hundreds of times from Koknese. And, approaching Riga the snow was no longer so thick. And I also remember thinking that in Abrene there was −25 degrees of frost and look, a few days later near Riga snow is only to be seen in patches. And when I arrived in Riga women and men were already walking in spring coats and with brimmed hats and there was no sign of our huge fur coats, only we were wearing them. And Easter was approaching.

He arrived in Riga to find that family life was following old traditions:

I remember that my cousin Mirdza's baby son was being christened and my mother telephoned the hairdresser. And everyone wanted me to stay at any cost but I had to catch the train for Berlin ... and so I didn't get to the christening because while everyone else was getting ready for it I was already on the train.

Andrejs draws the contrast between the dangerous and chaotic events in Rēzekne and the reassuring orderliness of family life in Riga. It is surely significant that he remembers that it was Good Friday in Rēzekne and Easter in Riga; winter in Rēzekne and spring in Riga.

A later part of the narrative places Andrejs and his fellow soldiers again on unknown Russian territory. They had nowhere to sleep and the temperature was $-25°$ C. They dug tunnels in the snow and burrowed into them in pairs, two soldiers per tunnel:

> We wrapped up and slept inside. But in reality we slept well and we weren't cold. Only afterwards I thought it over and thought we didn't do right. We got in head first and our feet were outside and perhaps we should have done it the other way round. Because the snow could have trapped us: it was quite heavy. And had we been nearer to the exit we would at least have had our heads out.

However, despite the hazards retrospectively perceived, they were fine. The incident is a further building block in a narrative of lucky escapes.

By the autumn of 1944 Andrejs was in Kurzeme in what has come to be called 'Kurzeme's katls' or the cauldron of Kurzeme. Battles were bloody and in the course of the winter months half the Latvian legion was killed. Andrejs was in charge of munitions which were drawn by horse and cart. His memories throughout the autumn focus on having to make judgements of life and death:

> It was a risky job because the Russians were quite astute. They were looking for ammunition because they knew we wouldn't be able to shoot without it. And that's why we were on the look out. And there have been many times when the horses have drawn the ammunition, but sometimes I've had to send the horses away and not given the ammunition. And then there have been times when the horses have all appeared running from the forest and I've handed out the cannon balls quickly and then the horses have disappeared quickly. It was a risky job and quite dangerous.

Risk and its successful circumvention are emphasized.

By the following spring Andrejs was transferred to an infantry division because the divisions were so depleted by deaths. His narrative contains the following description. He was awaiting orders to fight and knew that he had to cross a mine-covered field. A red rocket would signal advance and green that he was not required:

> It was dark and the soldiers were telling me where I should and shouldn't go because it was a mine field. But you understand, it's dark and a strange place and how should I know where the mines are and where not. But again I had such luck: the green rocket appeared and I didn't have to go.

After the capitulation in May Andrejs wandered around Kurzeme until taken captive by the Soviet army and imprisoned in Ventspils. He remembers that the prison was by the sea and that the distant horizon conjured up thoughts of freedom. He was very hungry:

> There was a terrible famine as always with Russians. They made soup with herbs because they didn't know that they were herbs. They thought they were vegetables. But the soups weren't edible because there was only dill and parsley and even these became fewer and fewer. But the good fortune was that we threw bits of paper with our name and surname across the barrier. The bits of paper were picked up and distributed in Ventspils. And people brought bread because they were allowed to give bread in half loaves. Prisoners were called out by their surnames. They pretended to be relatives and called out our names. And once I too got half a loaf of rye bread. I remember that she was a woman getting on in years. And then it's stuck in my mind how we were taken to the train which was to carry us to Russia. Through all of Ventspils right up to the train there were rows of people and they gave bread. And I was lucky again because I caught a whole loaf. The little soldiers [i.e. Russian soldiers] shouted and shouted at us but they didn't take it away from us. It was a terrible leave-taking. It was an unheard of farewell because they weren't throwing flowers but bread.

After several days travelling and apparent indecision on the part of the authorities as to where the train should go they ended up in Dubrovka near St Petersburg. A month later, in June, Andrejs was moved to Karelia:

> And there were a lot of lice. We were driven to the sauna but the lice stayed regardless. And there was enormous famine and enormous want. And then also there was a great deal of interrogation, both in the barracks and outside. They were looking to see if one had anything which wasn't allowed. I managed to hang on to three photographs, a five lat piece, both my rings, my wedding ring and the one Irēna [his wife] gave me and my cross and chain. The chain around my neck was seen by criminals not by the camp authorities. They pulled it off my neck but they threw the cross back at me. I have it to this day. They saw the rings as well. My fingers were bandaged and the rings were under the bandages. They grabbed hold of me, but I pushed them off and got away. And to my surprise I managed to save the photographs. I put them in my boots under the insoles. Nobody really examined my boots. They did examine whether we'd hidden anything on our bodies and organs, but somehow I managed it. It was my God-given luck.

However, despite his luck conditions were harsh. The shrapnel wounds in his back opened up and were suppurating. Famine made him weak and neither his arms nor his legs would obey him. Timber felling was beyond his strength. His narrative continues:

> Then I had the luck to fall ill with pneumonia. I was helped by a Lithuanian feldscher who put me in category five: they were the ones destined for St Peter. I had pneumonia and nobody took much notice of me. But then there was a young doctor from Uzbekhistan and she saved me. I don't know why she took an interest in me. And then there was a Lithuanian from Joniškis who could speak Latvian and who gave me medicine.

Andrejs recovered from pneumonia but was too weak to walk without a stick. He was passed as unfit and sent home. He attributes his release to his luck at having caught pneumonia and then at having evoked a sympathetic response from strangers. His return coincided with his name day, thus completing the magical protective circle which encompassed his travails.

> And on the 30th I arrived in Riga with the Leningrad train, exactly on my name-day. And it was early morning. And I still remember that I threw the stick on which I'd been leaning under the wheels of the carriage. I thought surely in Riga where I was born and grew up I can walk with my own two feet. And I started to walk along the platform as if with new feet. Probably that has a moral influence on a person. And so I haven't used a stick any more.

After two weeks with his uncle in Riga Andrejs returned home to his parents' summer house in the country south of Riga:

> Because my grandmother lived in Koknese. On 15th December I went to Koknese, that was late in the evening. I got out in Koknese station, I look, the station is bombarded, the culture building is bombarded. And quietly I go along the roads of Koknese, along by the old park. And then I entered it and saw those old alleys of trees, the old pond and then I felt that the old branches were like outstretched hands. That was exactly how I was welcomed. And then I knocked on the door and my grandmother opened the door. And then I lived there for two weeks. She waited for me, she told me everything, how and what and where and after ten days she died. And thanks to her, that she lived so long, the house had been left untouched.

In fact, she died on Christmas day. Had she not lived until Andrejs returned, the house would have been requisitioned. His reception by his old grandmother recalls Homer's story of the hero greeted by his faithful dog Argos.

The structure of Andrejs' account is derived from his 'God-given luck'. It enables him to negotiate the historical events which are the fate of the nation. In many ways his role in the narratives is that of the younger son of legends and stories. Indeed, in real life Andrejs is the youngest of three brothers. His luck enables him to preserve his identity: he preserves his most precious possessions and he is recognized, though with difficulty, on his return home. His paternal uncle greets him with the words: 'Could that possibly be you, Andrejs?'

An extreme example of the individual taking a lead in the moulding of his destiny is provided by Uldis. He was born in 1937 and remembers the war years:

> We were left living in my parents' flat. We were left four rooms. One couldn't speak of a normal life, because life had already left its mark. I was attracted by romance, by adventure. I had a decidedly extrovert psychological disposition. I was active with boxing for many years. I had read a lot of Main, Reed, Jack London. The war ended. In 1945 I participated in the street fighting. In 1941 I saw St Peter's church burning. In 1945 there were deportations. From our family, my godmother, cousin, grandfather, he was a craftsman shoemaker,

suffered. In 1949 my godmother was deported as owner of a large farm. I started experimenting with running away. But there was fear – Siberia. I was twelve years old and it started to interest me. They said that no one returned from there. My mind was preoccupied with Siberia, it was mentioned everywhere. All conversations finished with it. I listened to all that, people at home weren't aware of it. I exchanged Africa and America for Siberia – I had to see it. In 1947 I was thirteen years old. I had no money. I tried to hide on the Moscow train. I was befuddled, I was hungry, my spirit was flattened. I remembered Anna Brigadere, I remembered Sprīdītis.[6] I had taken with me some stamps, and I thought of selling them. In one square where there are two stations I sold them and got food. I hid in a train to Habarovska. I got as far as Molotova. There I was apprehended. I escaped. I got a few towns further, then I was caught before Sverdlovsk and beaten up. Then I realized I couldn't admit to being Latvian. I started to lie and say I was a White Russian or Pole. Then things went easier. I was caught again in Tjumen, I escaped, I got as far as Novosibirsk. I got to Krasnojarsk. It was already evening when I left the city. It was August. About midnight I got a lift in a lorry. We spent the night in a kolhoz. Others climbed onto the stove. I realized that I was in Siberia. That was a euphoric moment. It has stayed with me all my life.

In the morning I was taken as far as Atomanov on the banks of the Yenisei. There they knew what Latvians are. There I encountered for the first time a particular life style. They lived in holes dug in the ground with a roof. They were army *zemnīcas* [dug-outs]. I was looking for my godmother Milda Oseniece. I heard people speaking clearly in Latvian. I introduced myself. I waited for my godmother to return from work. She didn't recognize me. She fainted when I told her I was her brother's son Uldis. When she learnt that I had travelled there alone, she fainted a second time.

Uldis' narrative illustrates the way in which certain unusual individuals can wrest control from the master narrative by actively embracing what others fear and passively submit to. He was, he told me, steeped in the fiction of individual courage and adventure. When the execution of his own life plan is in danger of grinding to a halt he draws inspiration from the plot of a Latvian fairy tale play, *Sprīdītis*.

Indeed, folk tales provide a frequently used structure for narratives. In particular, there is the role of the disinherited son who receives magical help. In the typical folk tale the younger son, stepson or orphan is expelled from home and confronted by superhuman and evil adversaries. By a combination of luck, innate virtue and the acquisition of magical powers the hero is able to overcome evil. In the course of the tale the powerless unwanted son is transformed into a powerful and respected hero. Help is received from unlikely sources, good triumphs over evil. The chronological recitation of journeys through supernatural dangers is superseded by the establishment of timeless virtues and truths.

A personal protective destiny and the extraction of good from seemingly evil circumstances is characteristic of Solveiga's narrative. Her account is of the war and Siberia. In the summer of 1939 she was studying with a school friend in Berlin. The magical consonances between herself and the outside world are established at the start of the narrative: she returned to Riga on a ship called 'Solveiga'. The first year of Soviet occupation did not have a full impact on Solveiga because she was so preoccupied with her music:

> Well, yes, it was a very dark period, very sad, but my life personally was. . . . Well, I was young, maybe I didn't understand all the political situation as my parents did, because you know I was living in a kind of euphoria to do with my music. I was very successful. I had hopes of going to Paris in the autumn. My parents had lived through 1917 and the period after the First World War. They understood more. I only remember that I was very tense and sad.

Her acknowledgement of tension and sadness appears more as a concession to her parents than a true description of her feelings which as she herself acknowledges were euphoric. The family property was confiscated and they were living in a small flat in what used to be their house. Her father was given the job of boiler stoker and was responsible for heating the house. Solveiga continued her studies at the conservatory and upon graduating was given a teaching job. The arrest and deportation were sudden and unexpected:

> Suddenly one morning, I remember it was a Saturday and my class had an exam on that Saturday. I was due to go to work but it was not yet eight and there was a ring at the door. My parents were in the country. We were at home alone with my brother. There was a ring at the door and I went to open it. There were these strange men at the door; three men, one soldier with a long rifle and two others in private clothes. They asked for my parents. We said our parents were not at home. 'Where are they?' Like fools we told them where our parents were to be found, where they had gone. They came in, sat down and told us to get our things ready. 'Why?' We would have to go. 'Go where?' Well, they didn't know exactly, but we would be with our parents. That was alright then if we were going to our parents. And I remember one of the men to this day. If I saw him on the street today I would recognize him. He was a very good person. We heard afterwards that people were simply roped in from their work and made to do it [i.e. arrest others]. He comes up to me and he says take warm clothes. But it was June [June 14th 1941] 'I tell you take warm clothes'. And what did I do? I took a bed sheet and I put all my notes in the sheet, I put all my books in the sheet so that you could scarcely lift it. And I remember that like a complete idiot I took two summer frocks. And I said 'No, this belt doesn't go with the dress'. And he is repeating all the time 'Take some warm clothes'. And I say to him 'Why? There's no need'. And then I took some shoes out, but then I thought 'No, the colour doesn't go with the dress'. And that was all I took. As we go out of the door I remember saying, 'No! Come back all of you and sit down'. And I opened the piano and played Grieg's meditation. The man who had spoken of warm clothes was completely in tears: he sat and cried. I can't forget that. And then I closed the piano and I said, 'Fine we can go now'.

Thus Solveiga puts herself in a position of artistic control in the first stage of her journey towards exile. She finds kindness in unlikely places. At the start of her deportation those sent to arrest her are moved to try and help her.

She and her brother were transported by cattle wagon to Novosibirsk. Ordinarily men and women were separated:

> I don't know by what miracle my brother managed to avoid being called out. He was already eighteen and everyone of that age was called out.

Miraculous chance enables Solveiga to stay with her brother. From the rail terminal in Novosibirsk they were transported further by barge and then transferred to a small boat. They were taken to a church to sleep:

> And as we approach the church, we see mother standing by the door. It was incredible. Of course, we were overjoyed to meet. It was chance or fate, I don't know what. That's how we met and that's how we ended up all three together. About my father, they said he'd been separated and nobody knew where he was or where the men had gone. Later we learnt that he'd been taken to Solkanka, I believe there's a place with that name. It seems he was shot there.[7]

Meanwhile Solveiga and her mother and brother ended up in a village called Baravoja:[8]

> The local inhabitants were very good to us, very understanding and feeling. In so far as they could, they helped us, but they themselves were very poor.

The villagers there were earlier exiles. They had been taken to the forest, given axes and told that whoever managed to build a house before winter would stay alive, but those who didn't would perish. Solveiga's family sold their possessions in return for potatoes. They learnt to make 'Siberian pancakes' from potato peel and water and to drink 'kipetok' – boiling hot water which staves off hunger pangs. Local people showed them various plants in the taiga which they themselves had eaten when they first arrived. Despite such help their physical condition deteriorated and their bodies swelled from famine. Solveiga's mother and brother could not walk and a kind of indifference had overtaken them. Solveiga and a Jewish friend decided that they must escape. One hundred and fifty kilometres away was a small town, Kalpashevo,[9] where work was to be found in exchange for which one got a bread ration card. Solveiga knew that she had to get hold of a ration card. There was one path through the taiga and the two of them took it:

> We walked for about four days and on the way we stopped in various houses. But you know, I must tell you that none of the people where we stopped refused us. They had all suffered terribly themselves but they don't ask 'Where are you from? Where are you going to? Who are you?' They say: 'Here, sleep on the floor'. They give you that kipetok in the morning and evening and say 'Goodbye'.

Again Solveiga is at the mercy of strangers who turn out to be well disposed. Eventually Solveiga and her friend arrived in Kalpashevo and got work in a fish plant:

> During the war there was a terrible labour shortage because the men were all

in the war and the women were all overburdened working 12 to 14 hours a day. They took anyone who could work. On the first day we got a bread card. I remember that we took the bread, 600 grams, and stood by the kiosk and ate all the bread up. We couldn't take it back home. We hadn't seen bread for over a year.

The work was hard:

There were such enormous barges on the river Ob and they were carrying salt. They had constructed a plank from the barge to the bank and then the people who worked there, all women, walked up one plank to the barge and there they filled such sacks with salt and put it on their backs and they went down another plank to the shore, emptied salt and went back up again, you see, that's how it was. Twelve or fourteen hours a day.

Solveiga's long sentence structure mimics the monotony of the remembered work. The harsh conditions affected her health:

And do you know, something bad happened to me. I fell very ill. You asked me at the beginning about illnesses and I couldn't remember straight away what was wrong with me. I suppose my nerves froze because I had nothing to wear, I was without socks.[10] But it was already September and September there is like November with us in Latvia. And, for example, I had no socks and I remember I had an old cotton dressing-gown and I had that and it was all in tatters and I had a little knitted cardigan. And quite simply, I had nothing else. And it seems my nerves froze and such terrible pains started everywhere in my body and those pains were such that I couldn't, I couldn't breathe, I couldn't make a single movement, for example, I learnt to breathe very slowly, not quickly because every movement hurt terribly, I couldn't eat. We had one hour for lunch and we were given such soups. And the Jewish woman poured soup into my mouth with a spoon. I couldn't lift a spoon or put it to my mouth. And I wasn't released from work because I didn't have a temperature and only those who had a temperature were released.

Her survival is due to help from a woman whose social distance she emphasizes by her Jewishness, her distinct ethnicity. Solveiga was anxious for her mother and brother to join her. Her achievement in bringing this about is portrayed as the outcome of a fierce moral battle:

And do you know there was a very nice person there, he was a commandant, but not of this region but that one. And he really was very humane and he really wanted to help me very much, but he had a boss who was a wild beast, a real beast. And he wanted to send me back. And once I was handed over to the militia and put in prison and I was told that I had to wait for the result of what those two would decide. And then I heard – the prison was only a very simple affair of planks nailed together – and I heard those two shouting terribly. What hatred they had or what it was about that I couldn't understand. But after some hours, after a time, the good one, I still remember his name, Litvinovs, he came in to see me very excitedly and he said go quickly, go home and don't show yourself until I tell you.

The outcome of the battle was that the 'wild beast' was removed from his post and Solveiga was eventually able to send for her mother and brother:

> After about a month, they arrived with the last little boat. If they hadn't caught the boat they would have had to stay the winter there and they would not have survived. That is absolutely certain.

And then Solveiga was 'very lucky' again. Her mother became friends with a Russian family who were considered well off by local standards – they had their own house, a cow and hens and it was agreed that Solveiga would go there as a servant. In return, she would get a pail of potatoes a week and half a litre of milk a day. Her brother also got a job in a rubber boot factory in return for a bread ration card. But their luck was not to last, for rumours started that all the men were to be recruited into a labour army and that is what happened. One day all the men, including her brother, were rounded up, put on a barge and taken away:

> It was simply terrible. My mother had no strength and we had to go a long way on foot. It was already late autumn and muddy. Mother stayed at home but I went to see my brother off. And then I remember, I came back from the ship across an open space and I screamed 'I can't stand it'. I thought I would never see my brother again.

And so Solveiga carried on living with her mother until more rumours started that there would be a similar land army for women. However, Solveiga was asked to report to the culture centre where she learnt that a visiting theatre troupe required a pianist. At first she was reluctant to be reminded of the piano and everything she had lost. However she was eventually persuaded. The cold was again a problem. The orchestra pit was dug into the ground; the theatre itself was a disused barrack. Of course, there was no heating. Her legs got frost-bitten and swelled up so that she could not walk or stand. She had to be carried to the piano stool. After a year the theatre transferred to Tomsk and although deportees were not allowed to live where there was a railway terminal Solveiga went with the theatre troupe. It was autumn and her mother was reluctant to go because she had just bought potatoes to last the winter. However, Solveiga was determined to go with or without her mother:

> I said to mother, 'As you wish, either you stay here with the potatoes or you come with me without the potatoes. But I'm going.' I said, 'I'm going, I don't want to stay here.'

And so they left, and in Tomsk were shown to an enormous empty room in a deserted house on the banks of the river Tom. It was late autumn and there was terrible cold. The house was unheated, the room had no furniture except a huge table in the centre. She and her mother both slept on the same table at night. However, their continued stay in Tomsk was under threat because too many exiles had arrived in the city and the military authorities were planning to deport them. Meanwhile Solveiga heard a voice in her sleep saying: 'Go to Riga, go to Riga' and in the morning she got up knowing she would return to Riga. She had befriended a German doctor who admitted her mother to hospital. This meant she was unlikely to be sent back to Kalpashevo and would be given some food. Without passport or documents Solveiga set off across Russia. In Moscow she found she had unknowingly spent the night in the attic of the NKVD headquarters. Unwittingly she had again found shelter in the arms of the enemy. In Volokansk she was given lodgings by a deaf and dumb girl. In the final stage of the jouney she threw herself at the mercy of a locomotive driver:

> I go up to him, I say to him 'I badly need to get to Rēzekne. Help me, I have no money and no ticket'. He looks at me and says, 'Come get in the other side, not from the station side, from the other side of the locomotive'. I got into the locomotive and there is a coal-box. 'Get in the coal box and lie down so no one sees you'. I lay down in the coal and I arrived back in Latvia on that train.

She was scared of people, scared to ask for directions. She had forgotten how to get to her aunt:

> I went to the banks of the Daugava. I'd been there before the war and it hadn't been rebuilt yet. There was an old broken bench there and then my strength ebbed away and I sat down on the bench and howled like a dog.

Eventually she remembered a school friend living nearby. It was early morning and she found her flat and rang the bell:

> She did not recognize me. She said 'What do you want? What are looking for?' And you know when there is a difficult moment, some people don't cry but they have a certain smile. She says that when I suddenly smiled, then she recognized something of me.

Life was hard in Riga. Everyone was scared of Solveiga. It was difficult to find anywhere to stay. The concierge was always on the lookout, watching who came in and out. Solveiga could not stay more than a couple of nights in any one place. However, she managed to get a job as a pianist in a theatre and later as a conductor. However, her stay in Riga lasted barely eighteen months because the NKVD discovered and arrested her. She was stopped on the way to the orchestra offices:

> 'Show me your documents!' 'But I don't have any', I say. 'You know quite well that I don't have any documents'. 'Well, you'll have to come with me then' he says.

Solveiga was tried by the 'troika' (three NKVD members) and sentenced to three years' prison camp. She was sent to a prison camp on the edge of Riga where she had to operate an electrical saw. However, Solveiga made friends with a masseuse who worked in the prison hospital who offered to teach her massage so that she could take over her job:

> I was very lucky in that respect. . . . There was a tiny room next to the consulting room and I was allowed to move in. I was terribly happy because I was alone.

But her happiness was brief. A fellow prisoner was a theatre director and wanted a script of a play. Solveiga wrote to a colleague for it. It arrived with hand-written comments in the margin which were perceived as being anti-Soviet. As a result she was sentenced to exile in the republic of Komi. During her second period of exile Solveiga met her future husband and married. However, shortly after her marriage, her husband was arrested for anti-Soviet talk and sent to Vorkuta. Solveiga was left alone and pregnant. After the birth of her son she was transferred to Novosibirsk. During the long train journey her baby son caught dysentery from the milk which she brought along the way. In Novosibirsk she was taken to hospital. She had no feelings for the baby or, indeed, for anything else:

> I felt that the world was an enormous emptiness. Nothing existed for me. I spoke very little. I didn't know how others felt. I was as though half alive. And the only thing I have is the child. While I was pregnant I didn't have the feeling that I would have a baby, that I would be a mother. When my husband was arrested I didn't want either a child or anything else. I didn't want to live: I wanted to die. And all that time I somehow had no feeling for him. It was a bundle. Yes, I fed it and changed it, but I had no feelings either towards myself or towards him, or towards others, just emptiness. But you know when they told me that the child would not live, it was as though a voice from heaven told me that I had to fight. That child has to live. Only then did I realize that I had a child and that I must not lose him.

Solveiga spent a week walking with the baby wrapped in her husband's fur coat: eighteen hours a day around the hospital grounds. After a week the baby started to take drops of milk:

> You know then very gradually he started to drink drop by drop and today he is 41 years old and big and strong.

When the baby was on the way to recovery they continued their journey. One night they stopped at a station. The soldier accompanying Solveiga took her to the command centre to find somewhere to stay. He called a nurse from a nearby hospital and ordered her to put Solveiga up for the night. Solveiga could see that the woman was unwilling to take her, that she was forced into it. But neither of them had any choice. Solveiga picked up her baby and her suitcase and followed the woman:

> The woman was going at a gallop. We were walking along completely open land some three kilometres, and somewhere in the distance I could see a little light shining. The weight was heavy. I thought I couldn't manage anymore. I thought I would just lie down and freeze, so that there would be peace at last. But that child was so warm and so soft and so nice. And I walk some more and run after that woman. And then we are there at the house. The woman opens the door and we go inside. Suddenly, someone screams, 'Solveiga!' and can you imagine! That woman who took me there is looking at me round-eyed. How come that from the depths of that room someone is calling my name? And it turns out that there was a Latvian woman there who was imprisoned with me in Riga. And as I go inside the light falls on me and she recognizes me.

The light which falls on Solveiga and enables her to be recognized might almost be a spotlight.

Once again a potentially dangerous and threatening situation turns to Solveiga's advantage; an enemy becomes a friend. Solveiga's two periods of exile have left her indifferent to physical deprivations. It is as though her experiences of Siberian exile and imprisonment are perceived as the medium through which her self has been tempered to an indestructible hardness. Her life history is an account of the transformation of self. What she chooses to mention about her girlish self relates to a preoccupation with self: fashion, a musical career and a distancing from the politically menacing situation in Latvia. Illness, described as a freezing of the nerves, is an important turning point. It is similar to Milda's description (see pp. 136–8) of a deadness of the nerves. In both cases nerve death signals the death of an earlier self which has been enmeshed in the physical and social world and the emergence of a new and impermeable self.

Both Andrejs and Solveiga recount their lives as stories. Although they describe suffering and the threat of death the experiences are never presented without a literary frame. Throughout the personal voice seeks and finds support in textuality. The idea of a protective destiny is one of the chief ways of establishing a meaningful connection between an individual life and events in the world at large. It also transforms mere humans into heroes and heroines. It finds magical coincidences and unexpected acts of recognition and in so doing establishes parallels between the physical and the moral world. However, in drawing upon notions of life as destiny, both Andrejs and Solveiga are placing their lives alongside countless other tales of destiny past and present.

Much of Latvian history has been represented as the working out of a cruel destiny. This destiny also plays a part in folk songs. The themes of these songs are widely known. Individuals relate their own lives to these shared themes in several ways. Suffering and the destruction of meaning are often attributed to the very fact of being Latvian. Whether this makes suffering more bearable or a meaningless life more meaningful, might be open to question. But narrators certainly make the connection. Conversely, destiny singles out individual luck, opportunity and resourcefulness. Here, destiny empowers the individual. These reconstructions draw heavily upon literary 'quest' paradigms. Empty and terrifying landscapes are recalled, identity is sustained through recognition, and narratives end in home-comings.

6

THE EXPROPRIATION OF

BIOGRAPHY

'Simple Analysis of a Compound Sentence'

The children buried their companion's
   clothes
Who were they,
Who did the burying?
Children.

Children with white heads – linen,
Children with blue eyes – sky.
But what was the subject of the sentence doing?
Nothing much – burying the clothes.

With innocent hands
And yet – looking at each other
And even into the depths
At their companion without clothes.

In the mud grey fine sand
Steamers were puffing and gulls screeching
Defined as classificatory nouns
Plural nominative.

The description and the adjective
Were knocking around in all the farmsteads
Show me on the wall
Where is the sense.

My darling Anna Lisa
The analysis won't work.
I recommend this sentence to schools
And families in twilit evenings.

(Māris Čaklais)

In Soviet Latvia the control of history extended to the reconstruction of individual lives. The monitoring of personal memory took place through schools. It was both a way of instilling Soviet values and a recognition of the inevitable deficiencies of family histories. Often such lessons were exercises in the art of cultivating ambivalence. For example, one narrator recalled with evident pride his autobiographical description of exile: 'Circumstances forced us to relocate to Siberia'. The bleakly bureaucratic jargon aptly pinpoints some of the tensions of their experience. Many narrators perceived their so-called autobiographies as actively hampering their lives and obstructing their aspirations. The result is that their narratives are given in a passive mode. This chapter looks at the way in which the attribution of a culpable autobiography affects the retelling of lives.

Narratives are an essential tool for the construction of identity. In this process narrators demonstrate their relationship to shared values. Charles Taylor puts this succinctly: 'To ask what a person is, in abstraction from his or her self-interpretations, is to ask a fundamentally misguided question' (1989, p. 34). In the process of this narrative construction, the self aligns itself with various dimensions of history and society. Narrative is thus 'not an optional extra' (ibid., p. 47) it is the only way open to us for endowing our lives with meaning. Narrative displays the diverse ways of constructing identity.

However, although meaning can only be achieved through a narrative reconstruction of lives, its achievement is by no means certain. Some individuals are more successful than others in achieving a narrative identity, as the illness narratives record. Amongst the circumstances which impede success is the attribution of a politically stigmatized identity. The appropriation and reinterpretation of segments of lives render people less able to construct meaningful narratives with themselves at the centre.

In Soviet Latvia political language redefined autobiography, excluding vast expanses of human experience and specifying rigid areas of definitional relevance. This narrowing down of meaning reminds me of Maurice Bloch's description of political oratory in Malagasy: 'Communication becomes like a tunnel which once entered leaves no option for turning either to left or right' (1975, p. 24). In Latvia the term 'autobiography' was used in the sense of a curriculum vitae, a document for public and political consumption. It acquired a metonymic function, in that a document with prescribed areas of interest came to stand for a whole life. It has been argued that metonymy buttresses power, whereas metaphor can be used either to support or to challenge power (Paine 1981, p. 198). Metaphor nearly always involves an element of fantasy or imaginative escape – it expands thought. Metonymy is literal and, if anything, narrows and constricts reality. A large entity is represented by a smaller one. And so it is that a narrow political view of biography comes to dominate and constrain lives and their retelling.

Lessons in the writing of autobiography occupied an important place in the school curriculum in Soviet Latvia and support the metonymic view of autobiography. They were a standard constituent of Latvian language lessons.[1] Children were taught how to write an autobiography and advised on appropriate terminology for describing their family past and circumstances. All job and training applications required the writing of extensive autobiographies. Having family members living in exile or deported to

Siberia made admission to good schools, university and jobs difficult. It also reduced rights to accommodation and in some cases denied access to medical treatment. Latvians make frequent reference to their autobiographies and the term appears frequently in narratives. It does not, however, have quite the meaning associated with the western autobiographical tradition. The interchangeability in conversation of the terms autobiography and biography emphasizes the singularity of Latvian usage. Lessons in writing autobiography, like the proliferation of psychosomatic diagnoses, offered a compromise or safety valve. Both the teaching and medical professions acknowledged the universality of political fault and offered devices for its circumvention. Egīls, one of the letter-writers, summed up the post-war political atmosphere in Latvia with a quotation from Shakespeare, 'Use every man after his desert, and who should 'scape whipping?' (*Hamlet*: Act 2, scene ii, 561).

There is, however, an anti-language which employs metaphor to challenge this restricted view of life. This challenge resides in the notion of life as destiny, which empowers individuals and links them to past values and history. This counter-concept did not, of course, operate in public but was an internalized dialogue.

Meanwhile autobiography was assimilated to official biography. Lienīte's statement, 'I knew that those to whom I was interesting knew much more about me than I could ever know', shifts the source of authority away from herself on to the cheka. Such ideas depart radically from western traditions of autobiography. For example, Georges Gusdorf identifies the cultural preconditions for autobiography as 'a conscious awareness of the singularity of each individual life' (1980, p. 29). This characterization is not altogether appropriate for Communist societies, where an individual's past is of public interest. In this sense, people speak of having a biography or autobiography and distinguish themselves from others who do not have an autobiography. The use of these terms is somewhat akin to the way in which nineteenth-century novelists described a character, particularly a woman, as 'having a past'. Indeed, Latvian narrators also spoke of 'having a past' and the phrase is interchangeable with a biography. In Latvia autobiographies are constructed in public contexts: attributes are assigned which the individual may not wish to receive and others are extracted which she may not wish to reveal. For this reason I have used the term expropriation. Narratives of people singled out in this way are characterized by a difficulty in locating the self within the text. There is a similarity with women's autobiographical writing where the textual self may be decentred, allocated a subsidiary role or made to disappear altogether (see, e.g., Benstock 1986, p. 20). Latvian narratives which record official interest in their lives often display a concomitant decentring of the textual self.

The following narratives illustrate the ways in which the attribution of a past and a biography shapes the telling of one's life history. Both Malvīna's and Jānis' narrative illustrate a decentring of the individual within the text. They provide examples of what Passerini has termed 'the immovable obstacle of the "natural"' (1987, p. 9). Some lives have about them a quality of incompleteness and refuse to be subsumed within literary forms. Jānis' narrative is particularly interesting in that distinct styles of narrative correspond to the two major chronological periodizations. His early life in the pre-Soviet period is recounted in an intensely literary romantic fashion. His description of adolescent longings has unmistakably poetic associations. His post-war, Soviet memories are overburdened with facts to which he is able to give only the most minimal of structures. Words often fail him. Narrative coherence is provided by the themes of 'what might have been' – of regret and loss, but the literary feel of the earlier narrative disappears. Jānis himself acknowledges a turning point and change in his life and attributes this to the dawning of realism.

Jānis situates his own narrative within the context of a narrative of family history and a master narrative of national and world history. He begins with his parents' meeting and their marriage. (Indeed, he has produced a handwritten manuscript of some 300 pages on his family history.) He describes the inauspicious cirumstances of his parents' wedding:

> It took place under an unlucky star. My mother always wanted to show off with her husband. And my father finished the university with some sort of gold medal .[2] However, the gold medal wasn't for finishing the university, but a prize for taking part in some competition. And for that he got a gold medal. And mother was terribly keen for him to take the gold medal with him and to walk about with it during the wedding period so that everybody would see it. And on leaving St Petersburg he had fixed it to his coat and during this very long railway journey he had hung his coat on a hook and gone out himself. And during that time his medal was stolen. And he arrived in Sēlpils [for the wedding] terribly unhappy and mother was unhappy also. And in the end he always blamed mother that she was responsible, because she had said that the medal definitely had to be pinned on. So all in all it was quite a sad business.

This episode from the beginning of his parents' life together is built around three themes which are important for the later narrative, namely loss, regret and futility; the medal is lost but it might not have been if only his mother had not insisted on it being shown off. By prefacing his life history in this way, Jānis' own life takes on some of the unhappy characteristics of his parents' marriage.

At several points in the narrative Jānis situates his life in a broad historical context. For example he links his birth to the Russian Revolution:

> I was born on 1st September, 1917 according to the old calendar . . . no, no . . . how does it work out then?[3] But now I'm counted as being born on 13th October and the revolution took place on 8th and 9th October, according to today's reckoning. So that I have taken part in the revolution.

Jānis also lays claim to a memory from the first year of his life of the proclamation of Latvian independence:

> On 18th November the Latvian government was founded. My father was in the National Theatre for the proclamation. Mother and I were both standing on the bridge on that night, because mother was terrified, she thought that everyone

would either be arrested or shot. . . . They were those sorts of times. And mother had wrapped me in a big shawl and was standing on the bridge. And I remember quite clearly that mother was moaning and groaning and that someone approached us and it was my father and he cuddled me in that shawl.

These early involvements in world and national history serve as a counterbalance to later events which are perceived as crushing and demeaning. At the beginning of his life the intersection of public history with life history gives meaning and weight. In his adult life that same intersection robs it of meaning.

Jānis also remembers the following year, 1919:

Well, that was the year of famine. Things were terribly difficult in Riga and how people survived it all I don't know. All the inhabitants of poorhouses in Riga died.[4] It seems I was saved by an old man who was a teacher . . . he knew a little old woman on Zaķu island who had a goat and every day he would bring me a glass of goat's milk.

Years later Jānis was to meet this teacher unknowingly:

And it's interesting that I met this old gentleman during the year I was working in the laboratory at the school in Riga, after I'd returned from the concentration camp. And he knew who I was, but at that time I didn't know him. . . . And so at that time I couldn't thank him for his kindness. Now he is long since dead, but at that time I was a fool and didn't understand who he was. . . . And so all my life I have remembered that as a tremendous loss that I didn't thank him, because he saved my life with that goat's milk.

The salient feature of this whole episode picked out by memory is again loss. In contrast to Andrejs' narrative in the earlier chapter there is a failure of recognition, which combined with the feelings of regret and loss serve to diminish Jānis' identity.

At the age of seven Jānis was sent to the nursery section of the French Lycée in Riga. However he says:

It was my bad luck that the teachers decided that I was too clever for the nursery and after a few weeks I was transferred to the preparatory class. And that was my misfortune, because they all had one year of French language in nursery and I didn't and I always struggled with deficits in the French language.

A sense of loss again stamps the beginning of his school career. However, the term he uses – 'deficit' – has local associations with the shortcomings of a Soviet economy and suggests that his early school memories are influenced by his later experience of empty shops. That pervasive sense of loss also contrasts with his longings for freedom and broad horizons:

You see the generation in which I grew up, we were such strange people. We were the ancestors of these hippies. We dreamt of sailing around the world in sailing boats or walking. Our ideal was an educated wanderer, who could wander around. It's quite difficult to imagine – you can't even understand it. The world seemed so terribly beautiful that it had to be seen and felt. Not just to travel through by train. But one had to sit on the cliff edge with feet dangling over. And one had to sit like that watching for many hours. Those feelings were indescribable. That's what we were like in those days.... Here in Latvia, we speak of a fascist dictatorship, but it wasn't like that. But there were all kinds of rules . . . you weren't allowed to leave a plough on the field, in case it rusted. All the land had to be worked.... And at that time . . . to young people like us . . . we thought 'who can order me to put away a plough, I can do as I like'. Or if we had to go to work, 'Who can order me to go to work?' In the west one can sleep under a bridge and nobody.... You know, it was to an extent a kind of childishness, but the feeling was strange. The west seemed very beguiling. At that time Latvia seemed conventional and restricting.

Jānis summarizes it as a longing for freedom:

Those were my dreams about a perfect freedom, to travel about.... We were all educated, all poets. In the context of that time we were an educated generation, but so very childish and with unrealistic ideas. And I emphasize that it was only like that in the city and only in advantaged circles.... Take, for example, the madness with boats. There weren't a lot of people who could afford it. You understand, finding yourself in a boat on an expanse of water, that created a wonderful illusion of freedom. In that boat you were in a separate world. Round about was openness, there was no contact with anyone. It's impossible to describe. But at that time I felt it deeply and understood. And it was all connected with what I'd read in childhood of Jack London's travels among the islands of the Pacific Ocean, it was a kind of romance. We weren't really aware of what we wanted, we just longed for something.

This fluent passage of narrative is deeply imbued with literary qualities. His description of adolescent longing reminds me of Tennyson's poem 'Ulysses', although Jānis may not have read it:

> Yet all experience is an arch wherethro'
> Gleams that untravelled world, whose margin fades
> For ever and for ever when I move.

These longings for freedom serve to heighten the contrast with a progressive erosion of freedom, the loss of valued goals and aspirations and even the loss of his former self. There is one brief echo of these longings when Jānis refers to the beauty and fullness of the summer as his train travels through Lithuania on the way to the labour camp. He wants to throw himself from the train but resists the temptation:

And after the war when there was the flight from the bolsheviks and all that.... Then, I returned a completely different person.

Jānis dates the changes from 1941 and the invasion of the Russians:

Things were very low and rough. A bottomless pit appeared: all sorts of scum from prisons and the like.

His brother Pēteris was wanted by the secret police:

Pēteris began to hide in the autumn of 1940, that's when they started to look for him. He lived through the whole winter hiding and they only captured him in May. If he had managed to hide one more month, he would not have been taken.[5] They said that he had belonged to some organization involved in anti-state activities. The papers are with Andrejs. But I never heard anything like that from him. Just before Christmas I visited him in Vidzeme and during that night we talked about everything and then I asked him – 'Why you? There must be some reason?' And he said he didn't understand himself why he was being hunted. And I don't want to believe that he wanted to hide things from me. So that whole business was simply framed on him.

Jānis produced a letter from his brother dated March 10th 1941 which echoes his own yearnings for the freedom of unknown wilds. It addresses Jānis in an anglicized version of his name which is then transliterated back into Latvian:

Džounij! [Johnnie] I believe that during the war neither you nor I will disappear from the face of the earth.... But what if that weren't so? Even if the last fragment of consciousness were ready to leave my battered body, I'm afraid that even then, I would say, that that can't be right, you're joking, I still have so much to see. I have to cross huge territories with Džounij, the horizons which I've not yet reached are beckoning and inviting me. No, I can't go because who will be Džounij's loyal companion in these great adventures? Only me! And Džounij mustn't disappear because he has a contract with me which is written with the warmth of my heart and my enthusiasm, and it has stamped itself forever on my mind. Džounij, without life you can't reach the horizons! The far distances are calling.

Jānis' brother was twenty years old at the time of writing that letter, by May he had been arrested and shortly after that, at an unknown date, he was killed:

He was twenty years old. He was born in 1921. He had the most promise of all of us. He had a great deal of ability and he would have been the cleverest of us all.

The contrast is again between what might have been and what was, between unlimited potential and constraint. Jānis sees his death as partly related to the family's inability to grasp the complete irregularity and arbitrariness of the system:

You understand, we were so terribly naive, we thought there were some sort of rules and that those rules were obeyed.... He had to appear for military service. And so that they shouldn't search for him at home, he registered in some other place and the next time somewhere else. He himself couldn't understand why he was pursued. He had done nothing, had not been part of any organization, so that nothing could be pinned on him. And if he didn't do military service and didn't sort that out, then he was threatened with twelve years [imprisonment]. At that time we were counted as part of the Red Army, there was a territorial corps. [In other words, the family weighed up the relative risks of being caught for evasion of military service and of being accused of anti-Soviet talk and decided the former would carry a heavier penalty.] At the time we had such a naive view, twelve years seemed such a terribly long time.... And what possible consequences might there be if a person had said something wrong? What possible punishment might there be? A year or two of corrective education? But you see, the consequences were much more terrible than those of avoiding military service. Had we been as wise as we are now, then the whole matter would have been quite different. We didn't think that they were such beasts. We thought there was some order.... And at that time, we naively thought that everything has gone well so far, we've been lucky in everything and that even now nothing bad will happen.

Jānis links his earlier account of loss of freedom with the irregularity and unpredictability of life under Soviet occupation. Pēteris' death led to despair:

A terrible hopelessness settled on our family. We all felt totally battered.

Jānis occupies an active and central position in the text only when he is recounting his adolescent yearnings. Elsewhere effort and activity meet with failure. For example, Jānis recounts the following episode from the time when he was taken a Soviet prisoner of war:

There wasn't really anywhere to sleep and for two nights we simply slept on a table. I had a friend Zanders who had been guarding his bag all night long. But it was stolen nevertheless. I didn't have anything.

Jānis' narrative is about the way in which external events constrain and narrow down his life. This theme becomes more prominent in the post-war narrative. The restrictive force of having a past and a biography stamps his account of life in Soviet Latvia:

And then we were loaded into the wagons and we started the journey to the east. And I remember it was about 2nd or 3rd June we drove through Lithuania and it was full summer and beautiful and I so much wanted to throw myself out of the wagon doors and run into the forest. But we were very closely guarded there, they were sitting there with their guns and so on. And they were Lithuanians and a foreign country and I couldn't understand. If we'd been travelling through Latvia, then perhaps I could have risked it . . . and so on. But for example Indulis our neighbour pulled up the floorboards of the wagon, he got out and fell on the railway line and escaped you see. He escaped in Russia. And in Russia he had passed as a German, at first he had wandered about, but when he was arrested he had said he was German. And then he lived a year or so in a concentration camp for Germans. And then there was questioning, 'Who are you?' And he said he was a repatriate, that he was a German from Riga. But they had examined everything so carefully and something didn't match, you see. He couldn't be one of them. Because they knew every street – every street in which you've lived. And then he was taken to Riga and in Riga he was kept in the cheka. And then in the end he got consumption, you see. And then he had reckoned that there was no point, that he was going to die anyway. Then he had started to inform them that he was a Latvian after all. That he is a Latvian and that he has relatives here in Latvia. But nobody believed him. Because with the Russians, with the cheka it's like this – you're not believed at all. If you say something that is true, then you're definitely not believed. You must first tell some lies [laughing] and only then can you admit the truth. Otherwise you won't get to the truth. And so it was that he wasn't listened to at first, perhaps he was even beaten or something. And only later, they pricked up their ears and he was confronted with his wife and then when they discovered that he really was what he claimed he was sentenced to twenty-five years and he spent twelve years in Karaganda, in Kazakhia. That was our Indulis, our neighbour. So, all these things are interesting.

So I lived one year in Moscow from June to August of the next year and then I was released. Because I had got so lean, I was so worn down that I actually threatened to die. And then I . . . we, people who were completely worn down and who hadn't managed to die on the spot, then they were set free because they were good for nothing, not suitable for work. And I too was released. But shortly after that, a few weeks after I was released the concentration camp was disbanded, they turned it into a military construction camp [Russian – *strojbat*]. It was a very good thing that it was in Moscow. Because after all they were concerned that epidemics shouldn't spread to the civilian population.

Altogether, I was completely shattered. I had a complete depression. For example, a human being should be interested in his environment, in events, but I was in such a depression that everything was the same to me. I just thought that perhaps I might survive, perhaps I might live until . . . that there might be some miracle. I was in an utterly hopeless condition. But I was helped by the fact that I met one of my schoolfriends, a former schoolfriend, actually he was Andrejs' schoolfriend. There was a Dr Vētra, and he was Dr Vētra's son, a well-known lung doctor in Latvia. He had either studied or started studying medicine and he was a medical auxiliary in the legion and when he was taken prisoner he also got to the doctors and in the concentration camp he served as a medical auxiliary. And he . . . we got to know each other . . . he thought he was meeting Andrejs, but actually he was meeting someone else. And so we continued the acquaintance and he helped me a bit. And he also helped me to get to rehabilitation, when I was completely worn down he helped me to get to the group where the sick were taken in. And so later I got sent home as well.

Interestingly, Jānis mentions another non-recognition.

There were men who had been sent from Mordavia in 1941. They had already been hanging on to life for years. They died in rows. It was terrible . . . I was plagued with all sorts of ulcers [pointing to his legs]. You see . . . all over here. And my ankles hurt terribly I couldn't walk. I was completely emaciated, only bones were left. When you looked at people in the sauna, then you saw they had no bottom, only two large bones. We were completely worn down and, of course, I had no strength. But above all, there was the terrible indifference because everything had become indifferent. And so. . . . [Sighs] And so and so it was sad and that's what I can tell you. It was terrible. And most of all the famine. The famine and the cold. Even so I had managed to grab some clothes. It was summertime when we retreated to Königsberg that was in March I put on several layers of clothes – two pairs of trousers, I had a service jacket and dungarees and I had a coat. But lots of boys went virtually in their shirt sleeves. In the winter they froze terribly. They were terribly frozen, those poor sods. At least I had a few clothes underneath, I even had an old knitted jumper which

I'd managed to save and which they didn't take away. Although they did list everything and it was considered state property [laughing] but at least it stayed with me. Well, some of it was stolen. My blanket was stolen in the camp. But that's by the way, that was usual there. There was a famine and we were very cold – those were the main problems.

We had these kinds of dug-outs (*zemnīcas*). They were half dug in the ground. We ourselves built them during the summer. They were dug in the ground. Then at ground level there were windows to let the air in. There was a roof and the roof was covered with clay. The water would seep through in the spring. Every spring the water would penetrate. The clay didn't stop it. Inside there was a stove. There were two-tiered beds. We nailed together planks to make beds and that's where we slept. We built them ourselves.... It was all rather sad. But we weren't in a prison camp, it was much worse there. We were counted as being 'examined by the state'.... State examination ... state examination. We would shout, 'how long are we going to be examined?' That's how it was.

Jānis goes on to describe others who were sent to prison camps:

I met them after the war. Then they told me how they'd got on. They were sentenced to five years, one was Velands the other Ozols. Velands' father was a critic or some sort of artist. I remember he lived in Andreja Pumpura street and I met him on the street and he recounted how they needed workers and everyone was sentenced to five years. So altogether there were no rules. Whatever rule anyone thought up or needed was implemented. Over these years a lot has appeared in our literature, in newspapers and so on. For example, how the sentencing took place. Three party members, they are the judges. They decide whether to shoot someone or not, whether it should be ten years or twenty-five years. There's no so to speak.... We have here a terrible old bolshevik called Krustiņsone who was very famous and very industrious. She has written about it herself – how she participated in the so-called troikas. How they sentenced people according to a Communist conscience. You can imagine what the Communist conscience is like. Oh dear! It's all pathological. Whatever else, there should at least be some rules. [Sighs] I don't know.... It's even sadder than for a serf. I don't know, it's just mad how it's been. Only it's passed over and it's even been partly forgotten and somehow it's all behind one and it seems that it hasn't been so terrible.... But I don't know.... Altogether they are nightmares ... simply nightmares. They are nightmares. Just think that people have lived for forty years, however they've lived, whether they've had to work or not, but they've at least had some human rights and so on and so on. They've been able to do something....We ... for example, surely we could have started something up if we'd had the right to acquire even the smallest piece of land, if we could have grown something so that we could sell it and earn a bit of money. Or if we'd had the possibility of opening some little undertaking, even if it was a cobbler's workshop or something so that we could earn something. But all that was forbidden, just so that you wouldn't succeed in being better off than a serf. You had to cling on to life and be calm and quiet and work and not utter a squeak.... Oh, that's a devil's ... its devilish, devilish ... thinking. That's what it was. It's not worth talking about ... those things. One has to get hold of the literature, the facts such as they've appeared and then afterwards one can make judgements about the madness of the regime, no not the madness but the . . . the inhumanity.

Jānis' imprisonment left him demoralized:

You see it happened this way, that I was sacked from work here and for three years I knocked around being neither this nor that. I knocked around and during those years I was, how shall I put it so *misérable* [Jānis uses the French word] . . . so pitiable that I didn't dare to meet with people and maintain a friendship. I had changed when I came back home from military service. When I came home from military service in the autumn of 1941, from all those concentration camps . . . no, no from all that forest brother business and so then I was a completely different person. During the German period then I was neither a dreamer nor a . . . what should I call it? nor a . . . words fail me. In old age words fail, the right expressions fail. But in other words I became much more realistic and closer to everyday life. All that dreaming and all those things finished at that time. Not that they were necessarily good, but that's what life was like.

I was promised work. But the work could only be given if I was registered in Riga. If I'm not registered I can't get work. And so I waited for the work and the registration. And, and and it turned out to be very peculiar. One could be registered if one had work and one was taken on to work if one was registered. It was neither one thing nor the other.

Eventually Jānis managed to get a job as a laboratory assistant for a year from 1946 to 1947. But he soon found life in Riga intolerable:

But I began to hate Riga with all the Russians and so on and all the goings on. It was terrible there. A Russian tried to insinuate himself into my flat. He'd got some order and he wanted to put me out and so on. It was all quite terrible. And I got so fed up with life in Riga and then bread was still on coupons and that was the only thing you could get on coupons. You couldn't get anything else. For example, you were entitled to fish, you were entitled to cooking oil or some such. The whole month they weren't in the shops. On the last day, for example, on 30th or 29th they appeared. Then there were queues, you understand, so terrible. But I had to go to work. I had no time to stand in the queues. In practice one never got anything. It was an admirable state policy. Life was so horrible there and then a vacancy occurred in the school in Koknese. Andrejs had already got a job there. There was a . . . was it Pumpuriņš the head teacher? . . . And so I said there is a vacancy and I would like the job. Would he be willing to accept me. And I said, I said that, that that – I have a past, that I've been in the legion and so on. But then he said quite sensibly that they needed educated people in the country too. I was a graduate. And he accepted me at that time. So in 1947–48 I started to work in Koknese's primary school. Now it's all under water. It's been flooded.[6] I worked there for four years. And then there were all sorts of troubles. The so-called attestation took place. And then anyone who had any sort of past was sifted out.[7] And then my brother and I we were both sacked. We were both sacked and then the same situation arose that no work could be found in Koknese. Nothing was going on here, nothing was being built, there were no organizations where one could work. And then again I was in a trap. I didn't want to leave Koknese. Koknese has always been very dear to me. And I've always worked in the garden. I was sorry to abandon it. But then there was a doctor here whom I knew and he said, 'You know I have a vacancy, a vacancy for a disinfector. The wages are pitiable but the work isn't particularly hard'. I had nothing else so I took the disinfector job. Whenever there was any infectious illness one had to go to the house and disinfect it. That wasn't hard. But he was quite smart, he used me for all sorts of other jobs. For injections, practically all nursing jobs he made me do. At first I didn't even realize but he persuaded me with his politeness. And that's how I sat out those three years.

Like Jānis, Malvīna also sees herself as a victim. Her narrative contains episodes in which she herself adopts an entirely passive role. The sense of herself as a purposive human being disappears from the narrative text. Here is Malvīna describing the deportations from Pāvilosta in 1949:

They didn't deport many from Pāvilosta. Only from that little house on the corner on the way to Lielie. Simple labourers lived there. There was a little girl and a husband and wife. And people knew already that there would be deportations. I too packed a little bag and put my clothes in. I myself was a member of the Home Guard.[8] In the so-called Ulmanis period all the men who went to sea had to be members of the home guard. And the wives also had to be members. But I didn't get as far as complete membership. I saw that some of the home guards were, how shall I put it? . . . Time wasters, they would meet somewhere, go on excursions and so on. That played a part, because, of course, in my biography I had to write, 'three months in the home guard'. Then I took my little boy by the hand and went and waited. A lieutenant was standing there. I say to him, 'I know it's my turn', I could speak Russian of course. He said, 'Make sure you clear off, mind you don't get taken along!' Then they rounded them up. I don't even know how many people they took.

The knowledge that she has a biography robs Malvīna's account of a sense of agency and purpose. Malvīna assumes a passive role in her own life. Recollections of her earlier life are set in a similar mould:

My parents were caretakers in Aizpute, and then they came to Pāvilosta. We had this house before the First World War. Father had bought it. He had thought to go to sea but at that time there were no ships only little boats. We went with little boats . . . there was no other way. Then he went back to Aizpute. Then we fled to Russia. Then the Russians came in, there was all sorts of trouble, when he fled from Aizpute.[9] He worked in the forest and then he distributed English bibles around shops. There was an organization like that. At that time one didn't walk, one took them by horse. Cartloads of them around the shops. That's how he earned money. Then in the end Lenin got to power and there was famine. It was terrible. Little coupons were given out. We made stock from horses feet, all the bread that was given had mould and it was ground together with pine bark, that's what the bread was like. Altogether, it was difficult with food. Then the women, German women, went in huge crowds on demonstrations. All the shops where there was a German name. Then we saw that there was no air, no sustenance and we started to look for a train. We travelled a whole month in a cattle wagon. People were born, people died. They were buried right there by the track in the snow. And on Christmas eve [1920] we returned home.

In Latvia it was quite peaceful. You could say people were quite well off. The first people to give us help were Jews. They provided us with potatoes and bread straight away. In Liepāja we had to be in quarantine, there were barracks there. There were these store buildings where we were put, because many were ill and many had lice. For a whole month we had travelled in a cattle wagon, we slept high up and it was a good thing it was high because there was no air. There was just one small stove for the whole wagon. That's where we cooked each one in turn. Then we returned again to Aizpute and father became a caretaker.

I finished school in 1926 and then I came here. I went to peel timber props. Timber for England.[10] It was for the coalmines in England. They use it for props. It's called prop timber. And it had to be peeled so that not a single branch was left. So that when you ran your hand over it, it didn't catch on anything. Over towards the park, you know, when you drive that way there's a big chimney, all that yard was full of timber. Then both father and I would go. How much could I do as a young girl? The living was poor. We took everything on loan. They promised us that as soon as they got paid they would give us what was owing. At long last a Jew came who had financed it all and said the ship has sunk. Well what? We were left grounded.

It was very sad because for the most part we ate potatoes, cod and bread. Just after we returned from Russia, then we ate grains and gruel, we made a kind of thin soup. Then, of course, cod has liver inside, so-called '*lielmi*' and we melted that and added it to the soup, we grated potatoes and made pancakes from that. We got by like that. Milk could rarely be had. There were no pastures, no cows, nothing. Later father went to sea at times, with a little boat. At that time prices were very low. It wasn't as though the factories would buy the fish. There were private buyers but they would drive the prices so low that really there was nowhere to sell. But we would smoke the cod and dry them in the sun and then things were better.

One couldn't get work anywhere else round about. Because there aren't any rich farmers in these parts. It's quite sad really. When I went, when I went in the summer, then I got to know better off people, where the farmers were better off. Then I went and weeded sugar beets. I hoed everything. One sister fled to Germany first, and then from Germany to Sweden. The eldest sister stayed in Aizpute. She returned from Russia – there was no happiness there. They've both died now. Each in turn, first the eldest, then the younger and me I'm eighty-three years old, I'm left for the time being.

Her father's attempt to assert himself resulted in his loss of employment:

In truth he fell out with the Jews that's why he couldn't work. The bosses, well, let's call them simply Jews, they wanted me as a schoolgirl to kiss their hand every morning on the way to school. My father was a bit of a social democrat as we would now say, or something in that line. Father said . . . I didn't want to kiss their hand, every morning I had to kiss their hand. . . . Father said, 'No, my daughter won't kiss their hands. If she's given a present then that's different, but otherwise not'. Every time one met there was hand kissing. And with that he was given notice. And then he came to live here.

We were given half a hectare of land. At that time one could live well with half a hectare. At least we had enough to eat. Clothes had to be patched, but we had enough bread. We sowed carrots, sugar beet, everything. Then we could recover, so to speak. Then we asked for a larger piece of land [diminutive *zemīte*], father got an old horse, twenty-six years old. Then we kept him, and took him grazing wherever there was grass to fatten him up. Father would travel about, sometimes he would take fish to Cīrava and Tērgaļi. And then the farmer's wife would give him a loaf of bread or some butter. Then we could manage quite well. Later he put in a claim for land over by Grīni. The government officials met, the so-called elders of the parish [Latvian – *pagasts*], they met and interrogated father. I was with him precisely at that time. 'Well how do things stand? You have a horse, you have a cart, you have a plough'. We had got everything. We'd made a harrow, we made what we could ourselves. 'And after all you have a cow, then you can't have the land'. Instead the land was granted to an army officer.[11] And so we didn't move. It was difficult here, nothing grew. We were right on the dunes. Further inland things grow well, but here it was difficult, terrible.

The struggle to extract a living from unyielding and inauspicious conditions continued after Malvina's marriage:

I got married in 1932 and we bought a motor boat on loan. And then we bought nets. Everything was on loan. Every month we had to go to Liepāja and pay in Liepāja because the nets all came from Liepāja. Then another government came, the Communists came to power, they simply took everything away and left us the debts. We paid the debts only they don't give us anything back. Our boat was the best, it was the biggest boat, it had a Swedish motor.

It is interesting that Malvīna refers to the Soviet occupation of Latvia as yet another government. Her reference accentuates the polarity which she experiences between her own powerlessness and the global force of historical events. Her choice of words suggests that her expectations of any government are low. During the Soviet period, Malvīna finished a trawling course:

They taught us fishing techniques, about ichthyology. About catching fish and nets. How to repair nets. when I'd finished that course, that was in 1957, I took a mastercourse in trawling in Liepāja. That's when you catch fish the whole time. The nets were big. There were forty-five people on the trawling course and I was the only female. Yes, but when there are so many men then one woman is very much respected. And I worked hard, I wanted to complete the course and go to sea. When the course was finished it was time to get the documents so that I could go to sea, I had to write my biography as usual. Where were my relatives – my sister was in Sweden. Well then I wasn't allowed to sail to Sweden and so one woman was saved from drowning. Well, they simply didn't give me permission. Then my husband had his licence taken away. I have a son and his licence was taken away because my sister is in Sweden.

Then everyone was left without work. And then I was given the job of a net supervisor. There was a workshop next to the museum if you've been there. Now it's on the other side. And then things went well really well. Then I got a pension in 1976. I was lucky. At that time women got a pension from sixty, now it's from sixty-seven. But then when I was counted as a mechanic with the trawler, I was fifty-five. I was very lucky, I got a pension and then one could afford this and that, to mend the house a bit where it was necessary and to get some bits of furniture. But altogether my life has been so complicated, because my husband when his licence to go to sea was taken away, he started to drink terribly. Wherever he could get hold of it and he would carry things away from the house. And his friends would entertain him because of his sorrow. Then he sailed to Saulkrasti, in the bay of Riga to fish there and for a time I went with him to sea. You didn't need a licence for that. Then a ship went down. A day trawler overturned and they drowned. We got back and after that wives weren't allowed to go to sea.

Malvīna goes on to talk about why she stayed in Latvia:

Perhaps, I would have gone to Sweden but my mother was old and sickly, father had already died. I couldn't leave her alone to die. And so I stayed. I can't say that I've regretted it. Despite everything we survived. The only happiness was when I had work. This year everything has been so dry, everything has burnt out, the whole garden, not a single blade of grass is left. Now when it rains everything grows at a fantastic rate. I had cherries, I picked them, stoned them and couldn't think of what to cook any more. I could have offered you some. It's possible to manage. Of course, my pension is too small, unfair after so many years work. It should be more. We keep hoping. This new government is promising us more all the time. When they promise one feels a little better. But with promises one can't go far, because there's no money. [Malvīna uses the diminutive of money – *naudiņa*.]

Again, Malvīna refers to the restoration of independence as a new government, not a new regime, emphasizing again the indifferent effect that any political changes might have on a life such as hers.

And so it is that these narratives do not affirm the construction of an autobiographical self, rooted in and growing from a savoured past; instead, they record the dispersal, even at times the threatened disintegration, of the self as it falls victim to an alien system. The autobiography which should construct identity is filched from the grasp, and becomes at once a sign of and an element in a process of moral and personal impoverishment.

In the cases recorded in this chapter persistent political intrusion and the condemnation of their lives make it difficult for people to construct a personal past in an active autobiographical voice. Where narrators see their lives as entirely shaped by external circumstances and themselves as victims, the past is recorded as a series of events passively undergone. However, this passive mode, where individual lives are engulfed by historical events, has its own distinctive force, even though it does not rely on conventional structures of story telling. The overlap of the individual and the political erases the active voice, but it also seems, paradoxically, to isolate the narrator from the cultural resources upon which other, more optimistic, narratives draw. In this sense, it is true that violence thins cultures: political violence and oppression prevent the individual construction of a cultural world.

7

THE LIVED AND THE
REMEMBERED FOREST

> I want for nothing
> Living on the edge of the big forest
> I have five stags for ploughing
> And six deer for harrowing.
>
> Dark, dark are the woods,
> Dark in the daytime, dark at night,
> How could they not be dark –
> When there are only pines, only firs?
> (Latvian folk song)

> They left their homes empty and always sought dark forest hiding places, but even so they couldn't escape them; because they pursued them all the time through the forests, they captured them, murdered some and took others prisoner to their own country and they took all their property away from them. The Russians also fled through the forests and villages from the face of the Lithuanians, even when there were few of them, as a hare flees from the hunter and the Livonians and the Letts had become as food and sustenance for the Lithuanians and like sheep without a shepherd in the mouth of the wolf.
> (Heinrici Chronicon, 1225–1227, 1993, p. 128)

Latvian forests provided a physical refuge for many in the post-war decade. Their importance for personal memory, however, lies as much in their contribution to moral as to physical survival. Stories of forest life provide a moral structure to lives and enable others to achieve a sense of agency.

There is a long tradition which links the idea of the forest with refuge. Since the beginning of the century Latvian forests have provided shelter for political refugees. The term forest brothers (*meža braļi*) first came into use after the 1905 revolution when large numbers of men, particularly schoolteachers, took to the forests. However, the idea of the forest as refuge does not derive solely from historical association. The term forest brothers suggests that this notion of refuge derives from a complex of folkloric, literary and popular ideas related to the pastoral idyll. This interpretation is borne out by the kinds of narratives which former forest brothers (and sisters) gave.

Towards the end of the Second World War large numbers of men and lesser numbers of women sought refuge in the forests. Estimates put the peak number of guerrilla fighters at between 10,000 and 15,000 in Latvia and at 170,000 for the Baltic States as a whole (Misiunas and Taagepera 1993, p. 83; Plakans 1995, p. 155). During the post-war years the extermination of the forest brothers was a major political goal of the Soviet authorities, and, indeed, by the early 1950s most groups had been disbanded either through death or imprisonment. (The term forest brothers was used in all three Baltic countries.) [1]

I obtained accounts of forest life from twelve former forest brothers, five of them women. All of them had entered the forest because they perceived their lives to be endangered, although for some of them anti-Soviet resistance eventually came to assume equal importance. Narratives of forest life have certain features in common. They are structured around two interrelated themes. These can be broadly described as pastoral and adventure themes and both contrast with the bleak recollection of uncertainty, fear and famine which make an appearance in all forest narratives.

My identification of the pastoral theme in Latvian forest narratives is particularly indebted to Mikhail Bakhtin and his concepts of the idyllic chronotope (1992, p. 224–236) and the adventure chronotope (ibid., pp. 86–110). Bakhtin defines chronotope ('time space') in terms of:

> the intrinsic connectedness of temporal and spatial relationships that are expressed in literature.... In the literary artistic chronotope spatial and temporal indicators are fused into one carefully thought-out, concrete whole. Time as it were thickens, takes on flesh, becomes artistically visible, likewise space becomes charged and responsive to the movements of time, plot and history. The intersection of axes and fusion of indicators characterizes the artistic chronotope.... It can even be said that it is precisely the chronotope that defines genre and generic distinctions, for in literature the primary category in the chronotope is time. The chronotope as a formally constitutive category determines to a significant degree the image of man in literature as well. The image of man is always intrinsically chronotopic.
>
> (ibid., pp. 84–85)

For Bakhtin then time and space axes and the values which surround them provide the most important criteria for categorizing the novel. Chronotopes pervade the telling of the story, the presentation of character and event and the nature of the interrelationships between the elements which make up the novel. Although Bakhtin's theory is applied specifically to the novel, the idea of the chronotope also illuminates oral narratives.

Narratives of forest life blend personal memories of hardship with literary images of the forest. Forest narratives must be read bearing in mind Bakhtin's reminder of the partisan nature of language: 'Language is not a neutral medium that passes freely and easily into the private property of the speaker's intentions; it is populated – overpopulated – with the intentions of others' (ibid., p. 294). Latvian forests resonate with folkloric and literary associations. The forest figured in all primary school textbooks and formed part of every child's basic education. The forest forms an important part of a pastoral vision of the universe, which may also include the farmstead, family and childhood. Bakhtin characterizes the idyllic chronotope as consisting:

> in the special relationship that time has to space in the idyll: an organic fastening-down, a grafting of life and its events to a place, to a familiar territory with all its nooks and crannies, its familiar mountains, valleys, fields, rivers and forests, and one's own home......
> This unity of place in the life of generations weakens and renders less distinct all the temporal boundaries between individual lives and between various phases of one and the same life. The unity of place brings together and even fuses the cradle and the grave (the same little corner, the same earth), and brings together as well childhood and old age (the same grove, stream, the same lime trees, the same house), the life of the various generations who had also lived in that same place, under the same conditions, and who had seen the same things. This blurring of all the temporal boundaries made possible by a unity of place also contributes in an essential way to the creation of the cyclic rhythmicalness of time so characteristic of the idyll.
>
> (ibid., p. 225)

The specificity of place and the cyclical rhythm of time are important in Latvian narratives. Beyond these, however, two other defining characteristics of the pastoral tradition appear: these are nostalgia for the past and a polarization of the moral universe. Focus on the past is particularly important as a structuring device. Laurence Lerner makes this point with regard to nostalgia: 'Any emotion can provide the impulse of a lyric poem; but nostalgia can provide its structure as well. For nostalgia posits two different times, a present and a longed for past, and on this contrast a poem can be built' (1972, p. 44). We might add that this temporal contrast also offers a structure for narrative accounts, as the regular appeal to childhood memories shows. However, far more important is the underlying moral contrast, which manifests itself in a number of ways. Although the most common literary form of contrast may be between pastoral and urban life, the underlying message is a simple moral one. Renato Poggioli points out:

> The literary shepherd may still be a 'witness' in the ancient meaning of the term. The testimony he bears is simply that it is easier to reach moral truth and peace of mind (in other terms, innocence and happiness) by abandoning the strife of civil and social living and the ordeal of human fellowship for a solitary existence, in communion with nature and with the company of one's musings and thoughts
>
> (1984, p. 99)

In this extended sense the pastoral vision can be used as a vehicle of social criticism as well as accounting for the present hardness of life. Thus the pastoral theme contributes essential elements to the structure of narratives and provides a context for social and moral criticism.

Unlike literary texts constructed within a unifying mode, oral narratives shift between thematic styles of presentation or chronotopes. Forest narratives are also presented both in the adventure mode and in a mode which seems to defy literary categorization. I have in mind a certain intractability of physical and moral suffering which, from time to time, surfaces unceremoniously within the narrative. This movement between narrative genres creates a constant tension between contrasting spiritual and moral universes.

Many narratives about major biographical disruption are set in what Bakhtin would describe as adventure time. He characterizes this adventure time in relation to the Greek romance as follows:

> Greek adventure time lacks any natural, everyday cyclicity – such as might have introduced into it a temporal order and indices on a human scale, tying it to the repetitive aspects of natural and human life.... Thus all the action in a Greek romance, all the events and adventures that fill it, constitute time sequences that are neither historical, quotidian, biographical, nor even biographical and maturational.... What is important is to be able to escape, to catch up, to outstrip, to be or not to be in a given place at a given moment, to meet or not to meet and so forth. Within the limits of a given adventure, days, nights, hours, even minutes and seconds add up, as they would in any struggle or any active external undertaking. These time segments are introduced and intersect with specific link-words: 'suddenly' and 'at just that moment.' 'Suddenly' and 'at just that moment' best characterize this type of time, for this time usually has its origin and comes into its own in just those places where the normal, pragmatic and premeditated course of events is interrupted – and provides an opening for sheer chance, which has its own specific logic. This logic is one of random contingency, which is to say, chance simultaneity (meetings) and chance rupture (nonmeetings), that is, a logic of random disjunctions in time as well. In this random contingency, 'earlier' and 'later' are crucially, even decisively significant. Should something happen a minute earlier or a minute later, that is, should there be no chance simultaneity or chance disjunctions in time, there would be no plot at all, and nothing to write a novel about.
>
> (ibid., pp. 91–92)

This characterization of Greek adventure time applies almost without qualification to large segments of Latvian narratives. The notion of a logic of random temporal contingencies has particular relevance. However, forest narratives, in common with Latvian narratives generally, move between temporal modes and structures. Few narrators appear able to remain within the adventure mode without returning to the pastoral mode for varying lengths of time. However, Latvian pastoral provides not only a safe haven of the mind but is also linked, albeit not in a straightforward way, with social and historical changes.

Narratives develop a moral critique along three principal thematic dimensions. The beauty and moral order of the past is described. The goodness, beauty and strength of childhood and youth are emphasized. The innate goodness of earth, trees and animals and their communion with the forest brothers is described. Contrast and criticism are sharpened by periodic reversions to adventure time.

The sense of being surrounded by enemies did, of course, accurately reflect the reality of forest life. Tālis recounts:

> There was a bitterness felt by everyone, particularly during that autumn when everyone was living in hope alone. There was enemy all around, there was no hope.

Everyone who stayed in the forest was aware of the probability of death. Tālis describes a fellow forest brother thus:

> That same commander could have left [Latvia]. He was invited. But he said that it was better that his bones should be bleached here in his homeland.

Jānis' view of the enemy is more threatening:

> There is no front line here. The enemy can be all around. There was a reward issued for my brother and me. . .

Antonija's fear of the enemy is carried over to the present and is focused on those who betrayed the partisans:

> That can't be forgotten. There are those who are still alive. But those who died in the forest and who were shot by the checka, that can't be forgotten and forgiven. Now they are all old. But at least they could apologize, ask for pardon, be sorry, but they all deny that they have been guilty, they say it was necessary, that they cleansed Latvia of unnecessary people. But they are all at liberty.

And Antonija goes on to give a list of names.[2] She does not remember feeling fear in the forest, but first remembers feeling fear on her return to the city, to Riga:

> I was never afraid. Then when I returned from Russia, if I saw a militia man in a tram or trolleybus, then I got out. I had such panic from them, but up to then I was never afraid. I thought, if I stay alive I stay alive. I was never in a position where I was afraid.

Elza was in the same group of partisans as Antonija, but the forest she experienced was a different one. Her opening sentence about the forest links it to fear:

> You know, people lived in continual fear, the enemy was all around. As we read in the newspapers now, it had to be a terrible life where the enemy is behind every bush. All the time you have to be so tense.

For Elza that fear has had lasting effects:

> How shall I put it to you? On the nervous system, you feel that someone is following you the whole time. For a long time. You know, when I was arrested, I shouldn't really say this, when I was arrested, I felt freed. I was no longer

afraid of all those chekists, of anything. That's a completely different kind of fear. You know, I was liberated straight away, thank God I have nothing more to fear. I know that I shall be beaten now, that I shall be put in prison, I will be punished, I knew all that. We had reckoned with all that, we weren't afraid of all that. But exactly that moment of arrest, that's what we were afraid of. And it's terrible, all the time your nerves are tensed to the last. And when it was over, I thought I was as though completely free. I wasn't afraid of chekists or anything. They kicked me about with their feet and hit me, but it was nothing to me, nothing at all, because I had prepared myself for it . . . I was completely ready for it.

However, although Elza experienced capture and imprisonment as a release from fear, she continues to relive her early fears:

You know, at night I often dream. I dream that I'm going, I'm always going somewhere and then I fall down and I see that the chekist is following me with an automatic gun, and I'm falling into a kind of hole. It's often like that and the old war-time bunkers are there where the hide-outs were. And always I'm falling into the bunker. Inside is a chekist hide-out. I often dream like that. It has all stayed in my subconscious. Not the horror of the concentration camp, not even the famine. But living in the Latvian forest, your own forest and you need to be afraid. Like a forest animal, even worse.

Elza's emphasis on the fact that the forest is Latvian and her own suggests an expected incompatibility between fear and the forest. However, segments of Elza's narrative also take place in adventure time where fear is unknown. Indeed, Elza's account of her entry into the forest puts special emphasis on her lack of fear:

It was May. We were some fifteen people. We had to move to a new place. We had to go along a railway track across Lake Puzes. There was the railway and the big road to Ventspils. Across the corner of the lake was the forest again. It was night. In the morning, we went not along this side, but, as fate would have it, along the other side. We went up to the road. One person crossed, a second and a third. But the lace of my boot had come undone and I stayed behind. And that saved them because opposite was a hidden sentry post and they were waiting for us. They saw a man go past, then a second and a third and then they saw a woman coming. But women usually walk in the middle. But by the time we were in the middle of the road, they were still asleep although it was morning. And those who were on the left-hand side saw a woman coming and no one after her. As they shoot we run. And so we ran into the wood. And the others woke up and also began to shoot. And we still had to get over the tip of the lake and the railway and the road. A tree had fallen over to form a crossing. It was covered in morning dew and no wider than an arm. You could give me a million now and I wouldn't cross over it, but at that time the boys ran over without stopping and I followed. Then we ran over the road with them following. Then suddenly we saw a pile of branches and we realized that we wouldn't be able to escape. They thought we were under the branches. While they encircled the pile of branches and convinced themselves that we weren't inside, we had already crossed the railway. There was a hillock on the way to the big forest. But to surround the forest, they would have needed huge reinforcements. That was my first battle.

Elza's account of joining the group of forest brothers shares the principal feature which Bakhtin identifies as characteristic of adventure time, namely, the logic of random contingency. Elza's miscreant boot laces and the precise moment of their unravelling play a key role in the development of the drama.

In some accounts the absence of fear forms a narrative bridge with the pastoral idyll of youth. Here is Elza talking about fear again:

Only afterwards, when I remembered, I started to think, that I could well have been caught or shot. But at that time I wasn't at all afraid. But then, of course, I was young.

Jānis makes the same association between youth and fearlessness:

A young person does not feel fear.

The healthiness and strength of youth are also recalled. Several narrators commented on the fact that they never fell ill. For example, Antonija recalls how she lost her boots one winter and had to walk in socks:

But I could never fall ill. I don't know what it was, youth or what.

Although Emma was in her forties during her forest period she too remarked on the absence of illness:

We were six years in the forest. We came out in 1953.[3] We were in the fresh air, in famine, but we had no trouble from illness.

Fearsome unpredictability contrasts with the order and predictability of childhood memories. When I asked Elza what she remembered of her early childhood she replied:

Father taught us to work from an early age. When he returned from the First World War he had nothing. He started to work and only in old age did he manage to own his own house. That's why he got all the children to help him to work. He was the secretary of the *pagasts* and we helped him to work in the office.... In the summer we did all the farm jobs. Weeding ... father said that needs to be weeded, that needs to be mown, that needs to be done and in the evening he would come and look. If it wasn't done then we would be woken up at five and made to do it and allowed to sleep at mid-day so that we would ... we would ... from early childhood we were accustomed to order. Father always said, 'Don't hurry, do the job slowly at first, but properly. Speed will come later. The most important thing is for you to learn to do it properly from the very beginning and not in a slap dash fashion'. Of course, that was a characteristic of all Latvians, to do things properly and with love.

Elza links her ordered childhood with shared cultural values. Elza's mother died when she was five and she was left in her father's sole care:

He was never angry. If I'd done something wrong he'd call me into his office and say: 'You don't have a mother. I'm in place of a mother. If you grow up a bad child, no one will blame you, they'll blame me because I won't have known how to bring you up'. And he would speak for so long until I had a lump in my throat and I started to cry. And I've remembered that all my life. I'd rather he would have beaten me. That's how he brought us up. Father was a very good person.

The emphasis is on the ordered morality and love of her childhood. Talis' memories of his childhood are curiously lyrical and non-specific:

Everyone's childhood is dear to them. I dreamt of everything, much about history. About my young days, and what my mother and father taught me, about my ancestors, about the formation of the Latvian state. My parents were great patriots although my mother was born into a servant's family.

Apart from the detail about his mother's family of origin it is an impersonal reply which links happiness in an axiomatic way with childhood and childhood with national culture and history.

Both accounts serve as moral contrasts with later moral chaos. Indeed, a standard way of referring to the post-war period is by the term *juku laiki* or times of chaos. One way in which this moral chaos is conceptualized is as a kind of natural inversion. Descriptions of the country around the concentration camps in the taiga emphasize the inversion of the natural order. Elza's description of the country around the labour camp in Inta dwells on deviations and inversions of natural processes. Growth seems crippled or monstrous. Seasons are curtailed and temporal sequences distorted. Night swallows day:

Firstly, there were no trees there, only such crippled bushes. Then you can't go anywhere. Everywhere it's gone completely to swamp, you see. If you go one step.... A convoy sank in front of our eyes, in front of our very eyes.... The last thing we saw were arms raised like this holding an automatic rifle. One gets sucked in. You can see a field of red cranberries, but you can't get near it, because one step away from the tussock and cheerio, you're finished. Compared to the natural beauty in Latvia where you can walk in pine woods and birch groves.... And then there are the terrible changes, with us trees and grass grow gradually, but there it happens under your very eyes. But despite that, we longed for Latvia, even though there are not the excesses of nature. It's quieter, calmer, you see the tones are different. There isn't the sudden change; spring comes gradually, summer and autumn come gradually ... there it's sudden. In May the snow is falling, sometimes in June the snow is still falling. How do they reckon it? June is spring, July is summer, August is autumn. There's already snow in September. And then the terrible nights start, when night and day are one.

However, the most systematic use of childhood as a constituent of moral contrast is made by Lienīte. She spent four years of her early childhood hiding in the forest and her first memories are of life in the forest:

I have to say, I honestly don't remember whether those first memories of the forest bunker are when I was two or two and a half. My memories of a communal bunker are misty, but clearer of the time when we were alone, father, mother and us two sisters: my sister Ilze and I, she's two years older than me. Because, you understand, in that big bunker nobody wanted a man with two small children, because life in the forest is altogether risky. At that time and even now I didn't take it so tragically. Perhaps also I didn't take to heart the fact that there was nothing to eat, probably my mother and father took it badly – that there was nothing to give the children to eat. I remember feeding the tits, because we went out of the bunker sometimes in winter. I remember that father took us for a walk by the river. By the edge of the marsh there was a river.

Thus the opening segment of Lienīte's narrative counterposes the near famine conditions and the lack of support from other partisans with her awareness of the natural life of the forest. Her explanation of how the family first entered the forest emphasizes the arbitrariness and unfairness of political events:

In so far as I have to believe my parents we hid because my father had been called into the German army. He didn't go, because he was not cut out to shoot human beings. The same pattern of events repeated itself with the Russian army, and here too he didn't go. With the German army he managed to get away with guarding bridges, but with the Russian army it's not possible to get free. He had to hide. On my mother's side there were many relatives deported in 1941. Professor Šmits, perhaps you know him ... he was director of the English Institute. He was already deported to Russia in 1941 together with his wife. He died there, but his wife went to England or rather America. That was in later years. And there were many such occurrences. At all events in 1941 the year of terror, we knew everything.[4] We knew what the consequences of opposition would be and at that time people fervently believed that the war would end soon, that the English would come to our aid and that we would be free.[5] But there was no freedom and people simply fled, hoping that the Russian danger would pass away. That's how people went into the forest. My father was the first to enter the forest, but because my mother was alone at home, they started to visit her. Where is your husband? You can understand that my mother decided that she too would go into the forest. We were given away to my father's sister, but as a result, that house too came under surveillance. You understand, if there are children then where are the parents? How can you have spare children so to speak? ... At any event, there was this hope. I remember my mother listening to the English radio in the bunker and thinking that they would come and open up a second front. That at any moment they would be there.

The account emphasizes the randomness of events. Lienīte's father was wanted by the NKVD (People's Commissariat for Internal Affairs) despite the fact that he was 'not cut out to shoot human beings'. The interest of the NKVD extended to her mother and the children. Like many Latvians Lienīte's parents hoped for military intervention by the allies and her narrative moves from a consideration of the injustices of the situation to the image of her mother listening to the BBC and the betrayal of hope. The theme of treachery continues in the account of everyday forest life:

With food we had all sorts of experiences. At all events we did have food, because we have survived. I can't say that it was plentiful and there were times when there was nothing to eat. Once or twice the men from the bunker went on raids, and that's stealing. Once it was a shop and once a dairy. They simply went and took food. The local people did give a great deal. The men went to get food wherever they could. Those who could gave food to the forest brothers. As the saying goes, Latvians aren't like Jews who stand by one another. Unfortunately, we don't stand up for one another. And there were people whom everyone had to fear. Besides, the checkists weren't sleeping either. On the whole, people simply gave us food. I do know that father went to fetch it. Of course, they didn't come to the forest, we had to go to their houses.

Lienīte's unfavourable comparison of Latvians with Jews contrasts with the statement immediately preceding it which describes the generosity of local people. The negative contrast is essential to the development of her pastoral theme. Lienīte's account of forest diet is interwoven with her memories of human treachery and lack of solidarity:

I remember there were potatoes. We cooked at night. At night, in the hope that nobody would see. Because that's the only possibility. Or at dusk, when there's no one in the forest. One can't do anything else. You understand . . . during the day there might be some skier or other. During the summer it's altogether more dangerous, the cooking is done at night. I remember with food it was very difficult. When they brought milk, then I as the youngest was allowed to lick the cork, because the cream was on it. It was not just we who had difficulty getting hold of food, but at that time conditions in the Latvian countryside were not much easier.

Descriptions of physical hardship interlink with human betrayal:

I remember that we fell for it when mother took us out during the summer billberry season. She thought that a woman with children would seem ordinary, surely there were many like us? But a woman had approached us and mother realized that that meant danger. That same night we moved to a different bunker and two days later our bunker exploded because father had left it mined. That woman had gone straight to inform on us.

However, Lienīte emphasizes that she felt no fear:

My memories aren't dramatic, because I was a child. I was fed, I even had some clothes. I didn't have any feelings of fear. Adults may feel fear, but children don't. I know that my parents had many tragic moments, because I was bitten by a snake in the forest. You understand how it is for parents if their child is bitten by a snake. Where should they take her, because they need a doctor. Either that or they lose the child. But God really has stood by me.

The snake is part of Lienīte's pastoral vision:

The snake went back into the forest. I simply fell on top of the snake. It wasn't the snake's fault. See, here is one tooth-mark and here is another.

Apart from the snake bite Lienīte suffered no illness. Like some other narrators, Lienīte attributes her health to the harsh forest conditions:

You know, it's a peculiar thing with people, but in extreme conditions people are not ill. God helps them.

Lienīte's account of her forest childhood is set in a polarized world. Her pastoral vision links the beauty and goodness of nature with the innate goodness and wisdom of childhood and stands in contrast to the adult world of lies and treachery:

This satanism, I have read about it. I know that children shouldn't be treated as simpletons. Children are never fools. Perhaps their experience of life is narrower. At that time all of us who were the children of deported parents, we all knew perfectly well which is our fatherland and who we were. [Lienīte's parents were sentenced under the 58th clause for betrayal of the Fatherland, i.e. the Soviet Union.][6] We all knew how to keep quiet. One can't say that a child can give an account of everything. A child is just as wise, not more foolish by one kopeck. We knew with whom we could talk and with whom not, or whether to talk at all.

However, this innate wisdom is not nurtured by adults.

It is very sad and perhaps life would be quite different if we ourselves had had the courage to tell our children how it really was. But people were afraid for their lives and they simply lied. I consider that to be lying. People who as late as the 1970s said: 'No, I've never told the children that there were such deportations then. Why should they know?' Sometimes I've said to them, 'But have you never been afraid that one day that child will say, but, mother, why did you lie to me?' Those are my feelings of right and wrong. In my life I've been most oppressed by people's lies. But it's been like that for many and that's how one loses faith in other people.

Loss of faith in humankind underpins the entire narrative. Her memories of the deportations of 25th March 1949 give special emphasis to the hurt inflicted on animals:

When I start talking about the post-war years I remember them very well. The year 1949 and all that period of deportation. 25th March 1949. Morning, that literally ... never and in no way will that situation be erased, that enormous national tragedy. ... At that time I was living with my cousin. And the whole village knew that the chekists were coming, that they would be there at any moment. We stood by the windows and watched to see from which direction they would come. Then they came and our young men fled and they were shot at. There were cars and they were armed. In order to deport people they couldn't let them escape.

The last sentence reverses the chronological order of events and thereby distances the situation from human agency and motivation. The seemingly mechanical nature of events is contrasted with the animal pain:

The most terrible was the next morning. On that day ... those events: who was deported and who wasn't. The next morning when the cattle were driven along the road from the farmsteads of the deported. [A literal translation would be 'of the driven'. Lienīte uses the same verb – *dzīt* – to describe the cattle being driven along the road and the people from their homes.] That's made an enormous impression on my memory. In the morning, such a misty morning and the lowing cattle . . . not fed. Human beings understand something, but animals do not understand. And so they were taken away and driven together somewhere. Of course, those who had informed ransacked the houses looking for gain, to see what possessions there were and to appropriate them. And then all our post-war life began.

Animal innocence and suffering is contrasted with human cruelty and treachery. This polarized moral landscape is underlined by Lienīte's own role as victim or, more precisely, sacrificial offering. Her favourite game in the forest supports this interpretation:

What else do I remember from my forest childhood? I very much wanted to play theatre. In the evenings, who knows, perhaps also during the day I wouldn't give my father any peace. I said, 'Daddy, mummy let's go and play theatre. It doesn't matter what, I'll be the fool, you can be the wolf, I'll be the lamb that gets eaten. Just come'. I was very persistent, I didn't give up.

Lienīte bears the outward mark of her sacrificial role. Initially, the tooth mark of the snake, later it is the head wound inflicted when their bunker is discovered:

Yes, my childhood wasn't like that of other children. I don't know what it's like to ask for something. Give me such and such. I don't know whether that's bad or not. God knows better.

The forest sojourn is blasted apart and ends in violence and death:

It all ended tragically for some. I said earlier that God has always stood by me, and also on that occasion. A traitor insinuated himself into the group. He was simply sent. And this person betrayed us. It was either just before midsummer or on midsummer's day, I'll have to ask my father which it was. We were surrounded in the night. He simply came into the forest, as though he was hiding from the chekists, but he was an agent of the cheka. He lived with us for quite a time. . . . He betrayed us. One night I woke up and realized that we were ambushed, earth was falling on me. At that moment I felt blood pouring. I had no pain but I could feel it. It was mine, yes. After that I don't remember anything.

Lienīte was left with a metal splinter lodged in her brain and a big scar on her forehead:

Perhaps, God really knows what he is doing. I sometimes . . . sometimes I've felt sad I have no family and such like, I laugh that I am marked, I could change my surname twenty times, each person who has seen me once recognizes me, scar on the face, there aren't many such running around. Now it's straightforward, but it was very difficult to force oneself to lie all one's life. People ask you, 'Why do you have a scar on your face? Did a horse kick you?' 'No, not a horse. I fell'. In the end I thought, why should I lie, I hate lies, it irritated me. Then I said 'I was shot'. Because people didn't question me any further, because in those post-war years, there were very many shot people. So that's what I said, that the boys were playing and I was shot. Only these little boys were a bit bigger and the game was a bit more serious. It wasn't a game. But I say that God stood by me.

Lienīte was seven years old at the time the bunker was attacked and that event shaped the subsequent course of her life. Both parents were arrested, imprisoned and sentenced:

At that moment we were captured and simply taken away. Father and mother were taken to the central prison in Riga. Nobody asked anybody else any questions; they didn't know whether I was alive or whether I was dead. Of course, they were separated straight away, until father was sentenced, mother too. Vorkuta, Inta, Abezi. Finally mother ended up in Karaganda, father in Mordovia. That pleasure outing cost mother eight years and broken health. Father thirteen years in the mines of Vorkuta, but later he was also washing laundry ... he had stomach ulcers. Afterwards, when the uprisings started in Vorkuta he was sent to Mordovia.[7]

Lienīte's account of her parents' arrest and imprisonment draws upon shared notions of national guilt:

Mother told me later that everyone was the same in the labour camps, whether Ukrainians or White Russians, all in the same situation. There were Ukrainian women who could not bring themselves to utter the word Latvian, because Latvian red riflemen were so merciless.[8] No one could match them. Dumb terror. The nation has to suffer for the acts of the nation. They could go into a village and shoot everyone, just because they were the bearers of Soviet power. We can only pray to God that he forgive us our sins. That is the only possibility, that's how I understand it.

This interpretation of the Soviet occupation as a penance for past collective sins was frequently voiced.

After her parents' arrest Lienīte spent three months in hospital:

I was already cured, my forehead had healed and they couldn't keep me any longer.

Initially Lienīte went to live with two young cousins:

They weren't bad ... I think it was difficult for her as well living in these chaotic times. ... I went herding animals, because my cousin needed a means of livelihood ... I herded cattle. I also understood that it was difficult for her, my walking around the house with a shot face. As I said there are all kinds of people. Why should one pull a tiger by the tail? To tell the truth I didn't start school because my cousin had no one to herd the animals. Also I didn't have any clothes. And so at eight years old I still wasn't going to school. I turned eight in the autumn and the following year I went to school. But at that time at Christmas I was taken in by some neighbours.

The account of her stay with her cousins is also structured around a moral polarity. Hiding the truth and saving one's skin, 'not pulling the tiger by the tail' or telling the truth and by implication looking after the needs of the child. Lienīte carried the outward mark of forest life in the form of her scar and she thus posed a danger to anyone who took her in. Her early history posed difficulties and restrictions throughout her later life:

> It is very difficult to live after that. Because you have to hide something and there are few people to whom you can talk. Everyone wants to survive. I thank God that I learnt very quickly that one can either compromise one's conscience or reconcile oneself to not having a high position and not have such compromises. It's a much better feeling if you don't have to lie to anyone. You accept whatever position you're allowed. And in my biography I usually wrote as much, because I knew that those who were interested in me, knew much more about me than I could possibly ever know myself. Don't let's be naive, in the personnel departments there are only cheka agents. There were no personnel departments where that wasn't so. I understood that well and that's why I didn't particularly try to hide anything. I understood very well that I couldn't take up any position of power. If I am honest in my work, then there will always be people, even Latvians, who won't let me do it because of their selfish interests. For example, I want that person to do his work well but it's very easy for him to coerce me. 'You're a bandit's child, what do you want? You be quiet'.

Lienīte's unwillingness to compromise or lie about the past has led to her working as a gardener. Her comment on this occupation encapsulates the pastoral vision:

> Perhaps, it's wiser to dig the earth, because the earth [she uses the Latvian diminutive – *zemīte*] will not betray you. That's how it is.

The moral lesson drawn from this forest childhood and the subsequent course of her life in Soviet Latvia find an echo in an earlier pastoral vision:

> Blow, blow thou winter wind,
> Thou art not so unkind
> As man's ingratitude.
> . . .
> Freeze, freeze thou bitter sky,
> That dost not bite so nigh
> As benefits forgot.
> Though thou the waters warp,
> Thy sting is not so sharp,
> As friend remember'd not.
> ('Bitter Song', William Shakespeare)

The unreliability of human beings in contrast to the protectiveness of the forest is also evident in Emma's narrative. However, Emma was a mature woman of forty-two when she entered the forest in Kurzeme in 1947 and beyond the romantic vision her narrative also contains memories of the harsh realities of forest life from which a child such as Lienīte might have been protected. Emma spent a total of six years between 1947 and 1953 living in the forest of Vandzene. For three years she and her husband were alone in the forest. Emma had worked in the foreign department of the

Ministry of the Interior and her husband had worked in the war tribunal. Because of their occupations and because 'we could not forget the years 1940 and 1941' both felt unsafe. In 1944 they moved to Kurzeme. During the autumn of 1944 many refugees escaped to Sweden and Germany, 'But we stayed. There were no boats any more. We had no luck.' In Kurzeme they were sought by the cheka and decided to hide in the forest. Initially they joined a group of thirty men. Most of these men had local contacts and support, whereas Emma and her husband were from Riga and had no local connections: 'Everyone needed to eat and we felt that we were not wanted. We felt spare.' They then joined a smaller group of seven men:

> We knitted and knitted for the farmer, socks and cardigans. We crocheted, we worked non-stop. The men listened to the radio. They had nothing to do. It's difficult to find something to do on top of the cowshed. We kitted out the whole family with knitwear until the neighbours became suspicious. The neighbours turned us in and we had to go into the forest again.

At first they were with two young men but soon they found themselves alone:

> One night they agreed among themselves and disappeared while we slept. We were unnecessary ballast for them. We woke up to find ourselves alone in the bushes us two.

Emma's narrative of the early forest period charts a progressive fragmentation of solidarity. Each group in turn finds them a burden. At one stage they are suspected of being infiltrators.

Emma's memories of the forest form two distinct and interchanging narrative themes. Firstly her memories are of physical hardship and discomfort and these link back to her childhood dislike of the physical labour involved in farmwork. Secondly, she describes a spiritual unity with the forest and its animals. This pastoral theme provides a meaningful perspective on the past: a way of drawing together an otherwise painful life history. It appears to be unrelated to experience but rather has affinities with common Latvian literary themes. Above all this pastoral thread gives comfort and security to what would otherwise be remembered as an altogether bleak past.

Emma was born in 1905. Her memories of her country childhood lack any element of idealization or romanticization. Her parents were farmers who owned their own land:

> We were seven children, two died, five grew up. So we three brothers and two sisters lived. Now I'm the only one left of a large family. And so all of us were made to work. I was not yet at school when I was made to graze geese. The flock of geese lived in a shed in winter, but in summer they needed grazing. That was before I went to school. I started to go to school at eight years old. Children started by grazing geese. They were usually grazed on clover quite far away, the geese loved the clover. Then they grazed on the clover, but all around there was corn. I had to watch that they didn't go into the cornfield and I would walk between the clover and the corn field. When the geese went in the corn, I had

a stick in my hand and I used that to drive them back. The leader of the flock was the father. He would come towards me hissing. Then I had to watch out and grab his head and turn it the other way. Otherwise he would come on top of me, he would jump on my shoulders and hit me with his wings so that it hurt.

In contrast to lyrical literary evocations of shepherding, Emma did not enjoy her duties:

I didn't like it. I had to get up early in the morning. But altogether I didn't go herding for long. When I started to go to school father rented out part of the land and the house after the First World War. Then we had to start life all over again, because all our cows were taken away, of the eighteen cows we were left with just one. Of the four horses which worked the land just one mare was left and even she was ill with distemper. We had to give up everything. Russian soldiers left us that little mare. She died soon after. Then there was nothing left to herd. Then later when the cows gave birth father rented out a piece of the land and they rented rooms at the end of the house. Part of the agreement was that the tenants would herd two days a week and we would herd the third day. And so every third day I had to go herding. When I drove the cows out in the morning, my feet were wet from the grass. But when the neighbouring shepherds sang, I sang too.

I didn't like getting up so early, I desperately wanted to sleep in the mornings. Cows were usually driven out at four in the morning, at the latest at five. I was so sleepy that I used to lie down whilst herding.

Emma's account has little communing with nature:

We weren't of a mind to observe nature. We saw everything from a practical point of view. . . . We didn't go to the forest at all and we didn't have time to think about it, how beautiful it is. Yes, the wood was beautiful, it was all overgrown with huge trees. My father's wood too, he also sold firewood. But about the beauty neither my brother nor anyone said anything special. We didn't have time to think about it, we had to work. There was weeding in the summer. We had to weed the carrots, cabbages and then there were the pigs to feed. The pigs needed beetroot and that had to be grown. Towards autumn the leaves of the beets would bend over. We would pick the leaves and carry them on our arms like firewood to the cowshed and shred them in the trough and then give them to the pigs. To tell the truth, I didn't like country life even from early childhood. I found all those tasks difficult, I thought they were dirty. When I started to go to the city school that was the end. How I wanted to be in the city! When I got married and started to live in the city, I began to work there as well and only came on visits to my father. And when my father died my brothers quickly moved to the city. I don't know why but all our family dispersed and only the house remained. Then the house was sold . . . we don't have a house any more. We didn't have anywhere to live and so the two of us, my husband and I, built a little house so that we would have somewhere to live. And then I really enjoyed cultivating a garden. But in my father's house there was also a garden and it had to be tended. In the farmstead I didn't enjoy country life. But in the city when I went to the museum or theatre I enjoyed it so much, I remembered it and it stayed in my mind for a long while.

Emma's recollections of childhood and youth do not provide a basis for the later pastoral mode in which she recollects the forest. The countryside is associated with dirty and difficult work, in short with hardship. Some sense of this hardship persists in her later accounts of forest life:

It was hard, when there was nothing to eat. Then I started weaving the basketwork. Houses were watched. Neighbours watched neighbours, they observed one another and informed the cheka. Then I couldn't go there any more. So I went on the road to Roja.[9] There was a market in Roja and on market day the marketgoers would drive through the forest along that road. We would go by the roadside. My husband would stay in the forest so that he could see and I would come out onto the road. [To sell her basketwork.] But then someone or other would see [the basketwork] in a house and ask, 'Where did you get that?' And then the chekists would surround us with dogs in the forest, they would put out sentry posts and stay on guard for ten days or a fortnight waiting for us to come out. Once they found my basket hidden in a beehive. There were cranberries I had collected for the winter. They took the basketwork and the cranberries as well.

Their abiding problem in the forest was food:

We distributed potatoes over the forest and buried them. We slept on top of the potatoes so that they wouldn't freeze. We went hunting in Dundaga forest. We were sorry to do it, but the famine was terrible. When we were arrested they came to watch me in the sauna ... I was so thin. We roasted and boiled badgers. In the summer it was easier, but at other times we ate grass and leaves, there was nothing else to eat.

Emma likens conditions after their arrest, both in the prison and in the labour camps, to a sanatorium:

We were taken to the central prison, it was like a sanatorium. We could have a rest there.

Subsequent imprisonment in a labour camp is contrasted in a similarly favourable way with Latvian forest conditions:

When we got to the labour camp in Russia, it was like a sanatorium. It was hardest for us in the forest in our own homeland.

However, alongside these harsh memories of daily life in the forest is a mystical image of the forest where there is communion between humans and animals and where animals take on a protective role towards humans. She says:

The forest was like a refuge but we were not able to leave it.

The forest refuge did not, however, provide peace of mind:

It was a terrible time, continual fear of ambush. To the animals in the forest we were one of them. Like us the stags slept during the day, but during the night they would go to a clearing or a meadow to eat. They would go past us, but when there were chekists about they would bark re, re, re. The whole forest resounded and we knew we were being surrounded. Then we had to stay put. That's how God protected us. [Emma uses the diminutive of God – *Dieviņš*.] There was a spring and I went to fetch water from there. There is a wolf sitting at the side of the path looking at me. As I go past I say quietly to him: 'Go home, little wolf, go home.' And he laid his ears back and didn't touch me. And so the animals helped us.

A similar helpful role is assigned to animals in Ruta's account:

We had been given a little loaf of bread. We thought we would sit down and eat it. When we sat down to eat a squirrel above us goes chirp, chirp. Who's coming? A couple of paces away we see a man coming.

In this account the squirrel saves Ruta and her husband from the chekist. Tālis describes the forest as:

A dear friend. I have worked in the forest on amelioration programmes and dug ditches. I feel sorry for the forest. What it was once like! What firs and pines there were! Now it's all ragged and covered in bushes. Once I saw five little wolves [*vilciņi*]. I was on my own going to look at a grave. Then I met them. I felt strange that there were so many. But what could I do?

Tālis' use of the diminutive signals a relationship of intimacy and affection between himself and the wolves.

Latvian ideas about the wild and about forests have little in common with western traditions of thought. Roderick Nash's study of the conceptual development of wilderness in American history describes the moral and symbolic aspects of the wild. He writes of:

the long western tradition of imagining wild country as a moral vacuum, a cursed and chaotic wasteland. As a consequence, frontiers-men acutely sensed that they battled wild country not only for personal survival but in the name of nation, race and God ... wilderness was the villain, and the pioneer, as hero, relished its destruction.

(1967, p. 24)

Keith Thomas' study of the transformation of English attitudes to nature identifies a very similar constellation of ideas and attitudes in the early modern period. Thomas describes the theological underpinnings 'for the ascendancy of man over nature which had by the early modern period become the accepted goal of human endeavour' (1983, p. 22). Eugen Weber in his study of French attitudes to nineteenth-century rural society finds the idea of wilderness applied to rural populations (1979). In short, an opposition is set up between man and nature which is foreign to Latvian thought. In this respect, Latvian narratives are closer to eastern traditions. Roderick Nash characterizes this tradition 'as marked by respect, bordering on love, absent in the West. . . . And wilderness, in eastern thought, did not have an unholy or evil connotation but was venerated as the symbol and even the essence of deity' (ibid., p. 20). A good illustration of the close relationship between eastern spirituality and the forest is found in Michael

Carrithers' study of Buddhist forest monks (1983). Indeed, one narrator, Elza, described the forest as holy (*svēts*).

Latvian forest narratives, although they may share elements in common, do not, of course, draw upon eastern traditions. However, texts influence each other and also influence narratives. Forest narratives draw upon a well-established folk tradition which would form part of every Latvian child's primary education. Early anthologies of reading were standardized and limited in number throughout the period relevant to my narrators and all contained significant sections of songs and readings about the forest. In folk songs trees and forests are associated with singing and joy. For example, *Lokaties mežu gali, lai balsītis pāri skan* [Bend tree tops so that voices can be heard above you]. Trees are personified and attributed a variety of symbolic meanings. Oak and birch trees are associated with men and lime trees and wild cherries with women. The apple tree is associated specifically with motherhood and provides a refuge for orphans who are described as crying under the boughs of the apple tree. The term 'forest brothers' relates to this mystical tradition found in folk songs. The forest itself has a feminine aspect: there is mention of the forest mother and forest daughters. The rising and setting of the sun which is also a feminine symbol are associated with the sun tree which lives deep in the middle of the forest. Ideas about animals communicating with humans are, of course, found in all folk tales.

The contrast between the evil social world and the warmth and intimacy of nature is most poignantly expressed by Voldemārs, who entered the forest in 1944 when he was fifteen years old. Two years later he was captured and imprisoned. Was he sentenced? I asked: 'Yes. I managed to sit three months in the death cell. In the central prison in Riga. The trial itself was in Madona.' I asked whether the death sentence was often given. 'Usually people were called out at night, in the evening when it was dark.' Then in the next sentence the only use of diminutives signals a change of register as Voldemārs enters a personal and affectionate world:

> I had a view of the third block. A little horse [*zirdziņš*] was pulling something. It was a cart with barge boards. I wanted to know what was rattling. So I scrambled up to the window . . . there was a little light [*gaismiņa*] dawning. An old man was at the reins and the cart was covered, but underneath could be seen an arm and a leg. They were being taken for burial.

Voldemārs' account has particular relevance to my interpretation because of the way it introduces diminutive terms of endearment: little horse and little light used in the most terrifying context of the death cell. They recall the reassuring world of nature in a way that the words horse (*zirgs*) and light (*gaisma*) could not do.

These forest narratives draw upon established folkloric and linguistic traditions. In doing so they create a universe in which there is a fusion of natural and moral worlds. However, arrest and violent death were constant threats to this safe and harmonious life. The dangers and precariousness of survival are remembered in an adventure idiom, in which chance and coincidence furnish a connecting thread for identity.

8

DAMAGED LIVES, DAMAGED HEALTH

> I sat down and cried
> By the grey stone
> Let the evil day stay
> By the grey stone.
>
> Sorrow, what terrible sorrow,
> I didn't fret over my sorrow!
> I put sorrow under a stone
> And stepped over it singing.
>   (Folk songs)

> I wanted to place my unhappiness under a stone
> So that it would stay there for a long time
> Until I myself was underneath the stone.
>
> I wanted to place my unhappiness under a stone
> I lifted the stone – someone had beat me to it
> I lifted a second – occupied
> I lifted a third – occupied
> They'd walked over it singing.
>
> I lifted a fifth, sixth
> And ninth
> Occupied. Occupied.
>
> Keep it to yourself.
>   ('Latvian stones', Māra Zālīte)

Latvian narrators represent illness as a breakdown of values, purpose and meaning. Kleinman has written of illness, 'Acting like a sponge, illness soaks up personal and social significance from the world of the sick person' (1988, p. 31). In Latvia illness does not relate so much to a transfer of meaning as to a collision between the expectation of meaning and meaninglessness. Narrators locate illness at the point of intersection of memory and present experience, at the point where images of the past converge with and are undermined by the reality of everyday life. It is the disruption of the 'grammar of life histories', where this grammar is constituted in significant part by structures from the past. (The felicitous phrase is Zonabend's, 1984, p. 196) For narrators illness is the end result of processes which destroy cherished values. The incoherence of lives is equated with illness. Three sources of incoherence were repeatedly described and form the subject matter of this chapter. They are exile and homecoming, living accommodation and dishonesty at work.

This is not to deny the part played by real historical events in the development of psychological pain and illness. World events, the war and its aftermath are components of all Latvian narratives. However, the force of such events is mediated by concepts and values through which they are perceived and experienced. What is experienced as history by one generation becomes structure for the next. Paradoxically, therefore, structures inform the experience of historical events and, conversely, younger Latvians 'remember' the war at second remove through the memories and accounts of older people.

And so it is that the deconstruction of values central to Latvian social memory provided the structure for narratives of neurasthenia. The assault on the idea of a nurturing honest and orderly society, on the homeland, on the homestead and on the importance of living independently, on the value of work and on the importance of calmness and self control were described as leading ultimately to neurasthenia. Narrators affirmed a particular value, often linking it specifically to Latvians and then proceeded to describe how everyday occurrences and practices undermined it.

Narratives had an implicit and frequently explicit political tone. For example, Dzintra remembered being told 'If anyone is still dissatisfied with life then the only place for them is Strenči' (a notorious psychiatric hospital in north Vidzeme). The historical and political dimension of illness is expressed in ideas about its universality as discussed in the last chapter. Many narrators described Latvians as a damaged nation (*sabojāta tauta*), with damaged nerves (*sabojāti nervi*) being particularly widespread. One narrator, Māra, speaks for many with the term '*laikmeta vaina*' or ailment of the times. However, the English translation is unable to convey the power of the Latvian word which resides in its semantic polyvalence: *vaina* has a triple connotation of fault, guilt and illness. The term '*laikmeta vaina*' thus draws together widespread feelings that history and society are to blame in general as well as quite specific ways for ill-health. Doctors made specific links between neurasthenia and Latvians and neurasthenia and women. For example, Ilze claimed that neurasthenia was more likely to affect Latvians explaining this as folllows: 'They are a type of human being more easily broken'. Another casualty doctor related neurasthenia specifically to women: 'Probably there are no women who don't have it, in one form or another'.

Lay people do not talk of neurasthenia although they are willing to concede that what they are suffering from may be diagnosed as neurasthenia by doctors. Lay discourse revolves around the concept of damage. People talk of a damaged nervous system, damaged nerves and traumatized nerves (*traumēti nervi*). Narrators then go on to describe the way in which nervous ill-health results from the inability to put one's life in order (*nenokārtota dzīve*). For example, Silva attributes her illness to 'lack of order'. Her explanatory theory is it seems upheld by the medical practitioners although not in the way that she would like: 'I am dissatisfied not with any one doctor, but with the whole system. The doctor said I should rearrange my life in a more comfortable way. I didn't say anything more and just walked away.' The notion of disorder (*nekārtība*) provides a building block for all illness narratives. The disorder brought about by certain historical events and by unwanted social change is conceptualized as an assault on the nervous system. In many narratives damaged nerves are used as a political metaphor. Vizma offered a simple explanation: 'What I think is that with a hard life the nerves get worn down'.

Illness narratives situate the disorder and damage of life around certain recurring problems. Political repression is one aspect of the past which narrators link to nerve damage. For example, Heronīma who herself spent seven years in a labour camp said: 'I think that all these people from Siberia are traumatized to a certain extent'. However, the emphasis is not so much on the hardships suffered during exile and imprisonment, as on the dismantling of cherished notions of the homeland and family. The illness narratives of country people focus on the hardships surrounding collectivization and obligatory 'amelioration' programmes of the countryside. For city dwellers dishonesty and nepotism at work and problems to do with living accommodation are major topics of illness narrative. However, all the illness narratives share the themes of helplessness and lack of control which the metaphor of the meat-mincing machine captures. There was a widespread sense of being maimed by history and society. However, it was not simply the injustice and cruelty of events, but the inconsistencies within an unjust system of which narrators complained. They complained of the arbitrariness of a system which claims to be logical. It seemed that narrators were unwilling to relinquish their hope of salvaging meaning, consistency and fairness for their past lives, however arbitrary the events and unjust the institutions. Nervous damage is a narrative metaphor which replaces the hope for meaning. It is synonymous with the inability to find meaning. The idea of disorder is closely linked to meaninglessness. Inta put it thus: 'That's been introduced here: there are no contracts. Everything is done with bribery. Nothing is clear. Everything is twisted and upside down.' And she concludes with the statement already given: 'We are like meat in a mincing machine'.

EXILE AND HOMECOMING

For many narrators the experience of returning from exile in Siberia constituted a major assault on a central repository of meaning, namely the idea of *dzimtene* or homeland.[1] Illness narratives do not emphasize the hardships of deportation and exile so much as the difficulties of finding a place within Latvian society after returning from exile. The difficulties of reintegration were more difficult for children than for adults. For example, Anna's homecoming was made particularly painful by the contrast between her expectations and reality:

On waking the next day I felt I had woken up in a fairy tale land. At first, of course, there were difficulties with the time difference: I wanted to go to sleep and I woke early. And then problems started here. I just couldn't understand that here in Latvia where people were supposed to sing, that mother was crying again. That I couldn't be admitted to school, that no school would accept me because I had been deported – I was some sort of criminal. Of course, my relatives got involved and we persuaded them that it had all been a mistake; that a mother and child had been deported and then I was eventually admitted. I spoke with an accent and I wrote very badly. I should have gone into the fourth class, but, in fact, I started in the third. Of course, children are merciless. At school I remember that children called me a Russian. But at the same time they wanted me to help them with their Russian lessons. It wasn't difficult for me, I too wanted to be friends with someone. Later, things evened out somehow, but the first six months were psychologically difficult. My preconception of a bright and sparkling Latvia began to crumble.

The powerful image of the homeland which had sustained Anna and her mother throughout their period of exile received no support from the country which had given rise to it.

Antra situates similar difficulties in the wake of her father's deportation. He was a Lutheran pastor. Having lost his house and livelihood in Riga, he was offered a church in north west Vidzeme:

Well, let's begin with my childhood. Well . . . childhood. I don't really remember the early part of my life. Actually, my childhood memories begin exactly on the day my father was deported. Because up to then, I don't know maybe, perhaps it was so nice and so good together with my parents and brothers, that I can't remember it particularly.

However, when asked Antra is able to give a detailed account of her life before her father's arrest.

We lived in Gulbene.[2] There was a small river near the house. The greatest pleasure was by that river. Sometimes we would go with the grown-ups and at other times on our own – it wasn't far. We all liked that very much. We also liked the spring. I remember from childhood, the little ditch flooded and we could lie on planks and watch. And then there was a period when they started to give land to people who wanted it. And father also took four hectares of land. Well nowadays people have a lot of land, but to me maybe because I was small the land seemed enormous. And a lot of work had to be invested in it. Father himself ploughed and sowed, but all the same in spring and autumn people came to help us in return for money.

Actually, they worked not for money, but for grain and potatoes:

The house needed renovation. But after father renovated it and strengthened it, then it was a reasonable house. It wasn't altogether like a country house. [Antra means it wasn't quite as basic as Latvian country houses.] Father was very energetic. He very much wanted . . . he built a sauna from heavy timbers. And he dug a pond by the sauna. He wanted to fill it with fish. And that's how we started to live.

Antra's account of her early childhood in the harsh post-war years is of reconstruction and family harmony. Her father threw himself into the task of renovating the church:

> Lots of people came to work on it – they were enthusiasts. The Russians had been bombarded so I understand. As I remember it only the vestry was left. Only rooms and the church itself where people pray that was just in ruins, the walls were left. Well and then I know that people gathered the stones and the rubble and they built. My father still has a lot of photographs from that time. The church is now completely renovated.

I asked Antra what the parishioners and helpers were like:

> I find it difficult to characterize the parish because I only remember particular people who were more frequent visitors. They were such very sincere people. Some would bring us apples others would bring sweets to give to the children. So I remember particular individuals. Sometimes they came to our house after the service and they sat and drank tea and talked. And never ... I remember they were all kind. None of them was evil. Perhaps quietly when we couldn't hear they remembered the old times and the Russian deeds. But we children didn't hear about it, it was never talked about.

The harmony and supportiveness which she attributes to her early family life is extended to her father's parishioners. It contrasts with the violence of the arrest and the course of her subsequent life:

> Life started to become more regular again and we thought things would settle down but we were disappointed again. Father was deported.

I asked when that was:

> That was the year 1951. I don't remember how the chekists arrived. I don't remember how they came in the house, I only remember them there. I remember that they were in the room. The chekist officers were dressed in a way that set them apart. They were dressed in such long, black or dark leather coats. At their side they had a pistol or some fire-arm. Well, we children were dreadfully frightened by all that. We had heard all sorts of stories. And then suddenly, I can't remember how many there were, three or four. I only remember that they were in father's room. Father's case, the book case was wide open and they were leafing through nearly every book page by page looking for something. I wanted some explanation. I asked mother, 'Who are they?' Mother just said, 'Don't talk, don't talk. There's no time'. In other words, they were wanting to arrest father and looking for some excuse. And I was terribly frightened of it all. And then I also remember that I'd just had my birthday and grandmother's sister had given me a pretty little towel, in those days that was a rarity. I grabbed the little towel and said I wouldn't give it to them, because they were preparing to list all our possessions and take them away. But we didn't have anything to take. Father had made the furniture, the little beds and cupboards himself. We had no furniture. And by the way, there is still no furniture in my father's house. ... Well everything is quite basic. And at that time he had even less. And so even if they inventorized everything there

wasn't actually anything to take. Looking at it with today's eyes there was nothing to take.

But there were lots of books. They were digging around in those books. Father bought every book. He valued them. In one of those books was a photograph of Hitler. That was considered very good, factual evidence that my father is I don't know what sort of criminal. And then they immediately stopped their search, and interrupted everything else and arrested my father and drove off with him. It seems that at first he was kept in Gulbene and then I know that he was in Riga in the cheka headquarters, in the cellar. Earlier people were taken in cattle wagons, but in 1951, only individual people were arrested. And it seems it was on the basis of some information from some person and that that person was questioned. And it seems that somebody had written something. But that person was not always guilty. He might simply be forced to do it. The case was heard in Riga. I don't remember all the details about the hearing. But the long and the short of it was that he was sentenced to eight years. You must talk to my mother to find the reason stated.

In the event Antra's father spent four years in Vorkuta and six months in exile in Inta before being allowed home to Latvia:

Actually he was innocent. When he was released from prison he was recognized as being unjustly punished. Now he has all the documents, like most arrested people, showing that he really hadn't done anything. In court he had all sorts of witnesses from Salaspils concentration camp who, as a priest, he had saved from the Germans, but the court didn't take that into consideration. The people, those witnesses, got threats and that was the end. And when interrogations took place at home, my brothers were younger, but I was always quite alert and sensitive and I took it all very much to heart, because those Russian chekists were very rude and they stormed about and their behaviour. Later I understood that it had all had a terrible effect on me. Because later if a car like the one used by the cheka appeared on the road, I would already be running away from the house. We had a little meadow nearby and I was shaking with fear and actually in my subconscious was the idea that I had to flee from them. And I know that we had even taken some eggs from my grandmother and we had dug a little hollow in the meadow. And I, as organizer, had put the eggs there – my brothers were younger – in case they came again, then we would run and hide there. Actually, that would have been laughable and later the school year started. I started school in 1951.

Antra's mother was left with four young children to look after:

Well, when father was arrested, by that time I think the land those four hectares had already been taken away. . . . In that short time. But during that same time we were left some pasture. Grandmother had two cows and I think some horses were left. And when father was arrested mother had to travel to Riga often. The fares had to be paid for. Money was needed for everything. Mother didn't work. And then gradually the horses were sold, one cow was sold. And so we survived from what grandmother grew in the vegetable garden. Actually we lived only on that, because mother couldn't get any work. Because father was a pastor and on top of that he was deported. Mother looked very hard for work. Because we were starting to grow. And how many times can you patch the same clothes? They were sewing the whole time. I remember wearing old clothes for a long time. And then finally mother got work. Mother got work in the accounting office of a cooperative. And, of course, the wages ... she was taken on as an apprentice. The wages were very small. If I remember rightly it was 16 roubles. But at that time even 40 roubles was a very big wage. And the person who took her on was Jewish by nationality, her supervisor that is.[3] But despite that he tried to help mother in every way. He understood because at that time we were four children, my brother, the fourth had also been born. He tried to help mother in all sorts of ways, until he himself got into trouble for accepting mother. He had been called before the security organization and warned. But he had already accepted her and no action was taken. And after some time he fixed a job in the bakery. He was able to do it. The work was such that she had to hand the bread out to shops. And, of course, things were quite different then. We could get bread for free. And similarly the bakers who worked there, knowing our circumstances, they sometimes gave us a little bag of flour or a bit of sugar. And we children, when we went to the bakery to bring mother her lunch, we got bread. The bread was warm and tasted lovely. We could eat a bellyfull of bread and then sometimes the bakers had baked some buns for themselves and the they gave us some. So all in all we liked being in the bakery. But at that time I was already going to school.

Antra describes the material difficulties and how they were overcome with the help of the Jewish supervisor. However, her difficulties at school were very much greater and presented a challenge to her earlier assumptions about a supportive community. Antra was seven when her father was arrested and about to go to school:

I remember my father had just bought, just managed to buy a school bag. We bought the school bag in the shop. Father was proud that I was going to school, because to him knowledge was the most important thing. And we returned very proudly from the shop. I already put that bag on my shoulders. But that was before school. Because he bought that bag some time in the spring and even before the beginning of school he was already away, he'd already been sentenced. And then after he was sentenced he was sent to Vorkuta.

Antra describes his letters home:

Sometimes he wrote letters, but he never complained. Even in later conversations when I said to him, 'How can you consider that God is so good when you've worked for His good all this time, and really sacrificed your life. And He deported you. Where was He? Why didn't he protect you?' He says that God imposed that on him as a test. And he never considered it as a punishment. That it had been a test for him, that it had been necessary for him to learn about people and to see.

With the beginning of school Antra found it particularly difficult to reconcile her father's predicament and beliefs with the official teachings at school:

How shall I put it? Up to that time I hadn't noticed a bad attitude towards me from others because everyone behaved well. But when I started school, then gradually one or other teacher would throw a phrase at me. And gradually I became very sensitive to this issue. And I began to understand even from half a word or from a look. And children too would call me names. Firstly, because my father was a pastor and secondly because he was in prison. And naturally it's very clear for a child and we were taught at school and even at home it was sometimes said that only thieves and such like are put in prison. That's what we we're taught isn't it? And suddenly my father who has been so good and so on is in prison. And when my mother said that it's not true, that father hasn't done anything, that what has been done to him is all wrong and so on, I couldn't quite believe it. And how can it be that it's all wrong? It's difficult to understand. I didn't have enough sense to analyse it in detail or to test it out. But actually I did think that he probably had done something. I didn't say anything at home to my mother, but in my heart I somehow thought it. Yes, and then I remember at school it was definitely before the fourth class, that one teacher I remember his surname, it was Aizupietis. He taught us handicrafts and physical education. And I can't remember in what connection, whether we were having a conversation or whether someone had offended me or whether he'd heard something. But he came up to me. He said 'Don't worry. Your father is a good and honest man. And all honest Latvians are sitting in prison.' And he said for me not to take it to heart if someone said something ill-considered to me or offended me. Not to mind, that the time would come when everything would be cleared up. And that was a shock to me. Something that I remember to this day, because I was very surprised because no person outside the family had said anything like that to me. Everybody with whom I'd come into contact had said exactly the opposite. Father in prison. And a pastor and God knows what. Just the way children call names. One doesn't even need to say it aloud. An expression or a gesture may be enough. Well, of course, not all teachers behaved like that, but I was suspicious of all of them. Because I didn't know what they were thinking. There were teachers who said openly, 'What can you expect from a child like that, she has that kind of a father'. There were also other children in the class who had someone deported in the family. And then those children would be spread out [among different classes]. And then various things occurred, for example, they would not be accepted in the young pioneers.[4] But again, when the pioneer organization had to fulfil its plan, when it had to fulfil its plan then the pastor's daughter came in useful and even she was allowed to join the pioneers. But I didn't need any persuading. I wanted to join that organization so desperately, more than I've wanted anything else in my life. And when I got home I said that I'm going to join the pioneers. And mother screamed at me hysterically, and grandmother was even more set against it. She was totally against it. I go back to school. The teacher asks me, 'Well, did you talk to your parents? Are your parents willing?' 'Yes I did speak to them. Yes they are willing.' I couldn't tell that teacher, because firstly I wanted it so much and secondly because I was frightened to say anything. And then virtually the whole class had already joined. They had various activities and various little groups. And I wanted it too. I don't know, there were a few children who were left, probably the least trustworthy. And then the day arrived when we had to be enrolled in the pioneers. But I remember that there was a big problem with the pioneers. One had to buy a red kerchief and a pioneer badge. But at home I couldn't . . . my grandmother and mother would never buy that badge. And I thought for a long time about what I should do. And the day was coming closer all the time when I had to enroll. But I couldn't enroll because I didn't have the prerequisites. And then I decided on a very important move. At that time a pioneer scarf cost ten roubles . . .

Antra, in fact, decided to take the money from her grandmother's purse:

And now I take the money and go to the shop and buy the kerchief. And of course, grandmother to this day does not know that I took the roubles. But now I enroll in the pioneers. I go to school and on the way I pull out the kerchief and knot it, I come home and put it in my pocket. Once grandmother cleaning my coat finds the kerchief. And then all hell was let loose. At home I was scolded for being in the pioneers. At school it was the other way round.

Antra's narrative provides a powerful illustration of the confusion which deportation and imprisonment created for children. Punishment and wrongdoing form a logical unity which is difficult to take apart particularly for a young child. Antra was seven at the time of her father's arrest. The point of departure of her narrative is the arrest. She makes inferences rather than remembers the time before the arrest. It must have been a happy time: the family were together and the parishioners were supportive. By contrast those loving and supportive relationships disappeared after the arrest. Even within the family Antra could not express her thoughts as the incident about the pioneers illustrates. In Anna's previous narrative the confrontation between the notion of homeland (*dzimtene*) and reality is sudden and painful. For Antra the confrontation has been a more gradual and insidious but no less painful one. Antra's problems did not stop after her father's return:

Well, the interesting thing was that after he returned from prison, he had a beard and he'd never had a beard before, nor did he have one later. After he returned . . . when he came home, then I had the feeling . . . I was afraid to go near him. I couldn't understand if it was him, if it was my father. We children had been so longing for him, whatever the difficulties at school, a father is a father. We were waiting for him, but I had the feeling that a different person came back from that prison. To me . . . perhaps, in my perception he had changed into a different person. In a spiritual sense. There wasn't a spiritual closeness. Father, family . . . family, and yet there was something which pushed me away. Exactly that contradiction. And maybe I myself became guarded, I couldn't understand who to believe and who to trust. Sometimes I tried to confide in someone and always I was disappointed. And finally I understood that one has to keep oneself to oneself. And if something hurts, one can't entrust it to anyone because one doesn't want to be doubly embittered. And maybe for that reason . . . in my life I've never made particular friends. I don't have any girl friends or anyone else to whom I could talk about my life or anything like that. If I have some acquaintance visiting me, I can chat to them, but about my own problems, about things that hurt me I never talk. Nor about my family's problems. Others tell the last detail of what is happening at home or in the family. I never do. I listen but I myself can never talk.

Having described her inability to trust people, Antra's narrative reverts to her father's imprisonment in Vorkuta. Her narrative juxtaposes her present problems with the lack of loyalty and consistency of her father's friends. At the trial there were many who wanted to speak on his behalf, but in the end there was only one witness who was not intimidated by the threats:

All the others were intimidated, so that there was nobody to speak up for him. Of course, if it were today then I don't know how many people would appear.

The trauma of Antra's early family life have left her with the feeling that she has been robbed of a childhood which she cannot remember: she makes the paradoxical statement that she cannot remember anything prior to her father's arrest and that it must therefore have been happy. The arrest destroyed Antra's idea of a supportive community. It changed the relationship between Antra's family and the rest of the world:

I felt pushed out from society. For a child . . . for me that was very significant that all children are good but I'm on the sidelines, extruded and that created a reaction in me.

Many narrators recount similar childhood memories. For example, Jānis and Maiga were exiled in 1949 together with their elder brother and mother. (Their father had been shot in 1941.) Jānis was fourteen at the time and Maiga was twelve. They were collected and arrested from the school class room. Since their family consisted of a woman and children and no strong workers they were allocated to the worst kolhoz. Theirs was in the region of Molcanova.[5] It was swampy, ridden with insects and impenetrable forests. There was no food:

Mother had said there was nothing to eat. My brother promised to bring home a duck in the evening. He was hot, he'd gone in the water, swum and some five metres from the shore he caught cramp. And that's how he drowned.

The rest of the family returned to Latvia in 1957. Jānis was twenty-two and his sister was twenty. My question as to how things went on their return got two contradictory replies. Jānis' reply was: 'We had nothing to fear.' But Maiga contradicted him:

We were reproached and reproached. Even where I worked in the field brigade, I couldn't talk with the supervisor. We were regarded differently. When I was made to lift those heavy sacks and I protested, then I was given lectures. I cried and left. Even recently I heard someone, I won't mention any names, saying that all the deportees should have been shot . . . I thought, 'In what way am I guilty?' Then they realized that it applied to me and they were covered in confusion and said well, not quite all.

Other narrators remember being described as criminal children. Misiunas and Taagepera write, 'A regime which did not recognize hereditary wealth applied hereditary criteria of guilt' (1993, p. 98) and this claim was borne out by many narratives. However, guilt was imputed in everyday encounters and in the process of that imputation the child's concept of society was transformed.

Another problem described by many narrators was the change in character of those returning from exile or imprisonment. Vizma's father was an officer in the Latvian army, amongst the 540 arrested and deported to Norilsk on 14th June 1941.[6] He returned ten years later in 1951. Vizma was nine years old when her father was deported and nineteen when he returned:

> I remember every little nuance. I do remember, yes. I was finishing senior school. But to me . . . well, I suppose this belongs to the discussion of illness, but I have to say that when father returned he wasn't the same gay and bright person. I remember . . . those ten years had left their imprint. He had become gloomy, you could even say cruel, until he got over it. Now he is once again full of life and interesting. But those years weren't as pleasant as I'd expected. He didn't live with mother, he divorced. How shall I put it? He was simply . . . he didn't respect women, in the way that it was accepted during the period of Ulmanis. He behaved quite roughly towards mother . . . I don't want to go into the details, but he wanted to fight . . . 'How have you lived?' And he didn't pay any attention to me. That's how it was. In other words, it wasn't the way I had remembered it.

In common with many men returning from deportation Vizma's father had difficulties in resuming his place in the family. From the point of view of his family this was attributed to the transformation of his personality and his reluctance to acknowledge the material and psychological difficulties which his wife and daughter had experienced.

ACCOMMODATION

In the post-war years accommodation, along with hunger, was foremost among the problems experienced by deportees and their families. Returning to Antra's later narrative accommodation plays a key role and she links it with her experience of ill-health:

> No individual falls ill suddenly. Everything happens gradually. And round about that time I began to feel worse and that was the first time that nerve medicine was prescribed for me. There is no specific point in time when it starts. But I think it's everything that has built up and it's how we lived those first years. By the time I was nineteen my personal problems with my parents were over but then all the problems with my personal life started. Material circumstances: there was nowhere to live, if a person has nowhere to live it is a terrible problem. It is an indescribable problem. I rented all sorts of rooms. I was robbed time and again. I come home and I'm only left with what I'm wearing. It was only that kind of landlord who would rent out rooms. That's how it gradually developed.

Antra had left school at sixteen following an argument with a teacher and very much against her parents' wishes. She moved to Cēsis and eventually to Riga:

It was always my goal to move to Riga. . . . Of course, living accommodation is quite difficult in Riga. There have never been empty flats in Riga or for rent. But nevertheless I found something in one place. . . . There was no question of getting a separate flat or room. Only what you might call a bed space. Usually whoever rented out the rooms, they would rent one room but they would take several girls so that they would have more money altogether. I don't remember the exact rent, but at any rate it was quite high particularly in relation to the amount of money one could earn. It was a family who rented out the room. They had the one room which they rented out to us girls and they had the other room. Despite the fact that they were divorced they both lived in that one room. One could live there. We were some four or five girls. The number would change, because one would find somewhere else to live another would join us. The girls would change often, very often.

However, even this makeshift arrangement came to an end:

The people where we lived, their daughter got married and we all had to leave the room because the daughter was coming to live there with her husband. . . . And then after that I had to look for somewhere to live. At that time in Riga there was a stock market and all sorts of shady types mixed there and of course no honest people went there. But we didn't have any experience, I didn't know all the ins and outs. . . . And then a woman said to me that she had a room, that she lived with her young son and that she would be willing to take me. And then I went to live with her for a while. We all lived in one room with that woman and her son who was in the first class at school, a Russian school. She was a Russian. And then one evening I saw – they had a glass door – I saw her going out of the flat past the glass door, and I have the feeling that she's wearing my fur coat. I'd had this nice fur coat sent to me of the kind you couldn't get in Riga and I looked and I saw that she is wearing my fur coat on her back. And I get up and I see that my fur coat is missing. Of course, I couldn't sleep, I was very upset. After that, later in the night, I heard her returning with a man, and later living there it turned out that she was looking for men. In other words, she didn't work and those men gave her money. She slept with them and . . . in other words, that's what the woman was like. And she had chosen me.

Well, when the men weren't there she slept in the same room as us, but when the men came, she slept in the kitchen, in the bathroom. I'm ashamed to recount it. And I understood that that was why she'd chosen me. . . . And she had nothing in that flat. The flat was empty. She was very poor. At times she didn't have anything to eat. Well, and she'd chosen me because she'd noticed that I was the same size as her and she could wear my clothes. And, of course, I'd gone there because I had nowhere to go and I couldn't find anywhere to go and I was looking. And after that I noticed that I was missing two lengths of dress material sent from abroad.

Antra's mother's sister lived in Canada and regularly sent the family parcels. The material and fur coat referred to were sent from Canada:

She had taken them and then I started to look for somewhere else to live. . . . I had two cousins in Riga, but, you know, their flats were also small and if the worst came to the worst one could sleep the night there, but somehow I felt ashamed. I could go there once but not live there my whole life, nobody wants that. . . . One night I stayed with my cousin, the next night I stayed with my other cousin. And once I'd decided to go to one of the cousins and no one was at home. Somehow it came about that it was already the middle of the night and I was ashamed to approach anyone else, and I was walking around Riga from one end to the other and there is no one with whom to stay. It was already dark, but I was ashamed to ask anyone else and it got completely dark. Such a terrible situation developed and still I was ashamed and still I couldn't overcome my pride and I went to one house and I climbed to the top floor and I sat down on the landing and waited for the morning sitting there.

And then after that I started to look for a flat and then I was told that there was a family renting out a room in Ķengarags. And I went to see that woman. 'Yes', she said 'Come and live here', she was a Latvian woman, her name was Maija and her husband was Ziģis and their two boys. 'We'll rent you that room and that'll be fine'. Even from the appearance of their flat it was clear that they were drunkards, but I had no alternative, I thought I'll go anyway and have done with it. At any rate it will be better than the previous one. So I went there and it did turn out that there were frequent visitors and all sorts of drinking, they didn't get on between themselves, they had frequent fights. I called the police. I realized there was no future for me there. And it happened that I caught a cold, I got a very high temperature, the emergency ambulance came and they decided I had appendicitis and that I would need an operation. They took me to hospital and admitted me. I had an examination straight away. It turns out that I don't have appendicitis, I have an inflammation of the kidneys, something there. I was probably walking around with a half-naked bottom, the way one did earlier in shoes. We had no boots in those days. I remember. And then they treated me a bit in that hospital. When they had treated me they discharged me. And then when I came out from that hospital I realized I'd been well and truly robbed. A lot of things had been taken, all the better quality things that had been sent to me had been taken. And afterwards the neighbours told me that they had gone and sold my jumpers for a bottle of drink. At that time I think a bottle cost two or three roubles. And they'd gone round offering them to all the neighbours asking whether they wanted to buy a jumper in exchange for a bottle. So altogether they'd run up big losses for me.

And then after that . . . through an acquaintance I was taken to an old woman. And the old woman had a two-roomed flat and a big dog. And that woman was so terribly old, that woman was so terribly capricious that even today I think if I had to choose where to live, I would choose to live with the drunkard rather than with the old woman. Because on top of everything she was untidy and she had promised to rent me the room, but when I got there she only let me stay in the kitchen and only sleep in the kitchen. Yes, it was a long narrow kitchen and there was a so called *razkladuska* [Russian for camp bed] and then I slept there for a while, with that old woman. And altogether there was nothing there and then that old woman had a friend visit.

She also was Russian. Ivanova. At one time she had been the wife of a famous Russian opera singer. But it seemed to me that she was a little . . . that she was already on the verge of madness. And then there was another queer woman who came there. She had a little semi-basement flat in Pārdaugava and so we got talking and so she offered to rent me that half-basement flat. And so I went to that little half-basement flat. Of course, everything was terribly untidy there, but I put things in order. And that old woman sometimes came to sleep the night there when she had absolutely nowhere to go. That woman was the kind that was very helpful to everyone. She went to all the sick people. And she fed them and she herself was still working in VEF [a radio electronics factory] as a cleaner and she also wrote poetry herself. She had lots of notebooks full of poems. Altogether she was quite unusual. I said it was a one-room flat. So it had a kitchen and beyond that a room. And then she sometimes came – there was a place to sleep there and then she would sleep on that little bed in the kitchen. It was fitted out like a room, separate, with a cupboard and then she stayed there sometimes, but very rarely. And she practically didn't take any money from me. She was happy when she came and I always fed her well and I always kept something by so that I could give her a proper meal. Sometimes I would give her a present and she was happy about every little thing. She was a child of nature. She was an old woman but . . . [pause] she was very religious, she knew my father. And then, in other words, I lived there in that little cellar, I lived there until the time that I got our flat and all of my youth was spent in that cellar.

Memories of these earlier problems of finding somewhere to live continue to trouble her particularly at night time:

Those events were of all kinds. There is nowhere to live, altogether that is terrible, because that ruins one's nerves terribly, not just the war period, those terrors suffered, but all that knocking about in those flats. No one can understand that. That also is madness. Even now sometimes at night I wake in terror from a dream. I see a dream where I have no home and that's terrible.

Antra's narrative about finding a place to live is both a personal narrative and a political metaphor. Her personal memories are structured by shared social perceptions of the past. She moves from living with a Russian prostitute who literally takes the coat from Antra's back, to a Latvian couple who have taken to drink and have also turned to stealing and finally finds refuge with an other-worldly Latvian woman who wants no rent, who writes poetry and yet works as a cleaner. Antra's personal trajectory encompasses the social history of the past fifty years in Latvia. Antra's personal troubles, her experience of 'fleecing', serve as a metaphor for the political processes contained in those years.

For Vizma too accommodation played a key role in her illness biography. Before the war her parents had lived in the working-class Moscow district of Riga:[7]

Maybe that was the reason why nobody searched for us and deported us, maybe because we were very insignificant. Well, we lived very penuriously. My mother did not know how to sort things out or to earn a bit of extra money. So a piece of bread was really quite a big thing. . . . I stayed in that same flat until I was forty years old. That is sheer madness. My daughter was already born and still they would not give us a flat. They didn't give us one, the queues are long.

And some of the more powerful queues – I'm referring to the Russians – those move more quickly, but ordinary people, indigenous people they not only don't move forward but the queue gets longer all the time. And I must say I was reduced to hysteria crying … going there to the executive committee and realizing I had no rights where I stood. We were all squashed in that one-roomed flat, my daughter had been born. My mother had remarried, my husband had left me, gone away, we got divorced, but nevertheless to live in a one-roomed flat with my stepfather who was quite badly disposed towards me, I was a hindrance to him. It was terrible, I couldn't even buy a little piece of furniture, nothing new, just terrible.

My daughter and I were in the room but my mother and stepfather were in that little kitchen. Such a narrow little kitchen and that's how all my youth was spent, my best years. And as a joke I can tell you about the bureaucracy of that time, I can recount an incident. Below us in that house a little one-roomed flat was vacated, but it was generally known that the house would be demolished soon – it was in a state of utter collapse. It was about to be demolished and we would be given flats somewhere. Now it's long since been razed to the ground. And one flat was vacated, and now I go to the executive committee and I beg them, that I don't need to register that I shan't ask for anything else for myself in the future, only that I should be allowed to live there. For me to be able to live alone with my little child, to live alone. 'No and no.' And I started to cry. And the director of the executive committee left me alone in the office and said 'You can cry as much as you want but that will change nothing, because there are people living in sheds.' And then I asked him how they got to be in those sheds, in other words those who come from Russia, they stay in some barracks or sheds and they have to be given good flats. Then he said don't let's talk about that question. And do you know I really got that longed for little one-roomed flat. It's unpleasant to remember but one of my girl-friends had such a close relationship with one of the directors of Riga's trust. I asked her to put in a good word for me, to let me be on my own for a year or two. So that I can live like a human being. Because I'm a young person, and I can't wash in my own flat. 'Fine, I can't promise you, but I tell you, I'll speak on your behalf.' And what do you think, after a time I get an announcement, a call that I've been allocated a flat. Smiling at me, smiling ironically as though thinking to themselves that I was involved in some sort of relationship I was given the order for the flat. I thought 'Smile as much as you like, think what you like, at least I'll get a couple of years to live alone in a little room.' That's how flats were allocated with us.

And when did she move to her new flat? I asked:

I can tell you that exactly. It was my little girl's tenth birthday. My daughter too until the age of ten lived in terrible circumstances. In my childhood everything was well looked after, there was a good landlord, everything was clean and beautiful, there were gardens and flowers and flowering cherries. All that was broken down and uncared for and the house was left derelict, the sheds collapsed. But my daughter laughs and says that it was quite jolly to play hide and seek and that she didn't feel any hardship.

Vizma herself however feels she suffered a lot due to the cramped living conditions:

> I can't put it into words when every moment whether it's morning or evening you only feel discomfort, constriction, humiliation and embarrassment. What sort of effect can that have, well what? I couldn't even get married, I would have got married a second time. Everybody had difficulties with flats, but no man came along who had his own flat. They came, had a look round and then even that possibility disappeared of starting a new life. Those circumstances were terrible. And for my daughter too ... that constriction, she had to do school-work, she worked well. The constriction, everyone was pushing past her desk. I think that all that oppressiveness, all that greyness has made a specific impact on my health. There are women who are different, but maybe I am by nature more emotional, for me that was all very difficult.

For Vizma too her personal problems are set in a political context and contrasted with a remembered past.

Anna's first reference to accommodation is made shortly after she describes their return from Siberia:

> People were very intimidated here. They didn't want to socialize freely. It was difficult to find anywhere to live, although houses were empty. They didn't let us in. We lived with relatives for three or four months, then we found a little old woman, she lived in a private house and she gave us a room.

Anna also relates her neurosis as she terms it to her subsequent difficult living circumstances. I asked her whether she had sought help for her problems.

> Well, I think I could be helped with the nerve illness. But I think that while the cause has not been liquidated, the cause of my neurosis, the cause of my stress, until I have peaceful home circumstances, at work I am tense, I have to listen to different people, different complaints, different characters, I have to be calm all the time, and when I go home I can't rest and again I have to hear ... to be specific I have to hear various swear words addressed to me. Actually, I don't get any rest anywhere. Only the holiday, those seven weeks that we psychiatrists have. That holiday is not a month but a month and a half. And perhaps it's the summer time when I distance myself most from work and family problems. Well, family problems remain. Grandmother is still there, I have to go back to that same flat. That doesn't disappear anywhere. Perhaps I just distance myself from work but not from everyday problems. So to sort out this accommodation problem is not so easy. Because in every instance, wherever I've turned, I'm told 'You have a large living space. What else do you want? We have lots of people in the queue who have bad living conditions.'

Anna lives with her first husband's mother-in-law (her first husband died) and her two daughters from her second marriage. It is a four-roomed flat which was rented by her in-laws' family since before the war. In the early 1960s a Russian family was billeted in the flat. I asked what relationships were like then:

In principle they were the same, only then father and mother-in-law were younger and stronger, the neighbours also were younger and more energetic. At that time the conflicts developed more within the family and less with the neighbouring family. Later her husband left her and she was left with her son. It seems she had a restless nature, she had to be in conflict with someone the whole time, but they were more monologues, we didn't engage in arguments. . . . But at any rate she is a temperamental woman, who considers that what she does or says is important and she takes no account of others. If that other needs to get in the bathroom, then she goes in there and locks herself in and washes her clothes from morning 'til night, without considering that there's a family next to her. In the morning when the children go to school they need at least to brush their teeth or wash their faces, but nothing like that is ever taken into account. All of that is very disturbing, as we say anti-social, even the toilet room. . . . Maybe it sounds odd, but that woman has so much evil in her and she has no feeling. [Anna is describing her neighbour with whom she shares the flat.] She goes past an old person and pushes her. She sees that she's walking along holding on to the wall the way old people do. She does all sorts of swinish things like that, such childish hooliganisms. For example, she doesn't like the fact that my fur jacket is hanging in the hall, then she starts to cut it slowly and systematically with a razor. In a week's time she has cut a sizeable hole. She doesn't like our shoes in the hall, she considers them dirty, she will open the door of our room and without any inhibitions she will throw those shoes in the room.

But most of all I suffer from the fact that my children hear those rude Russian swear words. I'm not so concerned about myself however unpleasant it may be and the same goes for grandmother, but a child. Those children are growing up the same way as me – neurotic. A new generation of neurotics, because they're already afraid. A young child doesn't understand swear words. I remember that my youngest daughter was five years old. She comes in and calls me swear words. My daughter asks me what they mean. I have to tell her that those are bad words. It hurts me especially for the children, that a new generation will also suffer from accommodation neurosis.

For Anna the tension and constriction which she feels in the flat is contrasted with her sense of well being when she is alone in the country:

I have always been oppressed by large gatherings of people. I have never liked crowds. Maybe that comes from being Latvian, from the genes, from peasanthood. Yes. A peasant loves an isolated farmstead, he is more of a loner. I don't like one building next to another, one flat above another, I don't like that. I want open spaces, I want forests, fields. I consider myself to be a real country person and I think to myself that as soon as I can, if it's in my powers, although I'm quite doubtful whether it will be in my powers looking at it from today's perspective, I very much want to spend the last years of my life in the country. In the peace of the country, in the quiet of the country, at peace with myself and the environment.

Anna invokes the culturally constructed image of the lone farmstead and the self-reliant farmer. Set against this historical construct her present living circumstances seem to fall particularly short.

WORK

Work is another area whose transformation contributes to neurasthenia. The framework for Vizma's discussion is provided by the historical stereotypes of Latvians as determined workers:

> I remember I had a supervisor, she was a real Russian, a party member, but as human being very straight and honest. I worked with her as the head of a cadre of workers. We were some three or four hundred people in the collective. And she said, 'I, being a Russian, would rather take Latvians to work, because Latvians are responsible and industrious.' It was very pleasant to hear that from a Russian. Doing one and the same job, Latvians will definitely be more accurate. That responsibility and industriousness have remained. Russians are more superficial, they like to gather together to gossip, to laugh, to drink. Although that Russian untidiness has caught hold.

Dishonesty and lack of order at work are further aspects of society which disrupt biography, breach the boundaries of the self and threaten its integrity. Vizma describes her difficulties at work by contrasting Latvian with Russian styles of behaviour:

> You know that's how it is. I don't want to I don't want to offend the Russian nation, that loudness, that shouting has been taken over from them. It's not characteristic of Latvians, they're quiet. And if that shouting doesn't take place in the presence of the customers, then he'll go a metre away and shout behind the wall. If he's firm and says there won't be any shouting, but if the director himself is a loud-mouth and shouts at his workers well, then there's pandemonium. Many officials have told me – I can't stop myself from speaking my mind. I say in your own home, your family, behind your door, you can give free rein to your voice, but the rest of us we don't like your voice. Then she calls me *Latishka* [Latvian] and I'm turned into the bad one. Another replies,'I feel better that way', but I say 'I feel worse when you shout that way'. Well you see, it's even stuck to us that lack of control.

Vizma herself feels that she has managed to maintain her self-control:

> Outwardly I was calm. All the conflict situations I managed as calmly as possible, but then I went to my office and drank medicines or elenium to get over it. And that was an everyday occurrence. You see our collective was large. There were lots of men officials, women too. They didn't know anything. But a few who were closer to me, either Latvians or women my age, they knew, but they did the same themselves. The women who worked in the buffet they also had difficulties. They just threw some medicine into their mouths and that was all.

The proverbial stealing is also mentioned by Vizma:

> You know there is a saying that Russia, well, the USSR is the richest nation in the world, because everybody steals and they can't empty everything. Industry

had simply worked out loss percentages so that there was enough for the small-time thieves and the big thieves who carried stuff away in lorryloads. For example, I know very well how it worked in my own line – in state restaurants. There were the so-called *raskladkas* [Russian for rations] that is how much raw meat had to be given to fry one burger. The meat loss in the process of frying or boiling was calculated. In actual fact there wasn't a big loss but in that way one could steal, the cooks, the chefs, the director and the whole collective was fed. The whole system was arranged that way. The little wages, those were just. . . . For example the buffet worker. Do you know what a buffet worker is? Every restaurant had a buffet where you could get coffee, drinks. They used to steal something dreadful. The buffet attendant didn't even know when pay day was due, the wages didn't matter anything to her, it was such trivia. They made money. For example, coffee. Nine grams were worked out per cup. They diluted it. You were lucky if you got two or three grams. Just imagine, earning two for every one cup. That all adds up by the evening. Thats what the chefs did, the store supervisors and everyone knew it and no one blamed anyone else. And that became part of one's character. But that wasn't the worst of it. Controls. You never knew which official was cheating, which table he'd added up wrongly.

Another problem related to drinking:

In the evenings drunkards tried to break in the restaurants. At that time the prices weren't so high and the doorman didn't bow for people to come in. We were worried the whole time that the door might be broken down or something might be done to the doorman. And the drinking was terrible. After the war, on pay day in every district someone was lying drunk in the street. Later people started drinking in a more civilized way in restaurants. I hope I'll be forgiven but I have to say that that terrible drinking until loss of consciousness, that Latvians picked up from the Russians. It was terrible what we experienced.

For Inta the connection between work and illness is equally close and more dramatic. Inta contrasts her recent difficulties with her earlier success at work:

And then at that time the directorship changed. Up to that time everything was fine, I worked well, I related well to people, I was active and energetic, I had good contacts and I was in charge of various enterprises. That was in the theatre in Ķengarags. We had a company there and then a new director arrived. He was a person of Russian nationality, pensioned from the army. At that time I thought they were such firm people, then I had the view that we would have discipline and I was well disposed towards him. But it turned out quite the other way. And I felt very deceved. Orgies, drinking started. They were a bit afraid of me, they respected me, then they were afraid to do it openly. But then one of the replacement technicians, a woman, telephoned and complained. That call came at home in the evening, telling me that such and such was happening and could I as the deputy director and administrator take some steps. And I'm thinking now what shall I do, I can't do anything myself and I called the police. That's what we do here when those sorts of things happen. Then the police get called out. Well, I thought, let them give them a bit of a run around. And so that's what I did. After that it all came to light. That same woman. . . . Well I don't know whether it was done intentionally or what but it came to the director's attention and he started to eat away at me. Well, to speak openly he started to humiliate me in various ways. Then I started to complain.

It was unjust. Because in principle my responsibility was very great. He had even put his responsibilities on me. I had both the housekeeping responsibilities and responsibility for mass initiatives, the planning of various shows. And then on my own initiative I planned various exhibitions, so that people would find it more interesting with us, so that cinema would not be just watching a film. The responsibility was too great but I didn't complain. And that's how it all started. I went to look for protection from the union, I sought protection at a higher level, but they told me not to get into conflict with the director, that I should get on, that I should listen to him and if it went wrong, then go away. And so I didn't get any support for myself. And the final straw was that a piece of curtain material was stolen, and he libelled me that I had stolen it or somehow appropriated it. And that was the last straw for me . . . that I was the housekeeper in the cinema and that I provided everything every little piece of wood, with us we couldn't get anything, we had terrible difficulties getting anything, you had to take some sort of bribe, some smoked chickens and go from office to office, well it was simply terrible . . . I supplied all that. And then to tell me in such a way.

Inta tried to take the matter to court but got nowhere:

And then I couldn't stand it any more and then I simply broke down. And all my fighting spirit and energy simply collapsed. Even though I had two little children I couldn't stand it. It was a terrible pressure.

And what happened then? I asked:

I got tired, I felt a kind of weariness. Such exhaustion took over that I can't do anything any more. And I collapsed as it were. If that's how it is then I went to the chemist and ate two packets of relanium in the hope that I would fall asleep and that for me that would be simpler.

That occurred about five years ago and since then Inta has found it difficult to be outgoing, to work and to socialize:

I have tried to work again in a department store in the information office. Well, helping people to orientate themselves, offering goods, speaking on the microphone. I had good diction and at one time I was studying in the technical college for cultural workers and I organized various concerts and undertakings and I thought now it will be peaceful there. You know it wasn't bad, but I didn't like it straight away. I thought I wouldn't have any contact with retail workers, but first as soon as I arrive I'm confronted with a regulation. And in that regulation it's written that I as a shop worker that I have no right to go into the shop and buy anything – how was it – during working hours or whatever. Well fine, of course, I won't go. Well, but in real life everything was quite contrary. People behaved completely otherwise. One would take, another would take. Well, that system in retailing is terrible. What it's like now I don't know, but at that time it was terrible. They took and they carried in piles round the offices and for me that. . . . Altogether I've always felt that I don't live in the right period. It's been like that from childhood. Somehow I have the feeling that I'm not living in my time. I have the feeling that this is not my place. And then I left that work. I couldn't stand it.

For Inta the confrontation between the work ethos and her inner conscience is a direct and dramatic one and is articulated primarily in a legal rather than a medical idiom.

Nīna's narrative makes a direct connection between dishonesty at work and her illness:

I worked in the state bank as an inspector. That was a thankless type of profession. I came into contact with all sorts of dishonest people as you know in our Soviet period. I had constant differences of opinion with them. I had to sort out the irregularities but the current system would not permit that. And that's why I had those sorts of conflicts here at the bank in Kandava. They simply took revenge on me so that I shouldn't poke my nose there and even today they dislike me. Traders, you know, were speculating, they were carrying out all sorts of malpractices and the appropriation of state funds took place before my eyes and I wasn't allowed to identify it. Well that, that traumatizes me the whole time. . . . I want to work honestly, we weren't allowed to work honestly. You're probably familiar with things. You read the Latvian press, don't you? That wears down the nervous system the whole time.

Well I thought it over. I started to fret, I started not sleeping, I couldn't fall asleep. I thought why is it that I want to work honestly and I would like things to be better for the state, for the state resources to be saved, you see I was very upset by the accommodation fund. I observed that all these fifty years during the Soviet period the fund for renovating buildings is in a poor state, things weren't renewed. Buildings collapsed. This house is twenty years old, it has never had a major redecoration. See, all those joins are collapsing, all the window frames are rotting, they're fragile, they should have been changed ages ago. And that's not just in this house. The whole of Riga is collapsing, but Riga has no money, Riga is threatened with bankruptcy. The means of transport have not been renewed on time, living quarters haven't been renewed on time, but the money disappears. The funds are withdrawn from the bank, somebody personally appropriates them, the property remains unrenovated. We had those sorts of manifestations on a massive scale in our country.

These narratives offer a political critique in parallel with the narrative of personal injury. There is a shared language of damage, injury, trauma and exploitation which is applied to society as well as to individuals. Although narratives start with illness, they move on to address social and historical issues. Social injustices are closely interwoven with personal traumas. Thus medical and political narratives interpenetrate. Lay illness narratives and aetiologies are deeply political: political causes are sought for the experience of illness. In the process medical language is dismissed as irrelevant to the illness experience. This is not to say that political meanings are absent from the medical language of neurasthenia. Ideas about the incurability of neurasthenia and hence the futility of treatment also carry political meanings. However, medical language is unable to contain the full force and extent of the political critique.

MEANINGS LOST AND GAINED

Earlier chapters looked at the ways in which narratives succeed or fail to redeem suffering and produce a coherent life. The differences between success and failure need to be examined more closely. If human life is in part the pursuit of meaning, it must be added that not all pursuits succeed. Some fail and still others find meaning only to lose it. Most meaningless lives retain a narrative coherence, although on occasion narrative structures disintegrate into a complete loss of meaning. Latvian narrators are preoccupied with meaning in a quite explicit way: they complain that their lives lack meaning and purpose. Ordinary peasant women with little schooling shed tears over the meaninglessness of their lives. What were they grieving over?

Latvian has two words which translate as meaning: *nozīme* and *jēga*. *Nozīme* is related to the word *zīmēt* – to draw – and is partially captured by the English term to delineate. *Jēga* has a broader connotation. It is related to words such as *jēdziens*, a concept and *apjēgt* to understand. However, *jēga* refers to a particular kind of understanding which is also morally satisfying and acceptable. Švābe's encyclopaedia gives the following definition of *jēga*: 'The meaning of some spiritual/mental activity, which justifies the pursuit of an activity or of life' (1950, p. 870). In its use *jēga* is intimately connected to the notion of a goal or of purpose. Questions about *dzīves jēga* (the meaning of life) are not so much about the underlying meaning or point of life, as they are about individual goals and purposes and the extent to which they have been thwarted by historical circumstances. Hence, the repeated complaints that there is no order in life, that nothing can be planned, nothing relied upon. The underlying complaint is that individual goals cannot be realized; that human intentions are overridden by history.

The attempt to capture meaning for lives meets with varying degrees of success. Illness narratives record the systematic erosion of meaning. Other narratives succeed in retrieving meaning by setting their individual lives within shared structures of belief. The narratives of older people tended to have a greater sense of underlying purpose and meaning. They were more literary in tone and asserted their membership of a textual community. (For a discussion of textual communities see Chapter 10.) However, age alone did not, of course, guarantee access to meaning. Why some narrators are successful in this quest and others not, is difficult to answer. The closest I can get to an answer is to suppose that differences in narrative reflect differences in experience. This is, of course, a circular argument but it offers a plausible account of the variations. My knowledge of the narrators' past experience is restricted to the actual narratives I heard: I can only infer the quality of their experience from what they told me.

Although lives may appear outwardly similar the quality of the experience draws upon the individual's past life and resources. The precise source of difference is hard to pinpoint. Subjective experiences are elusive and move in an indeterminate way between a private autobiography and a public domain of shared concepts. Outwardly the illness narratives did not record events any more terrible than those of other more purposive narratives, and yet their tone was vastly different. Illness narratives record a progressive loss of meaning, in the sense of purpose, although they may do so in a meaningful and coherent way. Only a few narratives reached the brink of incoherence. Other narratives record a retrieval of unexpected meanings ordinarily hidden.

The difference between these two types of narrative reflects their relationship to shared structures of belief. Whereas illness narratives dismantle such structures they are interwoven into the life histories of purposive narratives so closely as to be barely identifiable. The kind of literary structures I have in mind are widely disseminated and available (in principle) for all Latvians to draw upon. However, not all do draw upon these available cultural resources. Although the paradigm exists, individual narratives do not simply provide the medium for its instantiation.

My interpretation of narratives has benefited from a reading of Propp (1968), although his morphological analysis fails to answer my most important questions. Why do certain paradigms appear in some narratives and not in others? And what is the significance of local variations? My own answer would be that these paradigms do not simply make an appearance but are actively and selectively enlisted because they help to make sense of the past. Moreover, it is the variation specific to Latvia, rather than the shared underlying structure of the folk tale, which makes it useful to the retelling of individual lives.

Beyond these specific shortcomings, however, an exclusively structuralist analysis cannot give an account of how structures are identified. Thematic content is after all important. Similarly, shared thematic structures lend a purpose to the lives of Latvian narrators. However, this purpose is achieved through the meaning which such structures carry rather than through abstract form. My aim has been to identify common structures without obliterating the specific meanings which they carry. My reading and interpretation does not, of course, preclude others. There are losses and gains to any approach.

My chapter heading is a variation on a theme suggested by the writing of Shirley Brice Heath. She writes: 'Just as in each writing ... there are senses lost and senses gained, so there are in every reading by every reader senses lost and gained' (1993, p. 256). In my work such losses and gains relate in particular to transcription and translation. Transcription, like all translation, wrenches words from their embedded personal and social contexts. To me Latvian has always seemed a peculiarly embedded language, a language subtly suited to intimate family transactions. No doubt this is because as a child I heard Latvian almost exclusively at home. Although most children learn to speak in the family this soon comes to be supplemented by other social contexts which for me, as for most Latvians in England, were few. Latvian words always seemed to me to be heavily impregnated with the sensory qualities to which they referred. Fieldwork in Latvia did not dispel that sense of embeddedness. The extensive use of diminutives to promote feelings of warmth and understanding played a large part in perpetuating my feelings about the language. Diminutives are notoriously difficult to translate (see, e.g., Bratus 1969). Part of the reason is because diminutives refer not only to the narrated events, but also to speech events. They contribute to the construction of a shared world to which both listener and narrator assent. In Jakobson's terminology the diminutive is at one and the same time a shifter and a non-shifter (1971). (For a clear exposition of these terms see Crocker 1977, pp. 33–66). The full force of diminutives, particularly that which relates to the speech events, is lost in transcription. Transcription also loses the physical qualities of narratives which carry meaning as much as actual words. The timbre and intensity of individual voices, tremors, sighs and silences can convey lived experience more powerfully than words on a page.

However, there is also the obvious truth that both transcription and translation open up the possibility of greater analytic understanding. Both processes involve an act of distancing: transcription moves away from individual voices, translation from the familiar embeddedness of words. I could only achieve any kind of anthropological understanding through intellectual distancing, and transcription and translation were essential for this.

I chose to transcribe and translate large segments of spoken narrative, knowing that this conformed to the intentions of the narrators. Indeed, the epic sweep of lives demands such a presentation. However, which particular segments were included was determined by the identification of smaller portions of text in which strategies for representing identity and unifying the past were developed. Thus the identity of the narrator is to be found both in small segments of the narrative, and also in the overall structure of the narrated life. It is, therefore, important to look at narratives both as a whole and in their particularity. Tracing a hermeneutic circle I moved from the particular to the whole and back again.

My purpose here is to highlight the ways in which the narrative lives of letter-writers, in other words – damaged lives – differ from the narrated lives of others encountered during my stay. The notion of losses and gains applies not only to transcription, but also to the way in which narrators record losses and retrievals of meaning throughout the course of a lifetime. The complaint of illness narratives is that events and circumstances have conspired to rob their lives of meaning. By contrast other narratives succeed in retrieving meaning and purpose under the most inauspicious circumstances. These retrievals of meaning are supported by folk, biblical and literary structures. For example, there is the idea of destiny which pulls together lives which seem outwardly chaotic and meaningless. Chance meetings and recognitions play a key part in these narratives of destiny. Some lives are presented as quests – their goal being a homecoming and the homeland. Other lives are presented as pilgrimages whose goal is the transformation of the self. However, these supportive structures are noticeably absent from illness narratives.

The crucial distinction which I found between illness and other more purposive narratives does not fit with the findings of other anthropologists. Recent work in medical anthropology has emphasized the importance of narrative for illness. Illnesses are emplotted within lives and derive meaning from this process of embedding (see, e.g., Good 1994, pp. 135–165). It is almost taken as axiomatic that narrative is able to yield meaning. For example, Howard Brody, in a recent work on the role of narrative within medicine, equates narrative with intelligibility: 'The primary human mechanism for attaching meaning to particular experiences is to tell stories about them' (1987, p. 5). Anthropologists use narrative theory to construct a relationship between narrative and meaning which has certain similarities with an earlier functionalist account of social institutions and the promotion of a cohesive society. Just as every custom and institution was thought to play a part in maintaining the overall equilibrium of society, so all narrative creates a meaningful history and identity for the individual, and for societies – the writing of history being the most obvious case. Each is thought to have a necessary contribution to make to a larger, more meaningful whole: the social equilibrium in one case, and individual equilibrium in the other. Neither theory can account for the way in which things go wrong: for conflict, challenge to established meanings or loss of meaning. Although Latvians do claim very strong links between lives and illness, in the course of establishing this connection many narratives fail to acquire coherence and purpose. Indeed, it seems almost as though the inability to transform one's life into a meaningful story contributes to making people ill. Whatever the direction of causality, illness and the inability to make sense of one's life are found together.

Byron Good reminds us that whereas disease is located in the body:

> The narratives of those who are subjects of suffering represent illness, by contrast, as present in a life. Illness is grounded in human historicity, in the temporality of individuals and families and communities. It is present as potent memories and as desire.
>
> (1994, p. 157–8)

However, the fact that illness resides in the human realm of subjectivity and meaning and is intertwined with memory and desire, may make the need for meaning more urgent but does not guarantee its presence. For Good one important aspect of narrative is 'subjunctivity' (ibid., p. 153), by which he means a commitment to the possibility of change. However, he also recognizes that 'narratives of the tragic and hopeless cases, in particular of persons who are severely mentally retarded, showed little openness of this kind' (ibid., p. 155). Latvian illness narratives are more likely to belong to this tragic genre, than the open-ended narratives he describes elsewhere. Such narratives record the progressive narrowing of opportunity and illness represents a closure of possibilities. However, absence of meaning is painful to live with. It may be for this reason that we attribute meaning to situations where it cannot be found. In my own work of interpretation and editing I found myself drawn initially to narratives which succeeded in embodying purpose and meaning. These offer the reader the reward of sharing in a spiritual victory. Illness narratives by contrast are admissions of failure of meaning: uncomfortable and painful for narrator and listener or reader alike.

Illness narratives are distinguished not so much by an expected concern with the breakdown of health (although that is there too), as by other thematic and structural features. Victorious narratives – in contrast to illness narratives – are characterized by symbols of belonging and recognition. Illness narratives are characterized by exile and expulsion both real and symbolic, and by an undesired transformation or loss of identity. These themes are present within narratives both in an implicit and explicit form. Explicitly, they form part of lay aetiologies of illness. Implicitly, they are interwoven in narrated lives. Howard Brody in his insightful study of literary representations of sickness documents the effects of sickness on identity and perception of time past and future (1987, pp. 90–104). His analysis accepts the illness as an extraneous event which impinges upon and alters narrative experience. Since he is considering accounts of life-threatening illnesses, such as those described by Solzhenitsyn in *Cancer Ward*, his analysis is perfectly proper. It does not, however, fit the Latvian situation where illness is a response to failures of narrative experience. Isak Dinesen has a much-used quotation to the effect that one can bear anything if one can put it into a story. However, not all lives fit comfortably into stories and it is these troublesome and unyielding lives which are perceived as making people ill. In other words the inability to enshrine experience within available narrative structures, to transform private grief into public sorrow, makes people ill.

Thematically, Latvian illness narratives are characterized by three cumulatively linked losses: loss of a sense of belonging, loss of identity and loss of meaning. Narratives record such losses in straightforward ways requiring little interpretation: for example, the pain of a meaningless life, feelings of loneliness and of rejection and interrogations about concealed identities are described. However, such meanings are also conveyed by various implicit features of the narrative. Chapter 8 documented the way in which such life histories record the progressive dismantling of cherished values, particularly those values which are used as ethnic markers. Here the narratives/texts seem to acquire an autonomous voice over and above that of the narrator/author. The structure and development of the narration convey additional meanings to those explicitly carried by the text.

The role of ethnic identity and difference in the unfolding of illness within individual lives illustrates my point about the implicit meanings carried by narratives. Love of solitude, of one's home, of the homeland, love of work and self-control are all consciously used to symbolize the boundaries between Latvians and non-Latvians. Conversely, non-Latvians are distinguished by the absence of these traits. Russians feature prominently in narratives of illness. Their contrasting values and ways of behaving are frequently mentioned. For example, Latvians' love of quiet and solitude are contrasted with Russian love of noise and crowds. References are made to the Latvian tradition of living in isolated farmsteads and contrasted with the Russian tradition of villages. The ideal situation for a house is thought to be one where no sign of human habitation is visible. The Latvian habit of speaking quietly and calmly is contrasted with Russian habits of loud talking and shouting. Latvians pride themselves on being self-controlled, whereas Russians are thought to lack discipline and self-control: they swear and drink. Latvians characterize themselves by their extreme attachment to locality and to the idea of a Latvian homeland. Russians are perceived as rootless, ready to move to where the going is good. Latvian love of work for its own sake is enshrined in folk songs. Narratives make frequent reference to Latvians as hard workers. It is, however, a double-edged attribute which promotes survival in difficult circumstances, but hastens death in extreme conditions. Shalamov makes a similar observation but offers a different explanation in his short story 'Survival':

> Estonians, Latvians and Lithuanians were always the first to die – a phenomenon that the doctors always explained away by claiming that peoples of the Baltic states were weaker than Russians. True their normal way of life was more dissimilar to that of the Russian peasant, and it was more difficult for them. The primary reason, however, was quite different: it wasn't that they possessed less endurance, but that they were physically bigger than the Russians.
>
> (1990, pp. 30)

Russians avoid work and if it cannot be avoided they do it badly. Latvians frequently express astonishment that anyone can fail to value what they value, for example, that Russians are perceived as having no love of Russia or desire to return to their homeland. However, although there are frequent references to Russians as 'other' in the illness narratives, this emphasis on difference fails to support a sense of distinctive ethnic identity in the way that is classically described (see, e.g., Anthony Cohen 1986, p. 11). Indeed, the narratives can be seen as a chronicle of the penetration and ultimate destruction of core Latvian values by Russian habits and traditions. Although illness narratives start out by asserting a sense of belonging and acknowledging a commitment to shared values, the development of the narrative demonstrates the undoing of those values and the eventual transformation and destruction of the identity of the narrator. Narratives break down the ideals of homeland, of home, of work, of calmness and self-control. Phrases such as 'We've learnt that from them', or 'That's been brought over from there' or 'That's what we have become' recur both in narratives and in ordinary speech. Identity is perceived as invaded by otherness. The new identity is one of which people are ashamed and which sets them apart. It results from a loss of shared ideals and a failure to match up to inner aspirations. For example, the ideal of the homeland is found to be a mirage; the ideal of self-control cannot withstand the onslaughts of everyday life. Narrators admitted feeling shame at their inability to control themselves, particularly to control their anger. However, control was frequently maintained in public but lost in the privacy of family and home. Thus although people might appear outwardly to have maintained their identity, they themselves knew that they had changed profoundly. Their self-confessed inner transformation marks a loss of belonging.

Narratives which chronicle endurance or what might be termed 'a coming through' use shared symbols to draw together seemingly random and chaotic events and suffering. (This is discussed more fully in Chapter 10.) They rearrange past pain and confusion by pointing to an underlying purpose and meaning. In this process they also link the individual to shared systems of meaning and thus create a sense of belonging. Individual identity is reaffirmed throughout these narratives, for example, in unexpected acts of recognition and parallels between individual identities and lives and occurrences in the world. The relation of identity to otherness is different from that found in illness narratives. There is a metamorphosis from stranger/other to friend.

The differences between these two categories of narrative raise certain general and theoretical questions about the nature of memory. Maurice Halbwachs developed a strong case for the collective nature of memory:

> Our memories remain collective, however, and are recalled to us through others even though only we were participants in the events or saw the things concerned. In reality, we are never alone. Other men need not be physically present, since we always carry with us and in us a number of distinct persons.
>
> (1981, p. 23)

This memorable claim, 'we are never alone' is true of situations where we might not expect it to apply and yet it fails to reflect the experience of some others. Narratives of exile and extreme physical hardship where an individual is literally alone bring moral and literary references and structures to bear on the interpretation of hardship and suffering. They see themselves as going along a path that others have trodden before them. By contrast the pain of illness narratives resides precisely in their inner solitude, their inability to connect with shared experience. If we cannot make sense of experience then we are indeed alone. By contrast, in purposive meaningful narratives there is a sense that the narrator is in charge and that events are subordinate to him or her. Although such lives are varied, common paradigms of narrative structuring are found.

The moment people talk about the past they remember it in the way stories are told; they are unable to ignore the conventions of story telling. One such convention is the quest. This paradigm of the quest underlies many narratives recorded throughout Latvia (although not the illness narratives). Some typical elements of this paradigm stand out. The hero is a disinherited younger son or orphan banished from home. He is set apart by an imputed inferiority: for example, lack of wealth or intelligence. He travels through strange and foreign lands. He encounters a people threatened by evil monsters. The hero makes use of secret and extraordinary powers to overcome the monster and in return he is rewarded by wealth, high position and marriage to the king's daughter. The operative local version differs from this paradigm in some significant ways. The text which I have in mind is Anna Brigadere's play for children *Sprīdītis*, first published in 1903. *Sprīdītis* has many of the elements of a conventional quest plot. It tells of an orphaned boy whose father remarries and who is hated by his step-mother. He decides to leave the farmstead and go into the forest in search of wealth and happiness. He meets Wind Mother and Forest Mother (Latvian deities) who give him a magic whistle and a magic stick. He next encounters a king who fears his youngest daughter will be carried off by the devil. Spriditis overpowers the devil with the help of his magic whistle. In fulfilment of his promise, the king offers Sprīdītis gold and the princess in marriage. Thus far *Sprīdītis* conforms to the quest plot. However, the play ends in a specifically Latvian way. Sprīdītis finds the princess Zeltīte arrogant and venomous and rejects the offer of marriage and of gold. He chooses not to stay in the foreign kingdom, but returns to his farmstead and is welcomed back. He has himself changed and has learnt to value his farm and family. This Latvian version of the quest can be read as a political allegory about peasant social mobility and the exchange of ethnic identities. (Although this is a local version of the quest, parallels can be found in other literatures. For example, Candide returns to cultivate his own garden.) The newly formulated sense of nationalism urged that Latvians could both transform themselves and yet retain their ethnic allegiance. Sprīdītis' return to the farmstead, his recognition of its worth, and his return to his old sweetheart all carry a more general meaning.

Although there are difficulties in establishing both the precise movement of texts within society and that a particular text has influenced individual narratives, we can nevertheless identify certain recurring paradigms. The Latvian version of the quest is one such paradigm. In some cases the task is made easy by an explicit literary reference on the part of the speaker. Thus thirteen-year-old Uldis on the train to Moscow is miserable and penniless and reminds himself of the courage of Sprīdītis. Andrejs describes his homecoming along the alley of trees: 'And then I felt the old branches were like outstretched hands'. His use of the simile suggests an unconscious modelling on Sprīdītis, who having been thrown out of the king's castle says: 'It would be better in the forest. It's quite different there. There it's as though one were welcomed with loving arms' (1956, p. 71). However, beyond explicit references and borrowings, narratives share an underlying quest structure. They are about journeys through foreign lands, about chance meetings, coincidences and recognitions. Unexpected encounters and recognition give factual narratives an air of fiction. Terence Cave puts it thus:

> To tell a story which ends in recognition is to perform one of the most quintessential of all acts of fictional narration – the recognition scene is, as it were, the mark or signature of a fiction, so that even if something like it occurs in fact, it still sounds like fiction and will probably be retold as such.
>
> (1988, p. 4)

Recognition scenes punctuate victorious narratives. They are important because the events described – deportation, imprisonment and appropriation of land – involve total dislocation and the transformation of individuals which threaten identity. Recognition scenes provide evidence of continuity of self despite terrible experiences and changes to the self. Conversely, failures of recognition are one means by which narrators convey a negative transformation of self. The local features of the quest story are found in the emphasis on national identity and the return to one's homeland. Soviet political oppression is perceived as directed specifically at Latvians. For example, Kārlis who spent ten years in various labour camps said: 'Wherever I went there were Latvians. In the far north there were Latvians...'. Uldis soon learnt that to admit to being Latvian in Russia made his difficult journey more difficult and tried to pass as a Pole. In extreme situations where cold and famine made death likely narrators refer to qualities of character associated with being Latvian as having saved them. Throughout, the image of the homeland is described as sustaining them.

Meaning and metaphor play quite different roles in these two categories of narrative. Narratives of illness dwell on meaning or rather the loss of meaning. Typically loss of meaning or anomie has been associated with too much choice and the absence of prescriptiveness (see, e.g., Bennett 1975). By contrast, in Latvia loss of meaning is associated with past repression. Old peasant women, who earlier in their lives were unlikely to have been preoccupied with meaning, complain about the meaninglessness of their lives. However the complaint is not about the lack of some underlying metaphysical principle to human existence but rather to an elementary lack of direction and hence absence of fulfilment: 'All my life has been destroyed and all for nothing' or, 'My life has been made a mockery'. Victorious narratives are not preoccupied with meaning. Both types of narrative use metaphor, but with a different purpose. In the celebratory narratives the core metaphor is often destiny which binds together what might otherwise appear to be a disjointed life story. In the illness narratives metaphor serves to mark off the individual from society. For example, the image of the heart on strike has metaphorical resonances and evokes political rupture and conflict. So too the complaint of suffocation, 'I am short of air' suggests an incompatibility between the individual and her environment. Needless to say these images are also literal expressions of physical complaints. Lakoff and Johnson have pointed to the way in which many western metaphors are spatial in nature and derive from our experience of embodiment (1980). However, Lawrence Kirmayer suggests that our relationship to the social body is also a rich source of metaphor (1993, p. 173). Illness narratives use metaphors to convey the oppressive relationship between the individual and the social body. In these instances metaphor may unify the narrative but sunders the life.

Thus seemingly similar lives may be experienced in radically different ways and produce contrasting narrative structures. Some of the features of purposive and illness narratives are illustrated in the following extracts from two lives. Kārlis and Valdis were both born at the end of the last century and as youngsters were sent to Russia as apprentices to gain further qualifications in their respective crafts. Both lived through the revolution, but the tone of their memories and the structure of their narrative are different. These differences of narrative experience hinge on the amount of control perceived as belonging to their past and present selves. For the young Kārlis the themes are of magical luck and a personal destiny intertwined with the meta-narratives of history. Valdis' narrative by contrast robs him of any sense of control or agency and culminates in illness. Kārlis was born in 1897 and worked as a sailor. In 1914 the Riga harbour director sent him to St Petersburg as an apprentice electrician. Latvians owned a meeting house there, where Kārlis lived at first:

> There were a lot of Latvians there, they came to meetings. Then they went to work on the kolhozes and I was thrown out on the street. I lived under a boat. Sometimes I managed to sleep on the stairwell of that meeting house. Then something went wrong with the ventilator. They said if I could manage to put it right they would believe that I was an engineer. I fixed it. Then I was given pocket money. Cognac and cakes.

This episode of Kārlis' life has a pattern which provides a unifying theme throughout his life. He describes an initial situation of belonging. 'There were a lot of Latvians there.' This changes abruptly and Kārlis is left homeless. He speaks of being 'thrown onto the street'. He has to fend for himself as best he can. He is then put to the test. If he can mend the ventilator, he will have proved himself and established his true identity as an engineer. He passes the test and as a result he is rewarded and given a place to live. Folk tales provide a structure for his memories of adolescent exploits. This is not to question their authenticity, but merely to emphasize the form in which his memories are cast. Indeed, Kārlis' account has a strong sense of history. When asked if he remembered the revolution his reply was emphatic:

> I made the revolution. Where shall I start the story? ... When there were all those battles I was working in a big factory, an ammunition factory. As I was the senior electrician, I wasn't allowed anywhere, I had to stay in the factory. And during those days I didn't get to the battles, but only later. We weren't paid our wages. The first revolution was Kerensky's revolution in February then I .... Then came Lenin's revolution.[1] Then six of us from the factory went as a delegation to him. When we entered he ran towards us. He said, 'Come in come in'. He ordered us to form a red guard.

This account places Kārlis at the very heart of historical events. He not only saw the revolution but he made it. He did not participate in battles because he was indispensable in the ammunition factory. This in turn led to his meeting Lenin who is decribed as running towards them and then entrusting them with a historically vital task – the formation of the red guard. Throughout, the narrative is in an active mode.[2]

Compare this with Valdis' narrative. Though outwardly their lives have a certain similarity, their remembered experience and hence their narratives are highly contrasting. Valdis was born in 1899. At the age of fourteen he was apprenticed to a master craftsman in Riga. With the outbreak of the war Riga was evacuated:

> I went home. My master was going to Moscow, but I couldn't speak a single word [of Russian]. We discussed it at home and I decided to go with him after all. I lived in Moscow until the revolution. I survived it there. I lived in the workshop.

Valdis' experience of the revolution is one of survival, endurance and keeping his head down and out of the way.

> I was seventeen years old. After the revolution we were mobilized. I too. We were young boys. We were to be sent for training. We were loaded onto a train. We travelled for two days. We were unloaded in some village. It turns out that there is no training here but we are at the front. The old Kazaks, Kalmuks and Chechens are advancing towards us, we have to go to meet them. In the first battle we got a sound beating. In one farmhouse we happened upon some Kazaks with swords, and it just flowed. . . . Few of us stayed alive. After the battle I lay for a whole day on a mattress in some house.

Unlike Kārlis, Valdis actually did participate in the revolutionary battles. His account, however, is presented in the passive mode and emphasizes anonymity. Unnamed houses and places occur. The verb he uses for getting on the train is one normally reserved for loading and unloading goods (Latvian *salādēt* and *izlādēt*). Events conspire to rob him of any sense of autonomy or control. He and his comrades are young and untrained. They think they are going to receive training, but end up untrained at the front. The false expectation of training emphasizes Valdis' unpreparedness for the course which his life takes. As a result Valdis is laid prostrate and eventually falls ill:

> Then I sensed that I wasn't well. I fell ill with smallpox [*melnām bakām*]. I was sent back to Voronezh with the medical train.[3] On the way I fell ill with typhoid. I suppose I was lucky because I reached the hospital. I was put in a sledge and pulled. Once on the way I even fell out, I think. I lay ill with typhoid for a week. At midday we were brought sour cabbage soup. My neighbour was lying unconscious. I ate up my portion and I ate my neighbour's. In the evening I felt something was wrong, I had a temperature again. I lay there for two months.

Valdis responds passively to the war by falling ill. His passivity and helplessness are emphasized by his falling out of the sledge. One illness is superimposed upon another. His use of the term luck is tentative, and rather than actively emphasizing a positive turn in his life, it refers to possible worse outcomes. There is no sense of personal luck or a protective destiny in this account. The role of the extra portion of soup is to make him ill. Eventually Valdis was given three months' leave:

> I said I wanted to go to Riga, even though the whites were advancing on it. It was about the year 1919, I arrived in Riga. Nobody recognized me.

Unlike Kārlis who is able to establish his true identity even among strangers, Valdis is not even recognized by his family. With the founding of the Latvian state Valdis was mobilized into the Latvian army:

Everyone had to go to war. Suddenly I fell off my horse. It wasn't too bad, but at night my legs started hurting. Finally I was sent to the hospital. In Ķemeri I was put in the baths. After that back to the hospital. Then I described it all to one doctor. He examined me, sent me for X-ray: the problem was with my back, not my legs. The nerve centre in my back had been damaged. They had to put me in plaster. The doctors all came together and deliberated about what to do. They put a harness under my chin, drew my legs up into the air, plastered me in. I lay with that plaster for eight months. It wasn't easy. I stuck it out for four months. Lice had taken a hold of me. They smeared me with some medicine, then they disappeared.

Valdis' experiences in the Latvian army are even more disempowering and humiliating than his earlier experiences in the Red army. His imposed passivity becomes complete when he is strung up and put in plaster. However, the plaster traps the lice which feed on his body as well as himself. Valdis produced a photograph:

Here I am plastered in. Everything was enclosed. I ate with a little spoon. I couldn't move my head. I had to sleep on planks. Then I used a leather corset. I was short of breath.

That photograph is one of his most treasured possessions. I think this is because it provides an image of Valdis' relationship to the past and to history. He was roped in with things he did not like and which discomforted and hurt him. Exile for Kārlis is linked to the preservation of identity, but for Valdis to its loss.

A third type of narrative construction of identity is to be found in Emīlija's account. Her narrative records a spiritual transformation of self: from a remembrance of the pain of imposed violence to its sprirtual transcendence. Her terse narrative supports Rosaldo's challenge to 'the common assumption that the greatest human import always resides in the densest forest of symbols and that cultural depth always equals cultural elaboration. Do people always describe most thickly what matters to them most?' (1993, p. 2). The Ilongot head-hunter simply cites 'rage born of grief' (ibid., p. 178) as the reason for head-hunting. Emīlija's early narrative packs together events with little elaboration. Benjamin has written of the 'chaste compactness which precludes psychological analysis' and the way in which this 'commends a story to memory' (1992, p. 90). In many ways her narrative exemplifies this compactness, letting the events speak for themselves.

Emīlija's narrative is concise almost to the point of obscurity. Her opening sentence refers to her brother:

He was in the Latvian legion and taken prisoner and then he was released home.[4] He came home and he started to work and he helped me a lot. And then when we were deported to Russia in 1949, then my eldest son stayed behind at school.

Imprisonment, release, deportation and break-up of the family are referred to in one breath and without interconnecting links. Her memories centre on March 1949 when she, two of her children and her mother were deported. To my question about her mother's age the answer was as follows:

> She was about seventy-five years old. Quite old. They said we should be packed in two hours' time.[5] I had a crying fit. I had the little girl on my arm. Well, what could one do? They rounded us up and took us off.

Her neighbour Milda narrates her life with equal conciseness but greater coherence. Milda was born in 1914. Her father was a farm labourer (*puisis*) who at some point in the 1920s was given land to build a farmhouse.[6] A sense of repeated loss imbues much of her narrative. Asked how many brothers and sisters she has, the answer is terse and unhesitating:

> One sister, four brothers and all dead. Two shot.

Her memory for dates is hazy:

> My head is so knocked about that I can't remember. It could be . . . 1946 was when I was arrested, then they were all alive. They could have been killed about 1949 or 1950. It must have been 1949. I was only given four years. When I returned in 1950 they were already dead.

Asked for the year of her husband's arrest and deportation her reply is:

> Oh darling! Why do you ask me? It must have been when the Russians came in.

Her husband and brother had deserted from the German army, but were nevertheless arrested by the Soviets. The sense of the inexplicable underwrites her narrative. Instead of being mobilized into the Soviet army, her husband was sent to the coal mines in Tula[7] leaving her with three young children aged two, four and six:

> But I came from a strong lineage. We were all accustomed to work, my parents were servants, we had all grown up in hardship, we had all herded animals.

One day Milda received a letter from her husband which had somehow slipped past the censors. It described the terrible conditions and how he had to sleep on an iron bunk. She showed the letter to her brothers who felt that they also were threatened. When their mobilization drew near they decided to join the partisans in the forests.

Milda begged the partisans to leave her alone, not to come asking for food or clothes, because she had three small children to look after. They promised to leave her alone, but by that time she was already compromised. The bunker in which her brothers sheltered was betrayed:

> They were Latvians who betrayed them not Communists. I was just given a notice by a certain Krāms on the village council, to arrive in Cēsis at the war office to settle my husband's case. I went with my little horse. I had to take a doctor Grūbe, I was going to do šķūtes [a term originally used for serfs' obligatory transport duties].[8]

In other words Milda herself had been enrolled to take a neighbour along the first stage of his deportation. In Cēsis she was confronted with someone who claimed to know of her contacts with the partisans:

> You see not everyone who went into the forest was honest. Nothing was holy. Just save your own skin. He was brought towards me. 'Do you recognise him?' I said I didn't know him. How could I know him? I'd seen him just once. He'd come in just that once. There wasn't much to recognise. I said 'No'. But if everything he said had fitted me? He said he'd seen a woman with two children in the house in the woods, but I had three. They put the house plan in front of me. I said I didn't understand anything of house plans. I've only been to school for three winters.[9] I have a house in the woods but I have three children and I don't recognize that man.

There followed six months of interrogation:

> I was questioned in all sorts of ways, beaten in all sorts of ways, they did everything. They took me where nails are pulled off, where people were writhing on electrical chairs. They said, 'you will get the same if you don't tell us where your brothers and the others are'. Dear lord! What can I say . . . I only know that when I was led for questioning their blows didn't hurt me, in front of my eyes I just had the image of the Saviour, I felt he was saving me. That's how I survived. When the interrogation finished, then the war tribunal sentenced me in 1946. They couldn't establish guilt, I hadn't done anything. My husband was counted as being in the Soviet army, put in the coal mines, three small children left without father, without mother. I don't know how I didn't go mad. Now there isn't a day when I don't cry.

She was sentenced according the 58th clause,[10] because she had not informed on the partisans:

> And for four years . . . children without father, without mother [crying]. We survived it all. It's already six years since my husband died. His heart was destroyed. Returning from Tula they say he was swollen. From that famine.

Her own sentence was a correction labour camp in Komsomolsk. The journey there was in cattle trucks:

> We travelled forty days and nights in cattle trucks. At night we were guarded by alsatian dogs. There were benches in two stories for sleeping like salted herrings one next to the other. I had nothing with me to eat. We were given something to eat on the way. But we arrived in such a place in Russia where we were short of bread, water as well. And it is standing still and not moving forward. . . . We were women there. We were hungry the first day, we were hungry the second day, on the third day we were no longer hungry, only thirsty. But there is nothing to drink. And there were such cold nights. We would scratch the frost with our fingers. Not all of us reached the destination. The more weathered of us women survived, but the younger ones . . .

Asked whether people died on the journey, Milda avoids a direct answer but nevertheless manages to conjure up a vivid picture of corpses being removed from the train:

Oh dear! What one could see through that little window and we didn't have the strength to drag ourselves to the window and look. My lathe was on the ground. When we arrived in Komsomolsk[11] then I could no longer walk. After all, we'd had forty days in those cattle trucks. Then we were given five days rest and then we had to go to work.

There were no children there, only grown ups. We had a Latvian barrack there. We had to go to work. We were led by guards. At first we had to build huts for ourselves. We had to saw wood in the forest.

They worked in brigades of about thirty women with a Latvian brigadier in charge:

If we managed to fulfil the plan then things weren't too bad. But then we had to dig telephone poles two metres, a metre and a half deep in the frozen ground. We were given pliers, our hands were in blisters, we weren't able to do anything. We couldn't do anything in that soil. Our brigadier was a teacher, she knew many languages. And then she went and asked the Russian brigadiers and asked how we should work. And they had said we should ask for lots of pliers, light fires, heat the pliers and then when they were hot one could work. Those pliers were the death of us.

To my question as to whether she missed her children, she gave the following allegorical reply:

Why do you ask me? When they led us to work, there were such Russians there, such primitive villages, they kept their cows and pigs outside, those children ran towards us called us names, showed us their bare bottoms . . . [crying]. Well, what can you do?

Milda's reply conveys more by what she leaves out than by what she says. The implied contrast between what she says and what she suppresses emphasizes the painfulness of her separation. In describing the Russian children's rudeness and feelinglessness, she is implicitly contrasting them with her own children who would not behave like that. In referring to the primitive Russian villages she is remembering the Latvian tradition of living in isolated farmsteads. In mentioning the domestic animals left outside, she is emphasizing the Latvian farmer's love of his animals and concern for their well-being. During her absence her daughter suffered from pneumonia and her brothers were shot:

It wasn't easy. I can't even remember everything and I can't describe everything.

Her own health held out until she suffered from what she describes as nerve deadness:

Nerve deadness finished me off.[12] I am surprised I am alive today. God leads me. If God had not led me, I would not be alive today. I would not see my grandchildren. It seems He really is helping me.

This episode of nerve deadness constitutes both the nadir of her exile and the turning point of her narrative. This early part of the narrative records the impact of historical events on her life. Biblical references, such as the forty days travelling into exile provide a thematic unity. However it is in the latter part of the narrative that an underlying meaning is worked out.

Ilga describes the transformed self as follows: 'After all the endurance and suffering, nothing in the future is a threat'. Ilga contrasts the pretence of everyday social life unfavourably with the authenticity of prison life and behaviour:

> There was no theatre, no acting, no pretence. There everything was exactly as it is. All the wounds were open. There was clarity and light. That evened out much of the evil which was about.

Ilga's account echoes St Augustine's *Confessions* in which his younger self is represented as rooted in a time-bound world of fleshly desire and weakness but viewed from the timeless perspective of his emerged spiritual self. Ilga's progression is also an Augustinian one, from a trapped physical self to a timeless spiritual self.

Uldis echoes Ilga's view about the truthfulness of prison life. 'Prisoners know much more about what is going on outside than free people. The free person is isolated – work, home. Everything is concentrated in the prisons. There are many people's destinies, many events. He can only be untruthful for a short time.' (For a fuller discussion of Augustine's influence on the development of the western autobiographical tradition, see John Freccero's article on 'Autobiography and Narrative', 1986.)

In Emīlija's case this transformation of the self is articulated in an explicitly Christian idiom. I shall resume her narrative at the point where she succumbed to 'nerve deadness'. With this illness a specifically Christian perspective is introduced and thereafter controls the narrative. She attributes her survival to divine intervention: 'God leads me'. Several narrators portray 'nerve deadness' in similar terms:

> I couldn't move a single joint, neither lift my arm, nor move a finger. I thought I wouldn't see my children again. The other women were all helpful, they poured food into my mouth. My husband also sent me parcels.

My naive question about her weight received the following reply:

> Don't speak of weight! Who would bother to weigh us? Nobody knew how much each weighed. But a nurse or doctor came every day with a big needle and gave me two injections. . . . I thought I would stay that way. But the women who spoke Russian said that the doctor said I would recover. Now when all my bones hurt and my back hurts I'm afraid that once again I won't be able to move.

Asked to describe what hurt during her illness Milda replied:

> It neither hurt, nor didn't hurt. I lay like a living corpse. I didn't feel anything. I didn't feel the needles, nothing. I lay there like a lifeless object. . . . Many doctors came. I was terribly thin. Then for a whole month I wasn't sent to work. I was left to work in the kitchen. Then I had enough to eat there. During that month I sort of recovered. And then there was a Russian woman who had a

heated greenhouse. She was from another barrack, also imprisoned, but she was allowed to walk without a convoy. She needed a helper. She was allowed to choose. She wanted one of the Latvians because they worked harder than the Russians. And then she came in and chose me. There were cucumbers and tomatoes to be watered. And that Russian woman also was very good. She cooked all sorts of porridge and gave it to me. God stood by me everywhere. Sometimes I wanted to tear off a cucumber or tomato. But, no, I refrained, I didn't tear it off. And when the supervisor came to gather the produce, all these generals, then they praised me terribly and then they gave me those cucumbers and tomatoes. She must have told them that I didn't take anything and they had understood.

After the recovery from nerve deadness moral principles organize the narrative. Milda is fed and nursed by others when she herself cannot move. Her self-restraint in the greenhouse is recognized and rewarded. After four years' imprisonment she was released:

It was exactly 1950. The ticket was free. I had some money too. We spoke Latvian, being all Latvians together. I couldn't speak Russian. Now the camp gates are open and I'm shown 'Go there'. I go to one place and my ticket isn't accepted. I go to a second, it isn't accepted. At last, it's accepted in a third place. I sit down and I think madness, how do I know where to go. The train moves a bit and then stops. Moves a bit and then stops. I am on my own. Everyone else was given at least ten years. Nobody had as short a time as me. I was the first to be set free. Because nobody proved my guilt … I didn't know the language. And then I thought 'Dear God, give me some companion who would take me to Moscow, to Riga. Once I got to Riga I would know from there on. I must have looked terrible. Two young people came in the carriage. Russians, of course, and they gave me such a look. I was sitting there alone. It wasn't a cattle wagon, it was a carriage for humans. I look, they are coming back, they sit down opposite me and start to speak to me. I tell them I don't understand, but they don't give up. One of them has been in Riga during the German time and he knows a few words of Latvian. And they were on an official trip to Moscow. And so he spoke one word Latvian, one word Russian and so in two weeks we got to Moscow. And that time we were travelling forty days and nights to Komsomolsk and we got back to Moscow in twelve days. They brought me back to Moscow and showed me the Moscow–Riga train. God has listened to all my prayers.

Milda's narrative reaches into the past with the help of biblical events and stories. Her deportation to Siberia is remembered as lasting forty days echoing the forty years of the Israelites in the wilderness. Her return is in the company of two unknown helpers and companions who point her in the right direction. It takes twelve days, thus evoking associations with the apostles. By bringing biblical structures to bear upon her narrative Milda is able to give shape and moral meaning to her life history. After her return Milda joined the kolhoz. The following incident typifies the course of her life:

I joined the kolhoz. There was a cow which had been rejected and thought no good and I went and asked for it to be given to me. I went to the doctor. There was that young rejected cow, she had a prolapsed uterus, but she was on the second milk. She had been very good on the first milk. If she will be well fed and well looked after she will be a good cow. She is pregnant. I got her cheap and on instalments.... She was a wonderful cow, everything came like a blessing from God. I can't stop thanking God that he has guided my life. That is wonderful.

There is in Milda's narrative a blend of personal and textual memories. At some points her personal voice fails to find support in textuality and is, therefore, dominant. In other cases the textual is dominant. There is a shift mid-way through her narrative, signifying a change of register from the personal to the biblical, from a chronological sequence of events which destroy her earlier social self to a timeless world in which she finds a new spiritual self. Her narrative demonstrates the way in which meanings are lost and retrieved in the course of a narrated life.

Common to the complaints of meaninglessness is the idea that purposes cannot be put into effect and goals cannot be achieved. The result is that people feel robbed of themselves as agents. Alistair Macintyre has pointed out that although we may play the lead part in our own lives, we may be discomfited to learn that we have barely a silent walk-on part in the lives of others (1992, p. 213). In such lives events crowd out and overpower the teller of the tale. The juxtaposition of illness with other narratives focuses on the way in which actors themselves construct and deconstruct meaning. Purposeful narratives are able to transform what would otherwise be a demeaning walk-on part into one rich with literary and historical resonance. Conversely, complaints about illness are simultaneously complaints about the incoherence of life.

10

HABITABLE IDENTITIES

Our native hearth
Is burning in the sky
To come home
We do not open the door
But the cover of a book.

We can't learn from a snail
Because home is not a refuge for us
But we will be a refuge for the homeland.
(*Our native hearth*, Māra Zālīte)

In listening to Latvians talk of the past I encountered recurring fragments of speech and feeling that seem to have broken away from some larger whole. It would perhaps be more accurate to say that I recognized these fragments in later listenings and transcriptions. These fragmented messages formed part of a cultural script in which both my older informants and I were well versed. The plots, their embellishment and my subsequent interpretations are rooted in this script. Why this should be so has a historical explanation.

The consolidation of Latvian national identity in the nineteenth century was closely linked to the development of a written language. The publication of folk songs, literature and history were all deeply involved in this process of identity construction. However, the assimilation of cultural texts was not some mysterious and historically unspecifiable encounter. It took place in classrooms as children learnt to read from textbooks which recounted an ancestral past and instructed them in who they now were. This chapter looks at the ways in which identities were constructed and passed onto children. In the process variations in degrees of concordance between public and private scripts occur. For older people who went to school during or before the independence period, there was considerable overlap between public and private worlds. For younger people schooled under Soviet rule there was conflict between the public and the private. The accounts of older narrators incorporate many literary elements. By contrast, narratives of those who learnt to read during the Soviet period do not belong to a shared literary tradition. The difference revolves around the presence or absence of a certain fictional quality to the narratives. The lives of many older narrators are cast in a legendary, mythical mode, whereas the lives of younger narrators are told as a sequence of unconnected happenings. However, the difference is not merely one of style, but of literary packages which carry social meanings and which position the individual in relation to a culture.

A POSITIVE SELF-IMAGE

The Latvian preoccupation with definitional problems about the essence of Latvianhood, *Latvietība*, with what it means to be Latvian, have a long and continuing history. One reason for this lies in the painfully unflattering and uncomfortable picture of Latvian peasantry presented by earlier accounts. These contribute to the identity Latvians have formed for themselves. The issue is sharpened by competition between histories each claiming to capture the past and to authorize Latvian identity.[1] One of the goals of the national awakening was to change this by providing Latvians with a habitable identity.

History writing depends of course on literacy. In Latvia literacy was associated with being German and history had been written by the Baltic Germans. In line with Gellner's ideas, 'Nationalism is about entry to, participation in, identification with, a literate high culture' (1993, p. 95), literacy became enormously important for Latvian identity, as well, of course, as providing a vehicle for the construction of that identity. Early printed texts were in Latin or German. Latvian first appeared in print in the form of cathechisms: the Jesuit catechism of 1585 and the Lutheran catechism of 1586. Indeed, the early printed literature directed at the peasantry was of a hortatory and morally didactic nature. In the process of exhorting Latvian peasants to work hard and to stay sober such texts also project an image of Latvian peasantry. Inevitably such images are of moral failings. For example, Georg Mancelius, whose sermons, published in 1654, include acutely observed glimpses of social life, also gives a horrific account of Latvian peasant life.[2] He describes scenes of superstition and moral debauchery.

'It is not right that you are angry, bark and jump about like a dog with your neighbour, that you fight with those nearest to you, it is not right, that night and day you drink and revel and roll around like an ale barrel' (quoted in Blese 1947, p. 72). Mancelius' sermons are written in the everyday language of Latvian peasants using the concrete imagery of daily life. However, the picture of immoral behaviour, although not unrelated to actual practices, also reflects baronial stereotypes of Latvian peasants as cunning, unreliable and lazy workers.

The first ABC for children, published in 1787, does not miss the opportunity to include several moral lessons. For example, O for *ozols* (oak) is accompanied by the epithet, 'The oak tree dries out from fire, and youth wastes away from brandy'. Or P for *pils* (a castle or palace): 'Even a palace won't satisfy the discontented; a righteous person is satisfied with his little farmstead'. R for *roze* (a rose): 'A rose is a pretty flower, but even prettier is a girl who works'. Or T for *tīklis* (a net): 'The net traps bold fish, but an inn ensnares and destroys drinkers'. U is for *ugunsgrēks* (a fire): 'Sometimes a fire is started by a pipe, when lads start to smoke, that is a big shame'. The subtext to this simple little alphabet is provided by the familiar complaints of Baltic landowners about serfs and peasants: idleness, drunkenness and discontent with their lot.[3]

Garlieb Merkel, whose revolutionary history of eighteenth-century Vidzeme was inspired by the ideas of Rousseau, urged the abolition of serfdom and the amelioration of the peasant condition. In the process he evokes scenes of utter moral as well as physical destitution. Although typically referred to in Latvian history books as a humanist and friend of Latvians the image of Latvian peasantry which he draws is one which calls for liberation but does not offer a comfortable identity. For example, Merkel describes the peasant distrust of innovation even when it alleviates their lot. He recalls an old peasant's words: 'Our masters fertilize us, so that we may continue to bear more fruit in the future' (1978, p. 29). Merkel also describes abandonment to drink:

> Tenderly sacrificing their share mothers offer a brandy glass to their unweaned babies. Fourteen year old boys and girls drink brandy without grimacing; and among men and women we will rarely find such as do not get drunk every Sunday, particularly after they have taken communion. If they lack money for this purpose then men take corn to sell and women take their clothes.
>
> (ibid., p. 30)

He also describes a callous lack of feeling:

> A Latvian will often calmly watch his children and closest relatives suffering and dying. He is too used to not finding sympathy for himself to be able to have any for others. And ties of kinship in the face of the iron grip of everyday want are but a spider's web.
>
> (ibid., p. 33)

Merkel goes on to give examples of this lack of feeling:

> In 1794 in manor house A. a Latvian drowned. As there was no doctor nearby I hurried there myself with two servants. While we were trying to revive the unfortunate man, all his family lay down to sleep. After an hour his brother woke up. He asked whether our efforts had met with success and when he heard the answer 'no', he took the fur coat from the drowned man, covered himself with it and peacefully went to sleep again.
>
> (ibid., p. 34)

He also describes mothers' indifference to their children's health and survival:

> Wherever smallpox broke out, mothers would carry their unweaned infants to the side of the sick person so that they would catch the disease or they would even give the smallpox poison to the child on bread and butter. If they are admonished about their rash behaviour

then they reply, 'If he has to die then it's better for the child to die now, than to eat up a lot of bread and then to die.'

(ibid., p. 34)

Merkel was writing in a polemical tradition and his descriptions were intended to shock. However, beyond the literary tradition of this writing, there is a core of truth which conveys a hopelessness born of destitution found in other histories of the family in other countries. This style of writing may also convey an inability to take on board the pain and horror of peasant history. If Latvian peasants had no feelings then their suffering could not be so terrible.

The nineteenth-century Latvian nationalist movement set out to expand Latvian identity beyond peasanthood and to reconstruct peasant identity. The earlier distinction lay between Germans and peasants: educated peasants were assimilated to the Baltic German classes. Berzholtz, a German priest at the Catholic church of St Jacob, put it thus: 'An educated Latvian cannot remain a Latvian because Latvians are only a peasant class. Their language is not needed – one does not need to speak the Latvian language in order to be able to plough.' (1861, quoted in Vike-Freiberga 1985) A similar view was expressed even more forcefully by Keuchel:

There has not yet been a highly educated Latvian. Whoever is educated and calls himself a Latvian is deceiving himself. They have not drawn their learning from Latvian sources. It is not possible to be both Latvian and educated – an educated Latvian is a contradiction in terms' (1871, ibid.).

The negative approach was also exemplified in the idea that Latvians were *Undeutsch.*

Thus the nineteenth-century nationalist movement had to overcome this Baltic German legacy of ideas about the peasantry. Latvian historians belonged to this nationalist tradition and wrote their histories with a view to rehabilitating peasanthood. Their histories were formulated in opposition to earlier views. Latvian peasant identity and language were highly emotive issues central to this movement. The idea of Latvian as the language of ploughing has been transformed from a slur to a source of national pride.[4]

However, it was above all literary work which offered Latvians a refurbished image of themselves. It is, with few exceptions, a literature about rural life and the hardships and sufferings of peasants. Much of it has a didactic tone – it seems to be telling Latvians what they should be like as well as what they are like. In a peasant society, the pastoral tone of the literature is not surprising. What is noteworthy is the extent of incorporation of this literature into elementary school reading books. Anthologies for very young school children contain excerpts from novels and autobiographies of the time. Conversely, many poets and novelists wrote autobiographical accounts of their childhood.

An underlying theme to much of this literature is that of the dignity of the peasant and his moral integrity in the face of poverty and oppression. For example, a novel called *Rich Relations* published in 1886 tells the story of a younger son without land or means, ignored by his rich relatives, reduced to poverty and destitution, who eventually enters a poor house in old age. An extract of this novel is to be found in an anthology for primary schools published in 1925 (Klaustiņš 1925, pp. 107–134). The exercises at the end of the reading pose the following questions: 'How does father Andris overcome hate, anger, possessiveness, envy, quarrels, life's adversities and sufferings?' or 'What impression does suffering leave on a good person and what on a weak or bad person?' (ibid., p. 122). These exercises for school children illustrate the way in which literary works could be, and were, used for character building and the promotion of a shared identity.

Literary representations have contributed to the matrix of popular ideas and feelings about peasanthood. Thus to be described as a real peasant (*īsts zemnieks* in Latvian) is a commendation. Peasants are thought to be deliberate, thorough, honest and kind. There are no similarities with the west European image of ungainliness, insensitivity or uncouthness. Concerted literary and historical efforts have succeeded in erasing such images. One informant, with poetic inversion, referred to peasants as aristocrats.

> During the Latvia period I was in quite a few of those country houses in Vidzeme and Kurzeme and in each house the farmer was just like an aristocrat. Very firm, deliberate and knowledgeable.

This transformation has been helped along by the open acknowledgement of peasant descent. For example, histories of literature emphasize the peasant origins of writers and their rootedness and loyalty to a peasant culture. Indeed, unusually large numbers of Latvian writers of note have produced autobiographical accounts of their childhood. These accounts are invariably set in the Latvian countryside and most often focus on seasons of childhood herding. Krišjānis Barons the collector of folk songs is among the many writers to have published his childhood memories. The accounts are literally pastoral in their subject matter in that herding animals was a typical task of peasant children from the ages of six or seven onwards. They are also pastoral in a romantic sense, fusing images of the innocence of childhood with the freshness and beauty of the countryside. Shepherds (*gans*) are always referred to in the diminutive (*ganiņš*), reflecting not only the young age of the shepherds but also the affection in which they are held.

The child shepherd as a symbol of Latvian identity is not fortuitous. Shepherding is associated with an ideal of freedom and song and has none of the negative associations of oppressed peasantry. Lidija, a painter, recalls her mother's childhood thus:

> My mother had to herd animals from about the age of eight. And she said, she remembered it for a long while, those cold autumn mornings when her bare feet froze. And she sang and sang to calm herself. And then once baron Gestenmeiker himself came by and stood for quite a long time and he said 'Sing, sing, my child.'

Renato Rosaldo describes the ease with which historians and anthropologists identify with pastoralists as opposed to sedentary cultivators: 'The characterization of proud freedom loving shepherds, as opposed to rapacious, oppressed peasants' (1986, p. 86). Some of these attitudes contribute to the elevation of the little shepherd to the status of a national hero. And the relationship of the anthropologist to the Nuer or Masai pastoralists or the historian to the shepherd of Montaillou finds an echo in the urban dwelling Latvian writer to his earlier, country-roaming self. Herding activities provide a focus both for literary and for personal narratives of the past. The honorific literary position of the Latvian shepherd relates to his affinity with the wild, with forest pastures and, hence, his freedom from the constraints of the farmstead and the peasant legacy of subordination. Krišjānis Barons usually remembered affectionately as father Barons, also wrote about his childhood and his reminiscences include herding: 'I have kept these pig herding seasons in loving memory. For days on end in the fresh, open air, the spoilt darling in mother nature's lap, I inherited physical strength and endurance of body' (1985, p. 14, 1924). Barons' reminiscences form part of a tradition which hallows country roots and in which childhood herding comes to epitomize those roots.

THE MYTHICAL FARMSTEAD

Twentieth-century Latvian literature continues in the pastoral tradition but focuses on the farmstead. In the process it is transformed into a symbol of Latvian ethnic identity. Perhaps the most exuberantly romantic portrayal is to be found in Edvarts Virza's prose poem 'Straumēni'. 'Straumēni' has as its focus a Zemgallian farmstead and its seasonal activities. It is a celebration of the rural idyll which has in the process transformed the way in which Latvians perceive and remember their country childhoods. Through such pastoral literature a generic notion of the farmstead was built up: it became a powerful social category which helped consolidate Latvian identity during the independence period. The ethnographic museum outside Riga further elevated the farmstead from a real entity to a timeless, mythical construct. The farmstead as portrayed by Virze is timeless. Time, to borrow Bakhtin's ideas about the pastoral, is fused with locality. In this way the painful history of serfdom and landlessness is concealed; the uncertain relationship of peasant to land, the migration of labourers from one farmstead to another, is replaced by a timeless and mystical bond between peasant and locality.

The farmstead as an ethnic icon appears in the following events. In 1942 during the Nazi occupation of Latvia the publishing house Zelta Ābele reissued 'Straumēni'.[5] The 1942 edition is a miniature, small enough to fit into a shirt pocket. It is beautifully produced with wood-cut drawings by the celebrated Latvian illustrator Jānis Pleipis.[6] Its special interest lies in its intended destination. It was issued free to Latvian soldiers serving on the eastern front. It was printed on thin cigarette paper of a size suitable for smoking. Its present-day rarity testifies to its actual use for this purpose. It is a kind of impossible object simultaneously representing transience and transcendence.

These symbols of enduring landscape such as the farmstead, the country childhood, and the shepherd are both private and public property. Because they belong at one and the same time to history, to fiction and to memory, their presence in narrative serves to bind together the various sources of narrative. Individual narratives too move between personal memory, fiction and history and at each level there is a re-encounter with the mythical farmstead. Its precise provenance, however, is never easy to establish: many entitlements to ownership can be found.

The farmstead serves as a theatre for memory both for country and for urban dwellers; for those whose childhood was spent on a farmstead and those who feel it should have been spent there. Lienīte's early childhood was spent hiding in the forest. In the context of describing her attempts to regain the family property she describes what 'home' means to her:

> All my life I was yearning, like a person without a home, but I didn't manage to regain this house. Although I live in Lielvārde, I constantly long for Piebalga. I feel as though my home is there. And I've never been able to understand those people who were able to leave altogether. I think that that's something that's put in the cradle with a person and God has laid down that he has to be in that one place. Unfortunately, all my life I'm just like a mad person or a melancholic.... I even laugh that I travel to church in Torņakalns [in Riga] from Lielvārde [some 50 kilometres away]. That's become a second home to me now.

This sense of yearning for the country home permeates the romantic literature of the early twentieth century. For example, Jānis Akuraters was forced to leave Latvia after participating in the uprisings of 1905.[7] He wrote *A Servant Boy's Summer* during his exile in Oslo which begins with a description of a city hemmed in with stones, and reminiscences of the beauty of the Latvian countryside:

> And I ask myself: where am I? And it seems to me that I am always out of place; I have left my homeland and I cannot return. My homeland? What is my homeland? Dreams entwine their arms about me and then I see my homeland. The scent of the wild cherries is in the air and once again I am walking along the green valleys and I hear the corncrake's cry on the edge of the corn fields. And wide and deep expanses open up and I am there where the white horizons are deep in their midday sleep and the trees are humming full of bees and the linden tree is in blossom by the luxuriant river bank.
>
> (1947, pp. 7–8)

Like many other Latvian writers Akuraters writes from exile and presents a vision of the past and the countryside sharpened by longing. His writing and that of other exiled writers supports Hobsbawm's contention that the nation was conceived from its margins. Akuraters offers a heightened awareness of beauty, but also a feeling of exile and disappointment, a fear that the remembered past may no longer be attainable. This matrix of feeling recurs in many narratives. For Lienīte it is the vision of an idyllic home which renders her a permanent exile. That sense of nostalgia is present in the accounts of other narrators, heightened at present by the very real legal and financial difficulties of regaining family property. For example, Anna speaks of her longing for the country and for home as follows:

> I have always been oppressed by large gatherings of people. I have never liked crowds. Maybe that comes from being Latvian, from the genes, from peasanthood. Yes. A peasant loves an isolated farmstead, he is more of a loner. I don't like one building next to another, one flat above another, I don't like that. I want open spaces, I want forests, fields. I consider myself to be a real country person and I think to myself that as soon as I can, if it's in my power, although I'm doubtful whether it will be in my power looking at it from today's perspective . . . I very much want to spend the last years of my life in the country. In the peace of the country, at peace with myself and the environment.

Lidija recounts her early married life and her dislike of Liepāja with its harsh winds and cold sea-water:

> I wasn't used to it and I always remembered Lielupe with longing. I have swum in all the rivers and lakes of Latvia and nowhere was the water so soft and fragrant as in Lielupe. When I washed my hair, then it would shine better than if I'd used shampoo. And the water would smell of the yellow water lilies. And all the banks were full of them. The water was warm. And I also remember all the grasses in the meadows, the flowers, they were all there. And when we went barefoot, the meadow flowers clung to our legs, the pollen, flower petals. It was beautiful.

However, beyond nostagia and idealization there was also the idea of lanscape as shaped by people, their work and traditions. This human landscape has a vocabulary of its own. For example, *vienzirgu zeme* – a plot of land small enough to be worked by one horse; *pusgraudnieks* – literally translated as a half-grain man, a share-cropper who pays rent with half his produce. Such terms specify the nature of the relationship between people and land. There are several words for path depending upon who walks there and for what purpose. For example, *olnīca* is the path used by shepherds, and its etymological connections with *ola*, an egg, suggest a well-worn and shiny surface. Such vocabulary evokes both a landscape and a way of life. The landscape lends a permanence to the way of life and the human activities infuse the landscape with a reassuring intimacy. This intimate and inhabited landscape is contrasted most sharply and painfully with the terrifying and empty landscapes of Siberian exile.

THE *DAINAS*

The sense of nature inscribed is captured in folk songs. For example:

> Our masters write, the sun writes,
> Marking my good brothers;
> Men write in books;
> The sun, in the maple leaf.

Indeed, folk songs played a central role in the consolidation of national identity. Barons' invitation to Latvians to send in their songs resulted in the collection of some 218,000 songs. These were catalogued according to subject matter and coded according to place of origin over a period of thirty-five years by Barons.[8] The first volume appeared in 1894 and the eighth and final volume edited by Barons appeared in 1915. The system of classification devised by Barons was based on the life cycle, thus inviting their use as identity markers. Traditionally the *dainas* constituted an important part of life-cycle rituals and of the cycle of agricultural activities. However, their publication and classification in this way increased their ability to shape and unify Latvian lives. Since then they have, indeed, assumed a sacred role both for the lives of individuals and for the nation. For example, christenings, birthdays and Christmas and Easter celebrations are accompanied by appropriately chosen *dainas*. For instance, the *daina* extolling effort and hard work at the head of my autobiographical chapter was inscribed on a foundation stone of my grandfather's house in Riga; it was also put in my cradle together with bread and salt at my christening. The *dainas*' revocation contrasts with their earlier reputation for being at best nonsense and at worst naughty.[9]

The *dainas* also played an important part in the song festivals. The first Latvian song festival was held in 1873. It and subsequent festivals were important to the movement of national awakening as indeed they were to the independence movement in the 1990s. Anatol Lieven describes how 'The sound of hundreds of thousands of voices symbolize national harmony in every sense, like Rousseau's "General Will" set to music' (1993, p. 113). In one sense, of course, such song festivals invent tradition. Although not in the sense of the songs being an artefact of the nationalist movement: they preceded it and were there to be collected. However, they were discovered, invested with new meanings and put to collective use. The nationalist movement transformed the *dainas* from an oral to a literary tradition. In the process they were rehabilitated and offered as a common source of national identity. Their unifying function is evident in the first song of the first volume of the twelve volumes of the *dainas*:

> One girl sings in Riga.
> A second sings in Valmiera.
> Both sing one song.
> Are they daughters of one mother?

This song supports Benedict Anderson's discussion of simultaneity as supporting nationalism (1991 pp. 22–36). 'Simultaneity is, as it were, transverse, cross-time, marked not by prefiguring and fulfilment, but by temporal coincidence, and measured by clock and calendar' (ibid., p. 24). The simultaneity of activities constitutes their sole commonality and link with the nation. Anderson describes the mass ceremony of newspaper reading:

It is performed in silent privacy, in the lair of his skull. Yet each communicant is well aware that the ceremony he performs is being replicated simultaneously by thousands (or millions) of others of whose existence he is confident, yet of whose identity he has not the slightest notion.... At the same time, the newspaper reader, observing exact replicas of his own paper being read ... is continually reassured that the imagined world is visibly rooted in everyday life.... Fiction seeps quietly and continuously into reality, creating that remarkable confidence of community in anonymity which is the hallmark of modern nations.

(ibid., pp. 35–36)

For Latvians songs and singing came to occupy a similar role to newspaper reading. They transformed individual songs and singing into a communion with the nation. The heading for that first section of the collected *dainas* – 'Songs and singing – the common property of the nation' – explicitly suggests that the entire published opus may act as a reference point for unifying Latvians. Whereas the *dainas* had belonged to specific localities their publication transformed them into both the voice and the property of the nation. Commentaries on the *dainas* also emphasize the common voice. For example, Jānis Andrups writes:

Having excluded everything that is personal or fortuitous or unacceptable to the community as a whole, the 'I' of the folk song does not stand alone – his song comprehends the voices of thousands who share his fate. Even more – we feel that behind the singer of the folk song there stand many by-gone generations of Latvians governed by the same strict concepts of community life. In this way, the experiences of the individual are generalized in the folk song, they are merged into the life of the community and assume the character of communal experiences.... The picture of community life given in the folk song is extended beyond the confines of time and place into universality, as it were.

(1954, p. 28)

Such readings of the *dainas* clearly contribute to the construction of national identity. Krišjānis Barons is always referred to as *Barontēvs* or Father Barons – a title which reflects his important role as originator of the nation. The collection and publication of the *dainas* offered Latvians an imagined community in Anderson's sense as well as an imagined identity.

Publication also contributed to the rehabilitation of the *dainas*. Earlier Baltic German views had been condemnatory. Paul Einhorn's was the most virulent attack: 'Then they sing such frivolous, unchaste and filthy songs in their language, day and night and without cease so that the devil himself could not match them in filth and shamelessness' (1649, p. 20). Georg Mancelius (1593–1654)[10] described the folk songs as '*blenu dziesmas*' which translates as stupid, foolish or naughty songs. In his sermons he too waged a war against folk songs: 'What foolishness is being heard? What shameless songs are being sung, so that an honest man's ears smart'; or 'If your neighbour has been overcome by the Devil or by the weakness of his flesh do not immediately sing about it'; or 'Many a father, many a mother do not themselves know how to pray to God, nor how to sing songs of God, they only sing with exultation about their mother and about their colt. What can such people teach their children' (quotations taken from Andrups and Kalve 1954, p. 60). However, Mancelius' own language had an earthy directness and relevance to country life. Jānis Andrups describes Mancelius as being 'in love with the world he fights against' (ibid., p. 62). Whether or not this was the case, the explicit message concerning the folk songs was a derogatory one.

The term *blēņu dziesmas* stuck and was later echoed by others. For example, Gotthard Stender (1714–1796), a pastor in Sēlpils for some thirty years, strove to wean the peasants away from their attachment to folk songs and stories.[11] Although his fame rests with his grammar and dictionary of the Latvian language, he also published stories and verses of a sentimental and morally didactic nature, which he hoped would eventually replace folk literature. Stender compares folk tales with old wives' tales, without a moral purpose and akin to a 'beautiful but blind horse' (quoted in Zeiferts 1993 (1922), p. 219). According to Stender's views folk songs were 'old peasant songs which are always sung to the self same tune, and in which there is no trace of wisdom or beauty' (Andrups and Kalve 1954, p. 81). It was the legacy of attitudes such as these which classification, annotation and publication of the *dainas* sought to dispel.

These views were not confined to Baltic Germans, but were held by Latvians themselves. They were linked to the idea of the Latvian language as an awkward and clumsy vehicle of expression rather like the Latvian peasants themselves. For example, the educationalist, Cimze, claimed that folk songs were as distinct from true poetry as wild flowers were from cultivated flowers. The idea that the *daina*s embodied and unified the Latvian spirit past and present only came to be accepted later. Attitudes of veneration belong to the twentieth century.

The rehabilitation of language and folk culture affected both the rural and urban population. For example, folk songs were printed in school textbooks which from the 1920s onwards were standardized throughout Latvia. They were important not only to the urban conception of what the peasant was like but also offered peasant children an attractive image of themselves.

Early school texts aimed to create a sense of belonging and connection with the past in their young country readers. One of the ways of doing this was to start from the child's own experience and memories and, indeed, much Latvian history has been written from the perspective of lived experience. It is particularly true of histories written for children. A primary school textbook for third-year children puts it thus:

> Primary children's first steps in history should be taken in subjects still alive in the nation's memory, to which they feel close and, therefore, find interesting and intelligible. And such material is to be found in the exceptional changes in our nation's life during the last century. Every schoolchild will have heard accounts of how our fathers and

fathers' fathers lived a few generations back. Similarly, at every step the schoolchild encounters other monuments of this historical period.

(Zālītis and Grīns 1927, p. 3)

This approach appeals to the authority of memory and lived experience and at the same time poses a challenge to earlier Baltic German accounts. Children are directed to scan their own and their family's memories:

Do you remember, what your mother and father told you about their childhood and youth? What nation did they live in? Who was the ruler? What were the teachers, priests and doctors like in those days? What associations were there? What holidays and other celebrations were there? What wars? What unrest? Do you remember what your grandfather and grandmother told you about life during their childhood and youth compared to life now: what were buildings like then and now? What were ploughs like then and now? How did they mow hay, thresh corn then and now?

(ibid., p. 5)

The sequence of chapters moves from earliest living recollections in the first half of the nineteenth century to the time of writing the book. Dealing with country matters and agricultural activities, it constructs a national identity rooted in the countryside. These history schoolbooks encourage an identification between the school child and the past, between family privations and national destiny.

My understanding of the literarization of folk traditions is, of course, different from that of Johann Herder, whose theories on folk culture as a vehicle of the national soul were suggested to him by his Baltic experiences. In particular, his experience of Jāņi, the midsummer festival on June 24th 1765 left a lasting impression on him. Herder sees peasants as spontaneously dipping into ancient sources of folk custom: 'You know that I myself have had the opportunity of seeing still living nations keeping alive the remains of ancient uncultivated singing, rhythms and dancing' (n.d., p. 85).

Herder saw folk culture as having a timeless and unchanging existence and as expressing the soul of a people. For this reason his ideas supported nationalist movements both in Latvia and elsewhere. However, in the process of rehabilitating Latvian folk culture it was transformed into a literary tradition which played a quite different role in the construction of identity. Rather than being based upon improvisation as Herder suggests it was set in print. In the process the folk culture was transformed into a symbol of nationalism, an umbrella term offering shelter to an assortment of people and from which they could draw inspiration according to their personal needs.

Life histories demonstrate that identities are not part of some abstract realm of national souls nor are they confined to the printed page. Instead they point us towards the idea of interpretative communities. By listening to personal narratives we can establish exactly how particular texts are being read. Early readings are fed back in the form of life stories and the debate about how texts are read and interpreted can to a certain extent be resolved. Life histories, as we have seen, embody specific readings of texts. They can provide us with a map of how texts move around in society. They also give an indication of the degree of congruence between public and private realms of thought and feeling.

In fact, narratives embody varying degrees of textual belonging. Illness narratives conspicuously lack a sense of belonging and hence the coherence which it brings to stories. Other narratives succeed in drawing upon the common fictional sources to produce a coherent personal story. At some very basic level, it seems that the ability and inability to make a coherent story of one's life are connected to health and illness. Steven Marcus says as much in his essay on Freud and Dora:

> A coherent story is in some manner connected with mental health (at the very least, with the absence of hysteria), and this in turn implies assumptions of the broadest and deepest kind about both the nature of coherence and the form and structure of human life. On this reading, human life is, ideally, a connected and coherent story, with all the details in explanatory place, and with everything (or as close to everything as is practically possible) accounted for, in its proper causal or other sequence. And inversely, illness amounts at least in part from an incoherent story or an inadequate narrative account of oneself.
>
> (1976, pp. 276–277)

There is it seems to me an essential mysteriousness about creating coherence from chaotic lives, and ultimately the answers as to why some people succeed and others fail eludes socio-anthropological explanation or, indeed, any other kind of explanation.

However, certain preconditions can be identified. One such condition is that of seeing one's life as part of a wider whole. One way of expressing this subordination is as a kind of textual belonging. This depends, of course, upon literacy and schooling. I and, as I subsequently discovered, others in Latvia were encouraged to study hard at school with the words: 'They can take everything away from you, but not your education' (*Tev visu var atņemt bet ne izglītību*). Testimonies share the themes of literary texts because such admonitions were taken seriously.[12]

Earlier chapters gave examples of literary paradigms used by narrators. A localized Latvian quest narrative which culminates not in the conquest of a princess and rule over a foreign kingdom, but in a homecoming, provides a structure for many recollections of exile. Lyrical evocations of the farmstead and of a pastoral childhood, of the enduring personal characteristics of Latvians and their relationship to Latvian destiny also recur. Such recurring themes and my familiarity with them attest to the power of childhood reading in the formation of enduring attitudes.

SCHOOL TEXTS IN SOVIET LATVIA

For the younger generation the relationship between personal and socio-cultural narratives is less harmonious. The tensions are well known and relate to conflicts between the public and private, between institutions and individuals, especially between schools and families. I want, however, to suggest a more specific source of hiatus between the public and the private. This relates to the nature of readings in school textbooks during the Soviet period. From 1945 onwards the contents of school books were dramatically revised. They were most systematically rewritten in the 1950s and 1960s. During these two decades Latvian fiction and poetry were by and large excluded from school anthologies. Instead, a new genre of Soviet folk songs was 'discovered', which attempted to build upon and develop existing traditions. Although outwardly mimicking traditional forms, their content was sharply different. They were concerned with military parades and festivals, with productivity and with exemplary work. Stories written specifically for school children had similar themes. There is little in these specifically constructed texts which connects with experience. The readings are about exemplary performance rather than about the tensions and contradictions of life as captured within a plot. Examples embody Soviet values in a static way with no chronological development.

Some examples will illustrate this genre. An ABC published in 1955 includes the following song:

> Strangers were amazed
> Is this Riga or Jelgava
> This isn't Riga or Jelgava
> This is the kolhoz village being built.
> (Lubāniete 1955, p. 79)

The grandeur of the collective is praised in lines which mimic the country person's admiration for large cities.

> Flags for the festival
> Are made by ourselves
> Now we're setting off for the parade
> The flag is flying bravely.
> (Lubāniete 1965, p. 25)

Although the format is of a traditional folk song these lines are attributed to L. Nekrasova.

Or in a similar militaristic vein there is:

> I hold hands with my dear father
> We are going to the festival parade
> This is all in honour of October
> The salute rings out as though today.
> (ibid., p. 27)

Such military themes are common. However, references to exemplary people and exemplary behaviour are more important for understanding personal narrative. Values are found embodied in particular persons and ready made rather than emerging from an interaction between people and their environment, in short from human experience. Some illustrations will demonstrate what I have in mind:

> Give me my books! To school!
> I will be a star pupil.
> Then daddy and mummy
> And my native land will be happy.
> (ibid., p. 7)

Or:

> We will be an example
> We will plant an apple tree
> (ibid. p. 32)

Stories also abound with examples. The following is an extract from a story entitled 'Preparations for the Kolhoz festivities': 'Rudolf's father is a chauffeur he drove to the pig farm and took Rudolf with him.... This farm is very exemplary' (Krauliņš 1946, p. 152).

Or: 'My mummy works in a factory. She makes electric light bulbs. Every month she exceeds the targets set by the plan' (Lubāniete 1954, p. 48).

Or: 'The pupils together with their teacher and headmaster drove to the meeting at the workers' club ... my father ... he is a worker. He is the best stonemason in our building enterprise' (Lubāniete 1950, pp. 35–36).

A final example illustrates the priggish unreality of the moral world portrayed. 'Vija is a pupil in the second class. She is a star pupil (*teicamniece*) from the very first day at school'. Her friend asks her whether she doesn't mind spending all her time on work, to which Vija replies: 'I have quite a lot of free time. Of course I'm active in our school group and in the dramatic club. I also help my mother' (Lubāniete 1952, pp. 66–67).

These extracts from school anthologies give an indication of the difficulties which children growing up in Soviet Latvia might have experienced in relating what they read to what they experienced. There is no sense of a dynamic struggle between the ideal and the real, between good and evil. These stories and songs assert values but do not embed them in a story which relates to real lives. This early reading has influenced personal narrative. In part, this influence derives from the rejection of the values conveyed by school books. Equally importantly, however, school texts have failed to supply form and structure for personal memories and accounts of lives.

Thus school texts both reflect and amplify the conflicts between public and private, between school and family. Rather than guiding behaviour, portrayals of exemplary behaviour served to sharpen the discrepancies between models of behaviour and actuality. Earlier Latvian authors – of the independence period and before – were confined to the home. They formed part of the private world of the family whose testimony was perpetually challenged by the public world of work and school and in particular by Soviet textbooks. By the 1970s a wider range of authors was being included in the reading material of school children. However, this still leaves a whole generation of Latvians born during and after the war whose school reading lessons were based on exemplary Soviet folk songs and tales. These early school lessons have left an imprint on the way in which many illness narratives challenge and eventually undermine dominant values.

What I have shown in this book is the interplay between socio-cultural structures and the individual human subject. People relate individual lives to shared historical, literary and biblical structures. However, they do not do so unthinkingly or mechanically, but so as to convey the quality of their particular life experience. For example, not every literary paradigm is equally useful and many narratives reject or skilfully deconstruct shared cultural representations. Even older narrators do not all draw upon the available literary paradigms in retelling their lives. For some, the awfulness of lived experience exceeds the boundaries of literary form.

For others there is a conflict between the values to which they aspire and their lived lives: between aspiration and experience, and indeed, between textual exhortation and experience. Neither aspirations nor textual examples find a home in lives. Part of the blame lies in the destruction of literary traditions and an entire textual community. However, the departure of meaning from individual lives is not simply the result of a breakdown of literary traditions of story telling. Meaning is lost through the contradictions of values and personal experience and it is these contradictions which narratives actively explore. In the words of one letter-writer Jānis: 'Whatever one sets out to do cannot be put into effect. People in command are thieves'. Illness narratives systematically document the inauthenticity and contradictions of core values. By contrast, other more purposive narratives represent their lives as literary texts, thereby gaining entry to a textual and moral community. Both are valid responses to overpowering experience. In each case narrators assert their right to decide what makes for an acceptable human life.

APPENDIX I:

HISTORICAL BEARINGS

The narratives transcribed in this book draw upon individual and social memory but also upon history in a way which makes it difficult to prise them apart. History gives shape to individual memory and creates affinities with events long past. For example, living memory of labour camps reverberates with earlier historical accounts of oppression and violence against Latvian serfs. Siberian exile during Stalin's reign draws upon other earlier accounts of exile under the czars and massive population displacement. Accounts of forest partisans draw upon the idiom of earlier revolutionary exploits. The importance of land and the farmstead reflects nineteenth-century tales of land hunger. The role of women in articulating experience, especially loss and pain, follows a long tradition of folk poetry. But above all martyrdom and suffering run like veins throughout Latvian historiography.

Narratives form part of an oppositional folk tradition. Latvian folk songs were collected in the nineteenth century because they provided an alternative history and identity for Latvians. The contemporary oral history movement and the collection of life histories in Latvia have a similar function. My fieldwork took place during a euphoric transitional period when individuals felt empowered to speak, and they did so in opposition to official histories which had denied their experience. Narratives of lived experience were given in the spirit of testimonies. Soviet history books were withdrawn from schools and history lessons were in some cases suspended.[1] Indeed, many histories compete to capture the past in Latvia. Present-day Latvia has long been a battleground for different peoples: the word most frequently used to describe its history is 'turbulent'. Moreover, physical battles are reflected in a contest over historical truth and its ownership, not least among Latvians themselves. Russians, Baltic Germans, Latvians and latterly Soviets have developed distinct traditions of history writing about the Baltic area. Each school of history has developed in opposition to alien views.

Latvia lies on the eastern shores of the Baltic Sea in the north eastern corner of Europe. Roughly the same size as Ireland it is dwarfed by comparison with its eastern neighbour Russia. Its geography is closely linked to its history. From a British perspective it lies in eastern Europe, yet for Russians it has and continues to represent the west. This ambivalence accounts for the turbulence of its past.

BLOODY CRUSADES AND SERFDOM

In the 500 or so years following the birth of Christ it was a sparsely populated and densely forested area inhabited by Finnish tribes who lived largely by hunting and fishing.[2] During this time, place and river names suggest that Baltic tribes lived in the region north of the Pripet marshes. Between 550 and 650 AD Baltic tribes moved westwards pushing the Finnish tribes into coastal areas and northwards. Early historical records are few. Fuller written records date from the medieval period and the invasion of the Baltic lands by the teutonic knights. Latvian historians often periodize their accounts according to the nationality of the rulers. The German period dates from 1184. In this year the German monk Meinhard built a church at Ikškile, a Livonian village on the banks of the Daugava.[3] The Germans had sought permission from the *knaz* (prince) of Polock to preach Christianity and convert the Livonians and Lettigallians to Catholicism. Thus the conquest of the Baltic lands was carried out in the name of religion. Ikškile itself, however, being some 28 kilometres inland from the Gulf of Riga, proved difficult to defend since access to the sea could easily be closed off by the Livonian tribes. Another and more easily defended settlement was founded by Bishop Albert in 1201, at what is now Riga.

The battles between the Livonian chieftains and the military monastic Order of the Teutonic Knights constitute an important part of Latvian identity. So much so that in the 1930s Estonian historians were supposedly expelled from Latvia for failing to uphold the Latvian view of their past, as the German historian Georg von Rauch recounts:

> The Estonians always retained a certain capacity for self-criticism which the Latvians who were much more volatile and easily swayed by their emotions, seldom displayed. The romanticized accounts of early Latvian history published in Riga were not taken at all seriously in Tallinn, much to the annoyance of the Latvian historians.[4]
>
> (1974, p. 184)

The medieval period provided the content of much nineteenth-century poetry and in doing so offered a vision of a dignified, harmonious and independent existence and bravery in the face of attack. As the Latvian historian Švābe writes: 'The Latvian nation must always remember Zemgale's heroic battles for its independence' (1990, p. 101). The emphasis given in history books to the enormous bloodshed which accompanied the crusades suggests why Latvians might have remained amongst the least Christianized of European peoples.[5] Folk lore is more central to Latvian identity than religion, although Christianity has perhaps influenced folk beliefs more than Latvians care to admit.

By the end of the thirteenth century the Livonian tribes had been subjugated, and most of the area that is now Latvia became part of the Holy Roman Empire. The German state of Livonia was established, made up of four bishoprics and the lands of the Teutonic Order. The Latin chronicle of Henry of Livonia records the battles between the crusaders and the Livonians before 1227. Although Henry approved of war to acquire converts he clearly loved the indigenous people and perhaps for that reason he is often assigned honorary status as a Latvian.[6] Henry's description of the sacking of Jersika conveys his sympathies well:

> About the burning of Jersika. On the next day when everything had been plundered, they got ready to return and set fire to the city. And when the king saw the fire from the other side of the Daugava he gave a great sigh and moaning and crying he called out: 'Oh, Jersika, my beloved city! Oh, my father's inheritance! Oh, the unexpected destruction of my people! Alas! Was I born for this? To see my city burn, my people destroyed!'
>
> (*Indriķa Hronika*, 1993, pp. 130–131)

The battle of Gruenwald in 1410 in which the combined armies of Poland and Lithuania defeated the Knights of the Teutonic Order marks the beginning of the dissolution of the Order. Between 1558 and 1582 the armies of Ivan the Terrible ravaged the Baltic lands. Latvian history books recount how at the end of the wars no dog could be heard barking or cock crowing between Valka and Riga. The population had been halved and fields lay fallow. The peasants had no horses and put their wives to the plough. The conditions of the the time are described by Georg Mancelius, a Baltic German pastor from Kurland.[7] He wrote in Latvian:

> Great Russia completely devastated Vidzeme and tormented those people: peasants, Germans, lords and servants. They cut them, flayed them, scorched them and impaled them on skewers. They roasted them like pigs, with whips they raked their eyes from their foreheads. They raped and mocked women, ladies and virgins. Some were killed, others were taken as slaves for evermore to Russia. Others were taken naked as the day they were born to the bridge and then beaten about the head with rods and poles and then pushed into the river to drown and left to be eaten by fishes and birds. Oh! How many were left on the dunghill! How many mothers' children were eaten by dogs at the roadside! How many ended up in prison! And who can speak of all those sorrows which those dear people, young and old, rich and poor, Germans and peasants, barons and other honest people saw and suffered during the time of the Russians?
>
> (Mancelius 1654, quoted in Andrups and Kalve 1953, p. 59)

These quotations are reproduced in histories and anthologies of literature, and they undoubtedly influence the Latvian image of Russians.

Although Ivan IV's invasion brought about the final dissolution of the Teutonic Order, the German landlords remained. Indeed, the Livonian landlords acquired a particularly evil reputation. For example:

> The petty landlords of the eastern Baltic seem to have been a particularly unpleasant lot, indulging in bouts of litigation with neighbours, and occasionally ending up in court themselves on charges of incest or adultery. The Baltic nobility believed they had a time honoured right to beat their peasants although they were also fearful of what might

happen should they revolt. . . . The evil reputation of the Livonian landlords and the wretched condition of the peasantry, was well known on
the other side of the Gulf of Finland, where the epithets 'Livonian dog'
and 'son of a Livonian tramp' were regular terms of abuse.

(Kirby 1990, pp. 157–158)

In the course of the sixteenth century peasants were tied more firmly to the
land and to their landlords. The bitter hatred of their German overlords
which such treatment engendered found an abiding voice in Latvian folk
songs:

> A black snake is grinding flour
> In the middle of the sea on a stone
> Let it be eaten by those masters
> Who force us to work without the sun.

A WINDOW ON THE WEST

An improvement in peasant conditions came with the Swedish conquests of
Livonia and Courland. The Swedes and Poles beat the Muscovite forces at
the battle of Wenden in 1581 and took Riga in 1621. The Swedish period
is looked upon as the golden period of Latvian history, especially because
of the development of schools and educational opportunities for peasants.[8]
It was, however, brought to an end by the Great Northern War and the
imperialist aspirations of Peter the Great. Latvia's access to the sea and its
ice-free western port of Liepāja opened opportunities for trade and made
it particularly covetable. Riga was captured in 1710 thus providing Peter I
with a window on the west and setting the course of history for the next
three centuries. Livonia and Courland were incorporated into the Russian
empire, in which they were to remain for the next two centuries. However,
the Baltic Germans remained as landlords and in return for loyalty to the
czar enjoyed considerable autonomy over local affairs. The nadir of
serfdom was reached in the eighteenth century in the Latvian lands as in
other parts of the Russian empire. Among the many obligations of peasants
was military service.[9] Folk songs attest to its duration:

> Going to war
> I left my sister in the cradle;
> Coming back from the war
> I found a great weaver.
> I asked mother
> Who is that weaver?
> That my son is your little sister
> Whom you left in the cradle.

At the beginning of the nineteenth century Latvia was a colonized society
owned and governed by a sizeable Baltic German elite. (Baltic Germans
constituted some 8 per cent of the total population.) In many ways it was
still a medieval society. Serfdom of a harsh variety existed throughout the
Baltic provinces. Latvians were tied to the land which they were not allowed

to own and were minorities in the towns. Riga and other towns were run by corporate guilds with a restricted membership. A famous landmark in Riga is the so-called Cat's house.[10] Built by a Latvian tradesman at the turn of the century it has a black cat perched on top of its turreted roof. Its significant feature is that its backside with tail in the air was originally turned defiantly towards the neighbouring guild building but was made to adopt a more decorous position. However, by the end of the century the assured position of the Baltic German barons was under threat. Serfdom had been abolished throughout the Latvian provinces by 1819 and a class of educated Latvian speakers was growing able to speak up for the rights of native Latvians.

In 1800 Riga had a population of some 29,000 (Švābe 1962, p. 104). Although small by comparison with other western european cities it must be remembered that cities in the Baltic area generally were small. St Petersburg had a population of 191,00 in 1787, but only four other cities (Danzig, Konigsberg, Stockholm and Copenhagen) had a population of 50,000 or more (see Kirby 1995, p. 49). By the end of the century Riga's population was more than a quarter of a million. Riga was ethnically diverse: in 1799 Baltic Germans constituted 46 per cent of the population and Latvians 32 per cent, with substantial Russian, Polish and Jewish minorities (Švābe 1962, p. 104). At the end of the century Riga was still a cosmopolitan city but the percentage of Latvian speakers had increased to 45 per cent, largely at the expense of the Baltic Germans.

THE LONGING FOR LAND

The reverberations of the French revolution were felt in the remote Baltic countryside. In particular, the writings of the Baltic German schoolmaster Garlieb Merkel (1769–1850) played a major role in disseminating revolutionary ideas. In Vidzeme the imposition of a new tax in 1784 paid in money not labour by all men, had prompted the peasants to try and throw off the yoke of the barons. Rather than pay the local barons, the peasants converged upon the town of Valmiera. Military force was used to stamp out peasant defiance.

The uprising most firmly imprinted on Latvian historical memory took place on the manorial lands of Kauguri near Valmiera. In 1802, in the course of the Sunday service, the pastor announced that peasants had to pay tax in money, not in hay and grain. This excited rumours that news of liberation from serfdom had been suppressed. The peasants refused to carry out their obligatory work. Some were arrested, others gathered to demand their release. In the end soldiers began shooting and killed ten people. The leaders of the movement were flogged and exiled to Siberia. As a result the uneasy relationship between the German Baltic landlords and their serfs became more sharply etched and antagonistic. Both exile and floggings have become part of social memory. Physical punishment of Latvians was introduced during the German occupation of 1941 to 1943, and the resentment which this generated drew upon centuries of physical punishment.

Widespread dissatisfaction and unrest eventually led to the 1804 land reform commission.[11] Although the outcome of the commission was the end of serfdom – marked by a law forbidding the sale of serfs without land, in practice the liberation of serfs between 1817 and 1861 left the peasants landless. In return for the cultivation of land they had to work the manorial lands. Referred to in Latvian as *klaušu laiki* (the times of the corvee), the lives of peasants actually worsened after the abolition of serfdom. The period from 1819 to mid-century was a particularly bitter and unsettled time. The expansion of manorial lands took place at the expense of peasant land. Peasant homes were destroyed: in Vidzeme nearly 1,000 and in Kurzeme some 3,000 peasant homes were destroyed in the space of some thirty years.

These circumstances gave rise to a passionate and unrelenting peasant longing for land. Much of Latvian literature is pastoral, but what land meant to the Latvian peasant is reflected above all in the writing of Jānis Purapuķe.[12] Born in Vidzeme in 1864 his novel *One's Own Small Piece of Land* (Savs Kaktiņš Savs Stūrītis Zemes) (1898) describes the plight of landless labourers of an earlier generation. Here is the protagonist, a landless labourer reflecting on the meaning of work and the land:

'What a hard life a farm servant has. . . . You're like a bird on the end of a branch: if the branch breaks and you're not killed you fly further and further. The world is so large and no-one has found its limit, but a farm labourer has no place where he can safely sit down and rest. It's fine so long as one has strength and one's hands and feet obey; but when evening comes and the unlucky hour strikes, or illness lays one low on a straw pallet – what then? How different it is for those who have their own corner of land, their appointed corner. Even if you just plant a potato it's – yours. No-one checks when you sleep and when you wake, what you eat weekdays and what you eat Sundays. If you are sick then rest. No-one will reproach you for needlessly taking up space and eating bread. Oh! If only one could achieve such a blessing. How differently one would then work and strive. In front of the window pale pink roses and dalias would bloom, along the wall michaelmas daisies and by the house corner a full artemesia bush [Latvian – *dievkociņš*].'

(1990 (1904), pp. 16–17)

The impetus behind present-day efforts to reclaim unprofitable ancestral lands has roots in these nineteenth-century longings for land. The farmstead and its land have a continued importance for Latvian identity.

RELIGIOUS DISAFFECTION

A run of cold wet summers with early frosts in the late 1830s exposed the vulnerability of the peasants. No longer the responsibility of the manor they were left without corn seed, fields remained unsown and by 1841 there was famine in several parishes in Vidzeme.[13] In this context rumours spread of the availability of free land in southern Russia. Fantasies of a warm and fertile land where giant vegetables grew and the misapprehension that land would be granted to the converted lay behind the mass conversions to the Orthodox Church. Between 1845 and 1848 40,397 Latvians converted to Russian orthodoxy (see Kirby 1995, p. 102). The siting of a Russian

Orthodox Church alongside the Lutheran church in provincial towns such as Limbaži stands as a testimony to that period.[14]

However, beyond the distress and land hunger to which the conversion movement testifies, it also speaks of the alienation of Latvian peasants from the official Lutheran Church. Perceived as a source of moral recrimination rather than spiritual solace, there were no psychological obstacles to its abandonment. Indeed, David Kirby points out that 'many of the converts believed it was possible to belong to both the Lutheran and the Orthodox church' (ibid., p. 102). The Lutheran Church was perceived as an organ of the Baltic German landlords – which in many ways, of course, it was. Sermons were used to instil habits of work, sobriety and contentment with one's lot and to berate bad habits. Folk songs capture the sceptical attitude of peasants towards the religion of their masters. For example:

> The steward was praying to God
> But his feet were dangling in hell
> What kind of God do you pray to
> When you beat the labourers?

No such reserve or hesitancy existed between the Moravian brethren and the Latvian peasantry. The Moravians had first appeared in Valmiera in 1729. By the early nineteenth century many small towns throughout Vidzeme boasted a Moravian meeting house.[15] The democratic practices of the Moravians and their austere yet emotional approach succeeded in tapping the religious inclinations of the peasantry. They instilled virtuous behaviour and restored self-respect to the demoralized, as well as providing opportunities for Latvian peasants to develop oratorical skills and leadership qualities.

In 1849, in the wake of the revolutionary movements in the rest of Europe, a law was passed to improve peasant rights to land. The need for a mobile labour force brought about legal changes and the law of 1863 allowed peasants in Vidzeme to choose their own place of residence. Two years later in 1865 corvee duties in return for the use of land were abolished. These changes fuelled land hunger and by 1912 90 per cent of all farmsteads formerly manorial property had been bought by Latvian peasants.

THE NATIONALIST MOVEMENT

The cutting of feudal ties to the land was a factor in the process of national awakening. New social structures created the opportunity for peasant sons to acquire new skills and a different awareness of themselves. The generation of Latvian nationalists who were active in the 1860s – men such as Krišjānis Valdemārs (1825–1888), Juris Alunāns (1832–64), and Atis Kronvalds (1837–75), were sons of peasants able to take advantage of changing social circumstances. They saw themselves as innovators and were referred to as the New Latvians (*Jaunlatvieši*). However, history has conferred upon them a unity and a definition which at the time they did not possess. Valdemārs saw the future of Latvia linked with Russia, particularly in the development of its maritime industry. Kronvalds had deep ties of indebtedness to his Baltic German patrons and their culture. And Alunāns appears to have had ambivalent and shifting allegiances to Latvian peasant and cosmopolitan culture (Plakans 1974, pp. 460–465). Their diversity and ambivalence is hardly surprising. The earlier division between Germans and Latvians or *Undeutsch* was one of social class. Social mobility for Latvians involved assimilation into the Baltic German classes and population statistics from Kurland as late as 1860–80 suggest that such assimilation was taking place at a substantial rate. Inevitably, much of the education of the New Latvians was in German or Russian. For Valdemārs, therefore, to describe himself as a Latvian whilst studying in Dorpat (Tērbata) was a revolutionary act, and it has been celebrated as such in the histories of Latvian nationalism.

Newspapers and the growth of a non-religious literature of fiction and poetry provided the opportunity for expressing the new nationalist feelings and ideas.[16] *Pēterburgas Avīzes* (1862–1865) was founded by Valdemārs and edited by Alunāns. One of the principal contributors was Krišjānis Barons. It was politically radical and caused consternation among the Baltic Germans. Governor Lieven put in an official complaint to the Ministry of the Interior. As a result the paper was censored and closed down. However, these events underline the fact that Latvian nationalism was as much the dream of exiles as of local inhabitants. After the closure of the *Pēterburgas Avīzes* the centre of Latvian radicalism moved to Riga where the Riga Latvian Association was founded in 1868. The activities of the organization were directed towards the promotion of national identity.

THE *DAINAS*

In particular, the Riga Latvian Association was responsible for organizing song festivals. The first song festival took place in 1872. During this same period folk songs (*dainas*) were collected and categorized. Their publication and dissemination through festivals played a major role in the consolidation of Latvian identity. Although they had been collected sporadically by German pastors – for example, two volumes of songs collected by August Bielenstein, a pastor from Dobele, appeared in 1874 and 1875 – their collection on a grand and systematic scale was undertaken by Krišjānis Barons. The enterprise was begun while Barons was still in Moscow and the first volume was published in 1894. Altogether more than 200,000 songs were collected. Their systematization was an attempt to provide Latvians with a unified image of themselves as well as an alternative history. The importance attached to the songs reflects a distrust of official histories. At a later date the folklorist Pēteris Šmits wrote:

> In recent times we often hear asserted that history cannot be studied from folk songs, with which one has to agree in an overall sense. But we can also go further and say that we cannot study Latvian history from the Baltic chronicles.

> (1937, p. 27)

The folk songs were referred to as the spiritual inheritance of Latvians.

'Our folk songs are for the most part an inheritance from the silver-haired, unfathomable past. From mouth to mouth, from person to person, they have been preserved in social memory to this day' (Smits 1923, p. 4). The *daina*s relate to all stages of the life cycle and in so doing reveal peasant attitudes to work, to their masters, to the land and, of course, to each other.

Thus the end of the century saw the emergence of a class of educated and more self-assured Latvians. It also saw Latvians, no longer a homogeneous peasant society, increasingly differentiated by money and property. The opportunity and drive to buy one's own piece of land accentuated the plight of the landless and the divisions between those with and without land. Švābe suggests that some 660,467 peasants, or 61 per cent of the rural population, were without land. Poor landless peasants no longer tied to a particular locality flooded into the towns in search of a livelihood. Between 1881 and 1897 17 per cent of the population of Vidzeme and 15 per cent of the population of Kurzeme moved to towns. Riga tripled in size in the last three decades of the century largely due to the growth of an industrial working class. Other landless peasants moved to Russia in search of cheaper land. Estimates set the number of land-hungry migrants during this period at some 200,000. After centuries of frozen immobility the last decades of the century witnessed a mass movement of country peoples.

RUSSIFICATION POLICIES

During the reign of Alexander III the Baltic provinces became the target of policies of intense Russification. The local administration, judiciary and education system was revised in line with Russian practices. This marked the end of the autonomy granted to the Baltic Germans since the time of Peter I. Instruction in schools was in Russian and non-Russian speaking teachers lost their jobs. Latvian books had to be printed in the cyrillic alphabet. David Kirby cites the fact that in 1889 only one of the district court judges in Riga was German. Whilst these policies had the desired effect of curbing the power of the Baltic Germans, they also introduced inefficiency and corruption. In these years, despite the systematic nature of the Russification policies, Latvian national identity was consolidated rather than dismantled. As Andrejs Plakans writes:

> Before cultural Russification had a chance to effect changes in the Latvian cultural world, that world had already matured sufficiently to withstand attacks upon it, whether planned or unplanned.... All of these manifestations of Russification policy had arrived too late to reverse patterns set in the previous decades among the Latvians.
>
> (1981, p. 246)

Indeed, the drive towards forging a Latvian identity derived an added impetus from the attempts at Russification. The many newspapers which appeared during the last two decades of the nineteenth century were deeply concerned with issues of national culture.

The newspaper *Dienas Lapa* first appeared in 1886 under the editorship of Pēteris Stučka. This paper gave rise to the name *Jaunā Strāva* or New Current, designating a new variety of free-thinking, socialist Latvians. Among them was the poet and playwright Jānis Pliekšāns (pen name Rainis) who used the paper to disseminate and popularize Marxist ideas.[17] In the spring of 1897 the authorities clamped down on members of *Jaunā Strāva*. There were many arrests and *Dienas Lapa* was closed down. Rainis himself escaped to Switzerland. Closely linked to the ideas of *Jaunā Strāva* was the Latvian Social Democratic Party, founded in 1904, which played a formative role in the 1905 revolution. Latvian society at the turn of the century harboured diverse groups with diverse grievances and the revolution was able to draw upon their disaffection.

THE REVOLUTION AND WAR IN LATVIA

As soon as news of the shooting of peaceful demonstrators in St Petersburg on January 9th 1905 reached Riga and the other Latvian towns a general strike was declared. On January 13th soldiers clashed with demonstrators in Riga, killing seventy people and injuring some two hundred. However, the epicentre of the revolution in the Baltic quickly moved to the Latvian countryside. Peasant anger was greater and had a more radical edge in the Latvian provinces than in the neighbouring provinces. Manorial servants went on strike. Church demonstrations took place with singing of revolutionary songs during church services. However, aggression was principally directed against property. Many hundreds of manors were burnt down as well as peasant farmsteads. One feature of this unrest was the leading role taken by elementary school teachers. The destruction of property was met by extreme and violent punishment. Czar Nicholas II sent punitive military expeditions, which in the period between 1905 and 1907 killed 2,500 people. Andrievs Ezergailis claims: 'The damage that the Latvians had committed until 1908 was basically against property while the damage to Latvians was mostly against people' (1974, p. 20). However, Anatol Lieven claims that the rebels killed 635 people (1993, p. 51). Here as elsewhere in Latvian history there is lack of agreement. Many others were sent to labour camps in Siberia. Latvians believed that the German barons were behind the punitive expeditions, and from then on 'the crust of social courtesy ceased to exist between the Latvians and the Germans' (Ezergailis 1979, p. 21). Following the revolution many people went into hiding in the forests and others were exiled.

The Latvian revolutionary spirit was forged by the events of 1905 which provided it with symbols and martyrs. Each turning of Latvian history has been experienced in terms of what has gone before: the outbreak of the First World War drew upon painful memories of revenge exacted by the punitive expeditions.

The war created greater havoc and destruction for Latvians than for any other group apart from Polish Jews. In the spring of 1915 German forces occupied Kurland as far as the river Daugava and the northern front remained there for the next two years. Ezergailis gives a figure of 800,000 Latvians displaced by the war between 1915 and 1917 – that is half of all living Latvians. In Kurzeme three-quarters of the population left, most seeking refuge in the interior of Russia, and some counties in Zemgale were left virtually uninhabited. The wiping out of inhabitants and the devastation of land recalled the ravages of Ivan the Terrible in the sixteenth century. Meanwhile self-help refugee organizations were set up in St Petersburg and one could almost speak of a tradition of exile. In St Petersburg there were an estimated 100,000 Latvian refugees. In August 1915 a central refugee committee was set up which was eventually to form the basis of the Latvian government.

The occupation of Kurzeme was envisaged as a prelude to colonization with plans for the settlement of some 6,000 Germans in the abandoned peasant farmsteads of Kurland and on the land donated by German barons.

The invasion of Kurland persuaded the Russian authorities to allow the formation of two Latvian rifle battalions or *strēlnieki*, made up of volunteers. Although now suspicious of the Baltic Germans, the Russian authorities were nevertheless not eager to set up national military units in the Baltic area. However, their spirit and military prowess brought about a change of policy. Throughout 1915 and 1916 these battalions fought to defend Mitau and later Riga. Casualties were disproportionately high and Latvian soldiers felt they had made needless sacrifices and that their military gains were squandered by the Russian army. The Christmas battles of 1916 to defend Riga in which the vast majority were killed have become part of national martyrology. As one primary school history book put it: 'The Christmas battles did not bring freedom for Kurzeme, they simply wove a new branch in the laurel and thorn crown of the strēlnieki' (Zālītis, 1947, p. 227) The following autumn on September 3rd the Germans occupied Riga.

By 1917 one reserve and eight regular regiments had been established. These regiments undoubtedly played an important part in the victory of the Bolsheviks although their motivation for fighting is subject to different interpretations. George Leggett's view is that:

> These battalions (later they became regiments) were largely recruited from men of worker-peasant stock; whilst their principal desire was to return to their native soil, they were prepared meanwhile to serve the Bolsheviks, whose broad social democratic slogans they found quite attractive, and who afforded them preferential treatment. The Latvian riflemen were well-disciplined, dependable soldiers, qualities which compensated for their indifferent Communist zeal and their ignorance of the Russian language.
>
> (1981, p. 263)

Latvian emigré historians have ruefully endorsed a similar position. For example, Edgars Andersons writes: 'Latvian leaders were not politically astute and the mass of people threw themselves too unrestrainedly into the whirlpool of events, sacrificing themselves in the interests of other nations' (1967, p. 173). Perhaps there is no answer to Ezergailis' question:

What is one to make of the Latvian drive from a province towards the centre of the empire? Was it in response to a call from Lenin or was it a spontaneous move? In October 1917, no one, certainly not the Latvian young men who marched into Petrograd (in a sense occupied it), realized the impact they were destined to make on Russia – the pivot of twentieth century history'

(1979, p. 241)

In any event, their centrality to the success of the bolshevik revolution is not under dispute. Latvian *strēlnieki* played a major role in the battles of the civil war and certain regiments such as the 6th Tukums regiment were responsible for policing and the maintenance of order.[18]

Although the motivation of Latvian soldiers may be conflicting and ambivalent, their role in forging Latvian identity is far more clear cut. They are the martyrs of Latvian nationalism and their sacrifice is commemorated in the monumental sculptures of *Brāļu kapi*, the national Cemetery in Riga.

THE FOUNDATION OF THE LATVIAN STATE

Meanwhile on the home front the collapse of the Czarist regime created new possibilities of greater autonomy for Latvia. The strongest political movement was represented by the social democrats, who had aligned themselves with the bolsheviks. By contrast the liberals and bourgeois representatives 'lacked much of the verve and organizational ability of the Latvian social democrats' (Kirby 1995, p. 229). The bolsheviks secured 41 per cent of the municipal vote in Riga and later 60 per cent of the Livland provincial assembly, creating, as Ezergailis claims, the first Latvian Bolshevik republic. Not only were land and property confiscated, but looting and killing were widespread. The German advance in April 1918 marked the end of the Iskolat republic.

The bourgeois parties were also struggling to assert themselves. On November 4th 1917 a provisional national council was elected in Valka including amongst its members the writers Kārlis Skalbe and Jānis Akur-aters.[19] Their aspirations were for complete national independence and for links with the western allies. The following year on November 18th, independence was declared with Kārlis Ulmanis, head of the peasant party, as president.[20] However, fighting continued between bolsheviks and Germans until the confrontation between the Estonian and Latvian armies and the Landeswehr at the battle of Cēsis. This battle in which companies of local school children from Valmiera and Cēsis participated marked the beginning of real independence.[21] David Kirby describes the defeat as curbing the influence of Germany on the international field: 'The twentieth-century battle of Wenden (Cēsis) was thus as much a turning point as had been the defeat inflicted on the Muscovite forces by a Swedish-Polish army in 1578' (1995, p. 279). The following year saw the defeat of German and bolshevik troops. Combined Latvian and Polish troops drove the bolshevik troops from Latgale, which was formally incorporated into Latvia in August 1920.

Between 1914 and 1920 Latvia lost one-quarter of its population. Half the population had fled as refugees to Russia and Siberia. Vast areas of the countryside were devastated and its industry had been dismantled. 1918 had been a year of famine when some 8,000 inhabitants of Riga died. During the years 1920 and 1921 many of these refugees returned to the homeland but many others remained behind. For many young Latvians this was to be the first of several dislocations in their lives. The new government was thus faced with pressing economic problems as well as the challenge of establishing political and administrative structures in a country with no traditions of political autonomy and democracy. The new constitution, revised in 1922, safeguarded the rights of all citizens and protected the rights of minorities.[22] Rights were conferred on minorities as a whole, thus safeguarding the cultural identity of particular groups. It was in many ways a highly progressive vision. However, the political landscape was constantly shifting and is all too easy to caricature as Hiden and Salmon note (1991, p. 50). Between 1922 and Ulmanis' coup in 1934 there were some thirty-nine parties represented and nineteen prime ministers. Proportional representation meant the constitutions 'were too democratic for their own good' in the words of Anatol Lieven (1993, p. 64). The agrarian parties played a dominant role in post-war politics with fourteen of the prime ministers drawn from the farmers' parties (see Kirby, 1995, p. 18).

LAND REFORMS

Radical land reforms between 1920 and 1924 transformed the nature of Latvian society.[23] Despite the peasants' freedom to purchase land, some 60 per cent of all land was still in the hands of big landowners, mostly Baltic Germans, but with a minority of Latvians – the so-called 'grey barons'.[24] As a result of the reforms big landowners were expropriated without compensation. They were allowed to keep no more than fifty hectares. Land was distributed to the landless, to small farmers and to those who had fought for Latvian independence. Although the reforms appeared to have a disquieting resemblance to bolshevik practices, they constituted 'an effective barrier to the spread of communism through the creation of a landowning peasantry' (Hiden 1991, p. 80). Some 70,000 farmsteads were created in this way. The new farmsteads thus created were small. The average size was twenty-two hectares with the majority being under ten hectares. Despite the precariousness of these small landholdings the rural economy flourished, sustained by a co-operative system and low-interest government loans.[25] The consensus of historians is that the brief independence period was marked by a fair degree of economic success, and certainly that is how most older Latvians remember it.

From a political perspective views are far more mixed and contradictory. Ulmanis' coup of 1934 brought parliamentary democracy to an end. However, in an era of dictatorships, that of Ulmanis was mild. Nicholas Hope argues that the Baltic states retained a democratic infrastructure which was not destroyed by the changes at the top. He writes:

It is crucial to stress positive features which continued throughout the

entire period of independence. These consisted of continuing enthusiasm for untested egalitarian and humanitarian constitutional arrange-
ments, the rapid extension of efficient national education systems, social
welfare provision, economic advance as countries exporting agricultural produce, and in the case of Estonia and Latvia, progress as
reasonably successful mixed economies of a Scandinavian type.

(1994, p. 53)

Schooling was made compulsory in 1920 and the illiteracy rate declined
from 22 per cent in 1920 to 10 per cent in 1937.[26] Particular emphasis was
put upon agricultural institutes. A system of compulsory insurance protected workers against sickness and accident.[27] Working women were
entitled to three months' maternity leave on full pay.[28] In 1922 the working
day of manual workers was restricted to eight hours and of white-collar
workers to six hours. The University of Latvia was founded in 1919 which
fostered international links and welcomed foreign academics.[29]

However, the weakness of Ulmanis' government lay in his relationship to
other political parties both of the extreme right and of the left. In the late
1920s the anti-Semitic organization *Ugunskrusts* (Firecross), transformed as
Pērkoņkrusts (Thundercross), appeared, but was subsequently outlawed by
Ulmanis in 1934. At the same time, Ulmanis' government became increasingly nationalistic – adopting *Pērkoņkrusts'* slogan 'Latvia for the Latvians',
thus moving away from the multi-ethnic commitment of the Constitution
1922.[30] Socialist parties too were outlawed and some socialists were
imprisoned. Although their fate was kind in comparison with that of their
brothers in Stalin's Russia and Hitler's Germany, Ulmanis' policy was
counter-productive. Indeed, Andrievs Ezergailis claims:

> Ulmanis in his anti-parliamentary, anti-socialist putsch came to be the
> biggest Communist-maker in Latvia since Pobedonestsev and Plehve,
> the Great Russian russifiers. Ulmanis drove all of the leftists of Latvia
> – Latvian, Jewish, or Russian – into the arms of communism.
>
> (1993, p. 272)[31]

Part of this intolerance of political difference was the censorship of the
press. In particular, Ulmanis was anxious that press criticism should
antagonize neither Russia nor Germany. The result was that Latvians were
not as well informed as they might have been about what was happening on
their doorstep. For example, there was little information about the winter
war of 1939–40 in Finland.

THE SOVIET INVASION

Following upon Germany's invasion of Poland a military base with 30,000
Soviet troops was forced upon Latvia in October 1939.[32] It took ordinary
Latvians who had turned their backs on the Soviet Union by surprise. In
fact, the secret clause of the notorious Molotov Ribbentrop pact signed on
August 23rd 1939 had assigned Poland and Lithuania to the German
sphere of influence and Estonia and Latvia to the Soviet sphere of

influence. Belated attempts at cooperation between the three Baltic states came too late. On May 26th the following year Molotov sent an ultimatum to the Latvian government accusing it of entering into an anti-Soviet alliance with Lithuania and Estonia and demanding the formation of a pro-Soviet government within eight hours. On June 17th 1940 Soviet troops crossed Latvia's southern and eastern borders. Elections were rigged and a puppet government was set up under Augusts Kirhenšteins which on July 21st applied for admission to the Soviet Union. On the following day Soviet decrees concerning nationalization of land and property were accepted. Land in excess of thirty hectares was confiscated. Rural dwellings which measured in excess of 170 square metres and town dwellings in excess of 220 square metres were expropriated. Moveable property such as furniture and linen was also appropriated. Farmers were obliged to give large amounts of agricultural produce to the state at nominal prices.[33]

Ulmanis had been put under house arrest, was deported to Voroshilovsk in the north Caucasus and died a year later. In November 1940 people's courts were set up – so-called *troikas* consisting of three party members without legal training. Torture and week-long interrogations were routine. Many went into hiding in the forests or lived itinerant lives of the hunted. During this first year of occupation some 35,000 people were killed and deported (Misiunas and Taagepera 1993, p. 42). Nearly half these deportations – some 15,000 – occurred on the night of June 14th. Among the Latvians deported during that first year of Soviet occupation were some 5,000 Jews (ibid., p. 64). Those deported in this early wave were professionals, administrators, business people, but also county elders, teachers and farmers. Latvian memories of this year are varied. For many middle-class city families it was a nightmare, whereas large sections of the rural population remained relatively unscathed. However, this first year of Soviet occupation has come to be known as the terrible year.

THE GERMAN OCCUPATION

The swift and unanticipated German invasion at the beginning of July 1941 met a stunned and demoralized population. This double occupation reversed a centuries-old fear and detestation: many Latvians greeted the German army as liberators. Misiunas and Taagepera have this to say about the two occupying powers:

> Of these the one coming second had an unfair advantage: it did not have to destroy the national elite, because that had already been done. Therefore, it generated relatively little resentment. The Baltic people could suspect Hitler of wanting to deport them east, but Stalin had actually started doing so. They saw no advantage in weakening Hitler against Stalin.
>
> (1993, p. 70)

In fact, an anthropological commission in Germany had laid plans for the deportation of some 50 per cent of the Latvian population to the interior of Russia and the assimilation of the other – racially purer – 50 per cent to the German nation.

However, the major victims of Nazi racist policy were the Jews. At the beginning of the German occupation there were some 70,000 Jews in Latvia. Of these some 4,000 are estimated to have survived. The Moscow district of Riga was turned into a ghetto and later an extermination camp was set up in Salaspils outside Riga.[34] Latvians did undoubtedly participate in the killing of Jews, although arguments based upon anti-Semitism in inter-war Latvia appear to be unfounded (Ezergailis 1993). Among the factors which have been mentioned are limited Jewish complicity with Soviet occupation (Gordon 1990). There is also some evidence that both the Nazi and the Soviet regime set different elements of the population against one another.

Between 1941 and 1944 Latvia became part of the Ostgebiet under the directorship of Alfred Rosenberg. The Germans played a double game with the Latvians – disguising their true intentions. Attempts by General Danker, head of the Latvian directorate, to achieve a measure of self-government failed. Hitler's initial policy was to disband non-German military and paramilitary organizations as untrustworthy. However, by the end of July 1941 the Germans were actively recruiting Latvian volunteers to police battalions and sending them to the eastern front. By 1942 the number of volunteers was drying up and the Latvian legion was formed in 1943. Adult men were conscripted to hard labour or the legion. Although part of the German army it was nominally under Latvian command. There were misunderstandings about the purpose of the legion; untrained soldiers who thought they were to defend Latvia's borders were sent to the eastern front. With the breaching of the front line the Latvian divisions returned to Latgale (eastern province of Latvia) in July 1944. By mid-August the Soviet army was moving towards Riga, which fell on October 13th. Soviet forces had already reached the Baltic sea on October 10th, thus effectively cutting off the province of Kurzeme and the 19th Latvian division which was defending it. It has come to be known as Kurzeme's *katls* (Kurzeme's cauldron), which powerfully conveys what happened there at the end of the war. Although it was apparent that the war was lost to the Soviets, Latvians continued fighting until capitulation on May 8th. After capitulation some 8,000 soldiers were taken as prisoners of war, but considerable numbers became guerrilla fighters hiding in the forests. Romuald Misiunas and Rein Taagepera estimate that there were in all about 40,000 partisans in Latvia.

POST-WAR CHAOS

The immediate post-war period is referred to by Latvians as *juku laiki*, or the time of chaos. Massive population losses – some 25 per cent of the pre-war population disappeared or were killed – affected nearly every family in Latvia. Homes had been expropriated or destroyed. Agriculture met with disaster and hunger prevailed. There was a scarcity of consumer goods. The history of the war and conscription of Latvians into both the German and subsequently the Soviet armies created fear and distrust between people.

Guerrilla activity was widespread in the countryside creating the feeling that the war was not yet over. Local country people who supported the partisans with food and medicaments were killed or deported for doing so.

Land and property was redistributed. Those who had actively supported the German occupation had their land reduced to 5–7 hectares. But as Misiunas and Taagepera point out, active support was a flexible term which covered the fulfilment of German requisition norms for agricultural produce (1993, p. 94). The property of the 100,000 refugees to the west was also appropriated by the state as was that of people killed and deported. Farms in excess of 20 hectares were also cut down. State land funds were created which included farm machinery and animals. Between 1940 and 1944 the state land fund all but doubled in size. Some of the land from this fund was redistributed to the landless, although this process was slow and haphazard. By the end of 1945, 42 per cent of the land fund had not yet been distributed. In practice this redistribution process was highly divisive, creating overnight a new class of beneficiaries with a vested interest in the system and setting them at odds with those who had been expropriated.

COLLECTIVIZATION

Collectivization was not implemented immediately, although unrealistically high taxes imposed on farmers in 1947 and 1948 gave an indication of what was to come. For farmers classified as *kulaks* a tax of 40 per cent of estimated income was imposed in 1947 and 75 per cent in 1948. In practice incomes were overestimated and farmers were unable to pay the taxes. Despite this softening approach only 8 per cent of farmers had joined the kolhozes at the beginning of 1949. On March 25th some 50,000 country people, men, women and children, were deported from Latvia. Many were deposited in the region of Tomsk. They constituted one-tenth of all farmers. Since land had already been confiscated the definition of a *kulak* was used retrospectively. In practice there was a large element of arbitrariness in the compilation of the lists for deportation and local envy and animosities were sometimes exploited. Those who survived deportation and exile often had no homes to return to and their return to the homeland could also be painful.

The deportations had the desired effect of speeding collectivization. Misiunas and Taagepera quote a figure for collectivized farms of 11 per cent on March 12th and 50 per cent on April 9th. By the end of 1951 more than 98 per cent of all Latvian farms had been collectivized.

The early years on the collective farms were difficult. Directors of the kolhozes were brought in from Russia. Their political beliefs were correct but they lacked relevant agricultural expertise. The result was extreme inefficiency and no pay for the farmers who worked there. Agricultural productivity slumped during the early 1950s. Grain production dropped from 1,372,000 tons in 1940, to 732,000 tons in 1950, to 436,000 tons in 1956. There was not enough winter feed for the kolhoz animals and in the spring workers recalled that cows were too weak to stand up by their own efforts and had to be hoisted up by ropes. In the course of 1950 problems were compounded by the increasing size of the kolhozes. The area of land under cultivation shrank systematically until by 1960 it was half of what it had been in 1939 (ibid., p. 190). These changes were perceived by the peasants as deliberate attempts to destroy Latvian agriculture and with it their identity.

Meanwhile the amount of land cultivated and the number of animals tended by individual households were strictly regulated. Country people had no enthusiasm for kolhoz work for which they were not paid, but obstacles were put in the way of their becoming self-sufficient through working their own patch of land. For example, in 1952 several generations living together were treated as one family, thus restricting the number of animals they could keep.[35] The cold wet summer and ruined harvest of that year made life even more difficult.

By the late 1950s limited improvements had taken place. The growth of sovhozes (state-owned farms) where workers were assured a wage was a small but significant improvement in the lives of rural dwellers.[36] Throughout the 1960s there were improvements in cereal yields which by 1965 reached and then surpassed pre-war levels. However, private plots of land continued to play an indispensable role in ensuring the survival of families. In 1960, although such plots represented only 5 per cent of the total land under cultivation, they yielded 66 per cent of all vegetables, 49 per cent of meat and milk and 71 per cent of eggs (ibid., p. 369). The rural standard of living in the late 1960s approached that of urban dwellers.

IMMIGRATION AND RUSSIFICATION FEARS

Plans for industrialization were rapidly put into effect after the war. Heavy industries such as metalwork, train and machine construction were concentrated in Riga. Light industries included textile manufacture in Daugavpils and Ogre and shoe manufacture in Riga. However, as Misiunas and Taagepera wryly point out, local markets continued to be short of consumer goods. The new industries corresponded to Soviet rather than local needs. Raw materials were brought in from other parts of the Soviet Union as was the workforce to man these new industries.[37]

War-time and post-war population losses led to an acute labour shortage. The movement of population from the country to towns which started and continued after the war was not sufficient to resolve the labour shortage. This led to state-sponsored immigration from other parts of the Soviet Union. Early immigrants fell into two categories: officials and managers whose job was to implement and oversee the new industries, and a much larger unskilled labour force. 1945 to 1947 was the period of most dramatic population changes, from a combination of reasons including exile, death and deportation, but immigration continued throughout the 1960s and 1970s. During this latter period massive housing projects were undertaken to house the incoming population. Between 1945 and 1959 half a million non-Latvians settled in Latvia – a quarter of the pre-war population – thus radically altering the nature of Latvian society. Part of the appeal of the Baltic countries lay in their higher standard of living compared to the rest of the Soviet Union and the offer of urban accommodation as part of the work package.[38] High-

rise residential blocks encircling Riga and other Latvian towns were constructed to house this new labour force.[39] The circumstances and timing of
the immigration were not the most auspicious for the development of
harmonious inter-ethnic relations. Large numbers of Latvians were in
Siberian labour camps and many of those who returned were not allowed to
live in towns.[40] The ethnic composition of Latvia and its major towns changed
as a result of this immigration. In 1935 Latvians constituted 75.5 per cent of
the population, but by 1953 the proportion had fallen to 60 per cent. Latvians
experienced a resurgence of anxiety about Russification.

Growth of Communist party membership was sluggish by Soviet standards although slightly less so in Latvia than in the other two Baltic
republics. In 1949 just over half the party members were Latvian. After the
death of Stalin in 1953 – and encouraged by the greater openness of
Khruschev's government – Latvian party members became bolder in the
expression of concern about local issues. Criticisms were voiced about the
direction of industrial development, its inappropriateness to local conditions and the absence of benefits to the local population. Following
Kruschev's visit to Latvia the official response was to dismiss both the
chairman of the council of ministers, Indriķis Pinksis, and the deputy
chairman Eduards Berklavs in July 1959, and systematic elimination of
nationalist members continued over the next few years. This process of
excising nationalist elements also took place at the level of municipal and
rural government bodies and affected Latvians in such professions as
teaching.[41] The purge reinstated Communists who were more attuned to
the expectations of Moscow and ensured that obedient party members were
in positions of responsibility throughout the country. There were no
comparable purges in the other two Baltic republics. The result was an
alienation of the mass of the Latvian population from government and,
indeed, from its quite lowly representatives.

The 1970s have been characterized as a decade of contradiction
(Misiunas and Taagepera 1993, p. 204). Political and economic centralization continued but material well-being increased. Western fashions and
life style came to exercise an increasing influence, particularly on young
Latvians. A generation of Latvians had grown up who had no direct
experience of the war or of deportations, and some had no knowledge at
all of these events. Many parents chose not to tell their children about
deportation for fear it would make it difficult for them to construct
successful careers and meaningful lives in Soviet Latvia.

During the latter part of the 1970s the promotion of the Russian
language intensified. Russian was to be taught in all nursery schools and
from the first year of schooling. All university lectures given in Latvian had
to be repeated in Russian, although the converse did not apply. Many
Latvians perceived this as an assault on the Latvian language. The moral
superiority attributed to the Russian language was most painful. The
Latvian minister of education Mirdza Kārkliņa is quoted as saying: 'Russian
safeguards the effectiveness of patriotic and internationalist education,
promoting the development of high moral and ideological-political qualities among pupils' (in Misiunas and Taagepera 1993, p. 212). Latvian was

used more rarely in shops and offices and became the private language of the home. Latvians complained that their language was described as 'a dog's language'.[42]

Writing about the 1980s Misiunas and Taagepera say: 'In terms of passive submissiveness, the Soviet rule gained further acceptance by simply lasting for another dozen years and sinking deeper into the collective memory' (ibid., p. 272). However, despite a seeming normality and acquiescence many aspects of life were rigidly controlled. Before major state celebrations psychiatric ambulance brigades had the task of rounding up those perceived as potential sources of trouble. Psychiatrists, like doctors throughout the Soviet Union, have a relatively low status, and this is reflected in their physical presence on the ambulances. This practice continued until the mid-1980s. The politically outspoken could and did end up in a special psychiatric hospital or prison. Political dissent continued to be brutally repressed, as exemplified by the treatment of a number of dissidents such as Gunārs Astra.[43]

LATVIAN LITERATURE AND LIBRARIES

A less obvious yet invidious aspect of this repression concerns the cultural life of Latvians. After the war libraries disappeared. School textbooks were recast in a Soviet mould. Censorship was fairly indiscriminate and there was a wholesale destruction of Latvian literature. When the texts reappeared in the late 1950s they came with Forewords which gave advice and cautions on their reading and in so doing robbed them of their earlier authority. However, some country libraries never reinstated the books which had earlier been destroyed. In such circumstances, the destruction of books constituted an assault of a peculiarly powerful kind upon a community which had hitherto defined itself in relation to those texts.

Nevertheless, literary texts, in particular poetry, continued to be important for Latvians. Poets such as Ojārs Vācietis, Imants Ziedonis, Māris Čaklais, Vizma Belševica and Māra Zalīte learnt to imply or suggest rather than to criticize or state outright. Many of their poems first appeared in the literary journal *Karogs* (*Flag*), which was from its beginnings in 1940 engaged in cat and mouse games with the authorities. It was a case of keeping the wolf happy while at the same time saving the goat and as such it required a fine sense of balance. Despite acquired sophistication in the art of compromise, many poets whose symbolism became too transparent were in repeated trouble with the censors.[44] For example, Belševica's poem 'Notes on Henry of Livonia's Chronicle', published in 1969, brought her to the attention of the censors through its implied parallels between the imperialism of Rome and the imperial intentions of the Soviet Union. However, the public thirst for poetic truth outstripped the censors, and the 16,000 copies of *Gadu Gredzeni* were sold out within hours of appearing in the bookshops.[45]

PERESTROIKA AND THE BALTIC

With the advent of Gorbachev the Baltic states took the vanguard in the restructuring of Soviet political life. There is evidence that Gorbachev wanted the Baltic to act as a showcase for *perestroika* and the restructuring of political and social life. However, with *glasnost* deep-seated resentments were unleashed which seemed to move the three republics inexorably away from the Soviet Union. In 1985 and 1986 there were extensive changes in Latvian government personnel and the introduction of younger party members. Anatolijs Gorbunovs (later president) became Secretary for Ideology in March 1985. What took place over the next few years was a radicalization of the native Communist Party members. The voices of dissidents were heard more clearly. In 1986 The Helsinki Group for the Defence of Human Rights was formed. On June 14th 1987 there was a gathering of several hundred by the Freedom Monument to commemorate the deportations of 1941. On August 23rd of the same year, 10,000 gathered to commemorate the Molotov–Ribbentrop pact. This public recalling of this embarrassing episode in Soviet history marked an important step in the growing freedom of expression. In October 1988 the Popular Front was formed from a coalition of forces including Communists within the government who demanded a range of reforms but primarily autonomy. In January 1989 legislation made Latvian the state language. The Russian population, understandably threatened by these moves, formed the Inter-front Movement in the summer of 1988. Claiming to represent inter-national as opposed to Latvian nationalist interests, they in fact owed much to the heavy military presence in Latvia.

In May 1989 elections were held at which the popular front candidates emerged as the winners. On August 23rd, again commemorating the Molotov–Ribbentrop pact, Latvians formed part of a chain of two million people from Vilnius through Riga to Tallinn, calling for independence from the Soviet Union. The following March Latvian Supreme Council elections led to two-thirds majorities for independence. In May President Gorbunovs met with the presidents of Estonia and Lithuania to renew the Baltic Entente of 1934. However, by the following January developments in the Baltic were threatening the dissolution of the Soviet Union and in Riga Omon special police troops stormed the Ministry of the Interior and killed six civilians in the process.[46] The *Independent* headline ran 'Bloodstained desperation of a dying regime' (22nd January 1991). Despite the regret expressed by Moscow over the violence, the January events intensified Baltic distrust and resolve to leave the Soviet Union. A referendum over the issue of independence on March 3rd produced a turnout of 86 per cent and a vote in support of independence of 72 per cent. It is estimated that two-fifths of the local Russian-speaking population also voted for independence.

However, throughout the spring the forces of reform and reaction were in collision. Already in March Peter Frank writing for the *Independent* feared a coup (10th March 1991). The counter-revolution when it came on August 19th was fearful but brief. Tanks rolled through the streets of Riga. Trains brought military reinforcements into Riga throughout the night. There was complete confusion and despair. Latvian Radio broadcast poetry and prayers before it went off air. By August 21st it was over, the main confrontations having taken place in Moscow. *The Sunday Times* headline on August 25th read 'Yeltsin sets Baltic Nations Free'. On August 20th the Latvian Supreme Council declared full independence, and this was given international recognition in the weeks that followed.

APPENDIX II:
PRINCIPAL NARRATORS

THE TWELVE LETTER-WRITERS APPEARING IN TEXT:

Antra (f.) b. 1944. Living in Ikšķile. Architectural assistant (pseudonym).
Dzintra Liepiņa (f.) b. 1940. Living in Liepāja. Office worker.
Egīls (m.) b. 1909. Living in Alūksne. Retired teacher (pseudonym).
Heronīma Mazule (f.) b. 1922. Living in Dobele. Retired accountant.
Ilze Sīpola (f.) b. 1941. Living in Mālpils. Typist.
Inta (f.) b. 1950. Living in Riga. Manageress (pseudonym).
Kristīna (f.) b. 1936. Living in Jelgava district. Emergency ambulance doctor (pseudonym).
Māra (f.) b. 1924. Living in Drusti. Farmer (pseudonym).
Nīna (f.) b. 1932. Living in Kandava. Retired bank clerk (pseudonym).
Olga Bakalinska (f.) b. 1927. Living in Riga. Retired accountant.
Silva Vētra (f.) b. 1957. Living in Jelgava. Bus driver.
Vizma (f.) b. 1932. Living in Baldone. Retired catering superintendent (pseudonym).

THE EIGHTEEN LOCAL CONTACTS APPEARING IN TEXT:

Andrejs Blese (m.) b. 1924. Living in Koknese. My mother's maternal cousin, school teacher, then after being sacked, kolhoz driver.
Anna (f.) b. 1945. Living in Riga. Doctor.
Antonija Žmuidina (f.) b. 1924. Living in Riga. Retired nurse.
Elza Glaudāne (f.) b. 1922. Living in Sloka. Retired hospital attendant.
Emma Priedīte (f.) b. 1905. Living in Saulkrasti. Retired office worker.
Ilga Pūpole (f.) b. 1932. Living in Riga.
Jānis Blese (m.) b. 1917. Living in Riga. Retired teacher, mother's maternal cousin.
Jānis Pormals (m.) b. 1920. Living in Riga. Wood craftsman.
Kārlis Baranovskis (m.) b. 1897. Living in Mazirbe. Retired railway supervisor.
Lidija Ubāne (f.) b. 1922. Living in Riga. Painter.
Lienīte Sestule (f.) b. 1941. Living in Lielvārde. Horticulturalist.

Malvīna Drafena (f.) b. 1911. Living in Pāvilosta. Retired fisherwoman (pseudonym).
Milda (f.) b. 1914. From Drusti. Farm worker.
Solveiga (f.) b. 1921. Living in Riga. Musician (pseudonym).
Talis Bāliņš (m.) b. 1930. Living in Ventspils district, no fixed occupation.
Uldis Vērsis (m.) b. 1924. Living in Riga, no fixed occupation.
Voldemārs Balande (m.) b. 1930. Living in Koknese. Retired labourer.
Valdis (m.) b. 1899. Living in Jūrmala. Retired shopkeeper (pseudonym).

NOTES

1 FAMILY HISTORY

1   Forty-four per cent of Latvia is forested. The highest hill, Gaiziņkalns, is 3,116 metres high. The principal rivers are the Daugava (1,020 km) rising in Russia; the Gauja (452 km) rising in Vidzeme; the Venta (342 km) and Lielupe (119 km) both rising in Lithuania.
2   My grandparents were part of a massive population movement from the Baltic towards the interior of Russia. There were an estimated 800,000 Latvians displaced as a result of the war.
3   That sense of security and ignorance of events in Russia appears widespread. Contemporary newspapers during 1938 and 1939 devote relatively little space to foreign news. For example, *Jaunākās Ziņas*, consisting of sixteen pages (thirty-two on Saturdays) devoted only three pages to foreign news. *Brīvā Zeme*, a daily paper of twelve pages devoted only a page and a half.
4   On that night some 15,000 people were arrested and killed outright or deported to Siberia.
5   The right of peasants to move to a locality of their own choosing dates from 1819 in Vidzeme, in Kurzeme in 1817, in Latgale 1861. The tradition of changing masters and moving on St George's day dates from an eighteenth-century Russian tradition. Previously this had taken place on Michaelmas day (September 29th) which marked the end of the agricultural year. All contracts were dated with reference to Jurģi (*Latvju Enciklopēdija*, ed. A. Švābe, Stockholm: Trīs Zvaigznes, 1951, vol.1\3, p. 917).

2 A CHRONICLE OF RESEARCH

1   There are several books which chronicle the disintegration of the Soviet Union from the Baltic perspective. The most gripping eye-witness account is by *Times* correspondent Anatol Lieven (1993). See also Kristian Gerner's and Stefan Hedlund's (1993) *The Baltic States and the End of the Soviet Empire*. An earlier account which covers the twentieth century and puts particular emphasis on Latvia's relations with Britain is by John Hiden (see Hiden and Salmon 1991).
2   The putsch occurred on August 19th 1991 and was over within three days. Following its collapse, independence was declared and internationally recognized in May 1992.
3   Soviet Latvian psychiatry was divided into so-called major and minor psychiatry, corresponding to the division between the psychoses and neuroses. By and large psychiatric hospitals and clinics practise major psychiatry, in other words they deal with psychotic illnesses. Neurasthenia is classified as a neurotic disorder and as such it is encountered in polyclinics, especially in the neurological subclinics, and to my surprise by the emergency ambulance services. It is within these latter settings encompassing general medical problems that diagnoses of neurasthenia figure so highly.
4   The Jugendstil architecture of Riga is the subject of Jānis Krastiņš' book (1980) now available in German translation.
5   New suburbs and districts were built: Bolderāja from the 1950s; Āgenskalna Priedes and Ķengarags from the 1950s and 1960s; Iļģuciems, Vecmīlgrāvis, Jugla, Purvciems;

Mežciems, Ziepniekkalns, Pleskodāle, Zolitūde, Imanta from the 1970s; Pļavinieki and Dārzciems from the 1980s (Latvijas Padomju Enciklopēdija, Rīga: Galvenā Enciklopēdiju Redakcija, 1988).

6 I am grateful to Professor Imants Eglītis for his interest. I know that his advice that I give a scientific definition of neurasthenia is evidence of his concern.

7 Latvians comprise 53.55 per cent of the population of Latvia (1993). These figures have been dropping, with the biggest changes in population structure occurring in the immediate post-war period. At present about one-third of the population of Riga is Latvian. Latvians who returned after deportation were not given residence permits in Riga or the larger cities.

| | | | Percentage of Latvians | | | | |
	1935	1943	1959	1970	1979	1989	1993
In Latvia	77	81.9	62.2	56.8	53.7	52	53.5
In Riga	63	79.1	44.5	40.9	38.3	36.7	–

Source: Mežs, I., Latvieši Latvijā, Etnodemogrāfisks Apskats, Rīga: Zinātne, 1994, Table 1,8.

8 The quality of the transcripts was uneven and was I feel related to my inexperience in narrative analysis. At any one time there were some half a dozen typists working on the tapes. I myself was busy talking to more informants. Were I to repeat or extend the research I would be more strict in checking the transcripts, straight away, thus saving myself the additional work of redoing the transcripts.

3 ORDER IN NARRATIVE EXPERIENCE

1 Namejs, a Semgallian chieftain, lived between 1200 and 1250. His death is recounted in the medieval chronicle *Heinrici Chronicon*. (For an English translation see Brundage 1961) However, the first mention of the Latvian flag is in the so-called 'Rhymed Chronicles' in connection with the battles around Cēsis in 1200. It seems that Lidija has conflated these two events and perhaps drawn upon some literary or poetical reworking of these medieval events which I have not been able to identify.

2 Adorno's much-quoted claim appears in *Noten zur Literatur* (1965). What he actually said was, 'Den Satz, nach Auschwitz noch Lyrik zu screiben, sei barbarisch, mochte ich nicht mildern; negativ ist darin der Impuls ausgesprochen, der die engagierte Dichtung beseelt' (ibid, p. 125). I translate this as 'I would not wish to tone down the statement that after Auschwitz it is barbaric to write lyrical poetry; in that sentence the impulse which animates politically engaged poetry is expressed in a negative way'. However, he revised his views later. In *Negative Dialectics* (1973) he writes: 'It may have been wrong to say that after Auschwitz you could no longer write poems. But it is not wrong to raise the less cultural question whether after Auschwitz you can go on living – especially whether one who has escaped by accident, one who by rights should have been killed, may go on living' (pp. 362–363). I am grateful to Colin Davies for helping me trace the source of these quotations.

3 My approach raises the issue of how meaningful narrative forms can be derived from arbitrary and violent events which have shattered meaning. The literature on the Holocaust confronts similar problems. For example, Young (1988) challenges the allegation that it is somehow irreverent to look at the literary form of Holocaust memories. The same could be said of Latvian memories. I would argue that the way in which people recast memories of a terrible past throws light on the necessary human and social resources for survival.

4 The challenge to the distinction between ordinary and literary language belongs to the wider debate about the relationship between non-fiction and fiction, form and content, truth and representation.

5 Paul Thompson's article (1989) describes the literary competitions taking place in Poland

for autobiographical essays. In Latvia autobiography is a popular genre. Many anthologies of autobiographical accounts of deportation and labour camp experiences have been published recently. For example, Līce, A., (ed.) *Via Dolorosa*, Rīga: Liesma 1990; *Atminu Lauskas*, Rīga: Latvijas Rakstnieku Asociācija, 1992; Janševskis, A., *Dzīvotgriba*, Rīga: Latvijas Kultūras Fonds, 1992; Kalnietis, J., *Ceļš: Baigo Gadu Vērtējums*, Tukums: Atauga, 1992; Bērzs, A., *Dokumentu Pārbaude*, Tukums: Atauga, 1993; Dauge, A., *Manas Dzīves Stāsts*, Aizkraukle: Krauklītis, 1994, *Es Sapni par Dzimteni Pagalvī Likšu*. *Latvieši Padomju Vergu Nometnēs un Izsūtījumā* in 10 volumes, Riga, vol. 1, 1993, vol. 2, 1994.

6   Deportation and mortality statistics are a contentious issue in the context of the Soviet Union. In 1953 Kalnbērziņš, first secretary of the Latvian communist party, reported that 119,000 people were deported, but no further information was made available. In Latvia the figures for deportation vary. According to recent Soviet data there were 64,500 deportations up to the year 1949; Andersons (1962–82, p. 318) gives a figure of between 108,000 and 216,000; Švābe of 540,000 (1950, p. 480). According to data of the Baltic Council there were between 180,000 and 200,000 deportations up to 1953. Of those deported in 1949 5,073 died during deportation. Discussions of these figures are to be found in Šilde, A., *Bez Tiesībām un Brīvības*, Copenhagen: Imanta 1965, Es Sapni par Dzimteni Pagalvī Likšu. (op. cit. n. 5 above) vol. 1, 1993, vol. 2, 1994.

7   Aristotle presents his ideas on dramatic unity in the *Poetics*.

8   Pauls Kundziņš, a Latvian exile living in Canada, has written a book on the architecture of the Latvian farmstead (1974). It is very much a memorial to the pastoral idyll. The open-air ethnographic museum outside Riga founded in 1924 is similarly a celebration of the pastoral idyll.

9   The association of cyclical with pastoral temporality owes something to Maurice Bloch's essay (1977), which links cyclicity with ritual and irreversible time with everyday perceptions. Within narrative there are, however, no simple dichotomies.

4 READING LETTERS

1   For an account of the Lutheran Church and its pastors in Soviet Latvia see: Ķiploks, E., *Dzimtenes Draudzes un Baznīcas*, Minneapolis: Latviešu Evanģēliskas Luterāņu Baznīcas Amerikā Apgāds 1987; Lange, E., *Latvijas Baznīcas Vēsture*. Latviešu Evanģēliskās Luterāņu Baznīcas Virsvalde 1872, pp. 63–68, 85–88, 91–92; Šilde, A., 'Baznīca Padomju Latvija un Ateitiskā Propaganda' in *Bez Tiesībām un Brīvības*, Copenhagen: Imanta, 1965; Lūse, A., 'Conversions to Christianity in Smiltene: A Discursive Transformation of the Self', unpublished MSc dissertation in Social Anthropology, London School of Economics and Political Science, 1995; Vardys, S.V. 'The role of the churches in the maintenance of regional and national identity in the Baltic Republics', pp. 151–164 in *Regional Identity under Soviet Rule*, eds Dietrich Loeber, V., Stanley Vardys and Laurence Kitching, AABS: Hackettstown, NJ, 1990.

2   St George's Day (Latvian – *Jurģi*) was traditionally the occasion for changing landlords or changing masters.

3   The Germans retreating from Vidzeme in September and October 1944 ordered the destruction of bridges, railways but less often houses. Agricultural land was burnt. Farmers were ordered out of their houses and made to dig entrenchments. In this way the church in Vecpiebalga was destroyed in Vidzeme.

4   Māra is referring to the taxes of 1947 and 1948. They were 40 per cent of estimated revenue in the first year and rose to 75 per cent in the second year.

5   Obligatory forestry work was widespread. The rules were issued by the Council of People's Commissariat for for timber felling, transmitted to the Latvian government and then to local executives. Local executives made decisions about the nature of requirements from particular individuals. Country people were forced to sign contracts promising to deliver stipulated amounts of timber. This obligatory forestry work was required between 1945 and 1949, with 1946 and 1947 being particularly hard years. The size of requirements took no account of transport at the disposal of households and timber often had to be transported without any mechanical help (J. Riekstiņš, unpublished material.)

Year	Timber export in cubic metres					
	1940	1950	1960	1970	1980	1982
Timber	1,344	2,735	2,465	5,012	2,110	2,212
Firewood	2,625	1,637	1,891	2,295	1,601	1,693
Total	3,969	4,372	4,356	7,307	3,711	3,905

Source: *Latvijas Padomju Enciklopēdija*, Rīga: Galvenā Enciklopēdiju Redakcija, 1984, vol. 5/2, p. 358.

6   According to the 1935 agricultural statutes of Soviet Russia each household could have one cow, two young calves, one sow with piglet (or two piglets without the sow), ten sheep and goats and twenty bee-hives. There was no limit on the number of poultry. In Kruschev's time, the rules were changed. Each household could keep one cow with a calf up to the age of one, one calf up to the age of two, one brood-sow with piglet aged up to three months, or two porkers, ten sheep and goats. From 1971 it was permitted to keep a brood-sow with piglet and up to two porkers with agreement of the general meeting of the kolhoz (Strautmanis, I., *Kolhozu Tiesību Pamati*, Rīga: Liesma, 1973, pp. 246–246; *Kolhoza Paraugstatūti*, Rīga: Latvijas Valsts Izdevniecība, 1953, p. 5)
        In the early years of collectivization there were some districts where each household had more than the 0.5 hectares allowed by the statutes. Gradually, however, each collective farm reduced the amount of land and animals allowed. The penalties according to regulations issued in 1965 were as follows: if the number of animals kept exceeded the permitted number, the owner was given an exact list of animals to be liquidated. If the animals were not destroyed, the militia were called in and the owner had to pay compensation to the state within ten days. Alternatively, the right to the use of pasture land could be withdrawn (*Kolhozu Tiesību Pamati* (op. cit. n. 5 above), p. 246).
7   *Stops* is a measurement of liquid and dry substances. The term comes from the name of a vessel. 1 *stops* is between 1.2 and 1.3 litres. Wood is measured by *sters*. 1 *sters* is equivalent to 1 cubic metre (*Latvijas Enciklopēdiskā Vārdnīca*, Rīga: Latvijas Enciklopēdiju Redakcija, 1991, vol. 2, p. 213).
8   Forty roubles a day or 0.4 roubles after the currency exchange of 1961 could buy 0.01 of a pair of shoes, 0.012 metres of woollen textile material, 0.16 pairs of nylon socks, 0.1 kilogram of smoked bacon (Šilde, A., *Bez Tiesībām un Brīvības*, Copenhagen: Imanta, 1965, p. 325).
9   School children from the age of twelve onwards were required to do farm work. For example, in 1955/56 grades 5 to 8 were required to work 33 hours during the summer season. Grade 11 were required to do a total of 68 hours throughout the year. By the mid 1960s this had increased to 144 hours per year. There was some variation between schools as the amount of time required depended upon local circumstances. Diplomas were awarded for the work. Children from towns worked in factories (*Mācību Plāni* (Teaching Plans) 1955/56, Rīga: LVI,1955; *Mācību Plāni* 1967/68 , Rīga: Zvaigzne, 1967).
10   Māra lives in the county of Drusti. Her house lying on the outskirts of the county was one of many which came to be abandoned.

5 DESTINY AND THE SHAPING OF AUTOBIOGRAPHY

1   The withdrawal of history books took place gradually from 1986 onwards as Gorbachev's reforms took hold. On October 1985 the minister for education announced new transitional education plans for 1986 to 1992. New history books were published from 1989 onwards. Berkerts' *A Short History of Latvia* (originally published during the independence period) was republished in 1992. As a result history teaching in schools was left in some confusion. In some schools this resulted in the temporary suspension of history lessons altogether (*Mācību Plāni* (Teaching Plans) 1986/87 *Mācību gadam*, Rīga: LPSR Izglītības Ministrija, 1986; *Vēstures Priekšmetu Mācību Plāni* 1991/92 *Mācību gadam*, Rīga: LR Izglītības Ministrija, 1991).

2   Māra Zālīte was born in 1952 in Siberia, her family having been deported on political grounds. She returned to Latvia in 1956. She has worked in an administrative capacity for the Writer's Union of Latvia and from 1989 has been editor of the literary journal *Karogs*. Her poem 'Latvia's Stones' was written between 1975 and 1978 and first published in 1979 in the collection *Rīt Varbūt* (*Perhaps Tomorrow*) (*Latviešu Rakstniecība Biogrāfijās*, ed. Hausmanis, V., Rīga: Latvijas Enciklopēdijas, 1992, p. 360).

3   Obligatory farmwork was required during the German occupation in 1942–1943 when school children and students were required to work a minimum three months on agricultural work (Aizsilnieks, A., *Latvijas Saimniecības Vēsture 1914–1945*, Stockholm: Daugava, 1968, pp. 911, 914–915).

4   Russian for 'Stop, who's there!'.

5   The bombardment of Rēzekne on April 6th, 1944 and over the next three weeks by the Soviet army left two-thirds of the city destroyed. Its population of 11,649 was reduced by 2,000. Nearly all dwelling houses were destroyed. The monument to the liberation of Latgale remained unscathed (Freivalds, O. *Kurzemes Cietoksnis*, Copenhagen: Imanta, 1954, p. 56).

6   *Sprīdītis*, a fairy tale play written by Anna Brigadere and first performed in 1903. The relevance of this play to Latvian narratives is discussed more fully in Chapter 13.

7   Solkanka (perhaps Solikamsk) is situated in the Ural mountains.

8   Baravoja (perhaps Borovlanka) is situated in Altai, western Siberia.

9   Kalpashevo is situated in central western Siberia, on the river Ob.

10 Solveiga refers to her nerves freezing and the symptoms which she describes suggest that she may have been suffering from Guillain Barre syndrome or acute infective polyneuritis.

6 THE EXPROPRIATION OF BIOGRAPHY

1   From 1974 instruction in the writing of autobiography formed part of Latvian language lessons for 8th and 9th grade children. Particular attention was paid to those aspects of life which confirmed appropriate ideological beliefs. The following extract provides a pattern taken from a Latvian language school book:

> I, Guna, daughter of Jānis, Lapiņa, was born into a family of collective farmers on August, 1, 1958. I studied in Pārupe secondary school between 1963 and 1973. I joined the organization of Pioneers when I was in the third year, and I have been a member of Komsomol since 1973. I have been a member of the school's dramatic club for six years. I am responsible for monitoring progress in my class. I have been successful in my studies throughout my period in school. Above all I am interested in literature and the theatre.
>
> My father, Jānis is leader of the field brigade in the collective farm. My mother Aina is a dairy worker. My brother Uldis studies in the fourth class of Pārupe secondary school.

> Pārupe, 4th June, G. Lapiņa.
> *Latviešu Valoda 7–9 klasei* (Latvian language text for 7th to 9th classes),
> 1974 Rīga: Zvaigzne.

2   Jānis' father, like many other Latvians, obtained his university education in St Petersburg between 1910 and 1918. At that time there was a sizeable colony of Latvians there. Since the middle of the nineteenth century St Petersburg was a centre for Latvian intellegentsia, in particular the so-called New Latvians. The Latvian welfare society of St Petersburg was founded in 1879. In 1899 it had 162 members. A Latvian Singing Society was founded in 1908 with 151 members.

3   The Gregorian calendar was finally introduced in Latvia during the German occupation of 1915–1918. From the sixteenth century onwards old and new calendars had been used concurrently at different times, places and for different purposes. The Gregorian calendar when it finally gained precedence made a difference of thirteen days (*Latvju Enciklopēdija* (op. cit. Ch. 1 n. 5), vol. 1/3, p. 932).

4   Some 8,000 of Riga's inhabitants died during that year.
5   Jānis is referring to 1940, the first year of Soviet occupation and the German occupation in June of 1941.
6   The River Daugava was flooded in 1961 in order to build the power station at Aizkraukle. In the process the Latvian mythical landscape was destroyed. For example, Staburags, the cliff from which the mythical/national hero Lāčplēsis plunged into the depths was covered by water. The River Daugava itself came to assume the massive proportions of Siberian rivers rather than its more modest earlier ones.
7   Jānis is again referring to the purges of 1959.
8   The home guard (*Aizsargi*) were formed in March 1919.
9   Malvīna's family contributed to the massive exodus from Kurzeme to the interior of Russia during the First World War, leaving the province with a quarter of its earlier population.
10 Britain was the principal importer of Latvian produce during the independence period. Timber constituted the second largest category of exports after food products. Tons of timber exported from Liepāja increased throughout the 1930s:

| | Tons of timber exported | | |
	1933	1934	1939
Plywood	1,771	2,149	3,450
Timber	55,984	50,934	71,944
Wood for matches	596	311	–

Source: Liepājas Statistikas Gada Grāmata 1934, 1935 and 1940.

11 The Land Reform Act gave special priority to those who had fought for Latvian independence (Agrarian Reform Act, P I, cl. 19).

7 THE LIVED AND THE REMEMBERED FOREST

1   The Soviet literature of the period projected the forest brothers as bandits and German fascists and their supporters as enemies of Soviet order. See, for example V. Lācis' novel *Uz Jauno Krastu* (To the New Shore) and history books such as the *History of the Latvian Soviet Socialist Republic* (LPSR) of 1959. Soviet estimates of the numbers of forest dwellers appear in accounts of the activities of extermination battalions. In 1945 Captain Piļķis of one such battalion identified 17,657 and killed 1,314. Estimates by Latvian historians range between 10,000 and 15,000 (Strods, H. 'Nacionālais Partizānu Kaŗš' in *Lauku Avize*, January 8th 1993, p. 23; Kostanda, O. ed. *Latvijas Vēsture*, Rīga: Zvaigzne, 1992).
2   Among the names which Antonija lists is Alfons Noviks, currently on trial for genocide.
3   Partisans were granted an amnesty after Stalin's death in March 1953.
4   1941 is typically referred to as the year of terror.
5   Lienīte's parents, like many other partisans, listened to the BBC World Service, and had a strong, but as it turned out misplaced, faith in the British power to save them.
6   The 58th clause of the Soviet Criminal Code lists offences against Soviet power together with their punishments. These include contacts with foreign countries for contra-revolutionary purposes (58.3) and collaboration with international bourgeoisie (58.4). The notorious sub-clause 58.1c refers to 'Families of persons sentenced by this clause who if found promoting this offence or hiding information are to be punished with imprisonment for five to ten years, with confiscation of property and deportation'. In 1961 a Criminal Code for LSSR was introduced. In this new version clause 59 corresponds to that of 58 in the previous code. Punishment became milder. In the post-war period clause 58 was invoked most frequently to justify deporation and imprisonment (Criminal Code, pp. 20–24, Criminal Code LPSR, pp. 28–29).
7   The uprisings in Vorkuta to which Lienīte refers took place between July 22nd and August

1st, 1953. They involved miners of Vorkuta camp. Revolt had already broken out in Norilsk and Karaganda with the slogan 'Death or Liberty'. The revolt began in the seventh mine and spread quickly throughout the other mines. On July 22nd a message came to the workers in mine seven that thirty workers had been arrested. Two thousand workers marched to the prison demanding they be liberated. The administration agreed but meanwhile called in the army. Troops from the red army and the ministry of the interior blockaded the camp and prison. The thirty prisoners broke out. The army was ordered to shoot but to everyone's surprise refused. In the event an officer from the ministry of the interior grabbed a machine gun himself, killing two and injuring fifty people. The administration of the camp was taken over by the workers, who demanded a wage, the possibility to see relatives and an opportunity to meet with representatives of the government. General Maslennikow, Vice-minister of Internal Affairs was sent. However, no agreement was reached and 500 soldiers blockaded the camp. Rudenko, General Procuror of USSR himself opened fire. On August 1st 100 miners were killed and several hundreds injured. Others were imprisoned or sent to other camps (Šilde, A., *Pa Deportēto Pēdām*, New York: Grāmatu Draugs, 1956, pp. 233–246).

8 Lienīte is referring to the role of the Latvian *strēlnieki* during the Russian Revolution.
9 Roja is a small market town situated on the northern tip of the peninsula of Kurzeme.

8 DAMAGED LIVES, DAMAGED HEALTH

1 Latvian concepts of the homeland have often been developed in exile. Their power and poignancy derive from longing. For example, the national poet Rainis spent much of his life in exile: between 1896 and 1897 he was in Berlin, in 1897 he was in Panevežys, between 1897 and 1899 in Pskow, in 1899 in Slobodsk (province of Vjatka) and between 1905 and 1920 he lived in Switzerland (*Latviešu Literatūras Vesture*, ed. Bērziņš, L., Rīga: Literatura, 1936, vol. 4, pp. 153–213).

Jānis Akuraters wrote one of the most lyrical accounts of the countryside *Kalpu Zēna Vasara* (*A Servant Boy's Summer*) whilst he was in Oslo during the years 1907 and 1908 (*Latvju Enciklopēdija* (op. cit. Ch. 1 n. 5) vol.1/1, p. 36).

Jānis Jaunsudrabiņš wrote two accounts of his country childhood. Volume 1 of *Baltā Grāmata* (*The White Book*) was published in 1914 while he was still in Latvia; the second volume was published in 1921 after his return from exile in the Caucasus between 1915 and 1919. However, in the opening sentence of *Baltā Grāmata* Jaunsudrabiņš has already set himself at a distance and views his childhood from the exile of adulthood and the exile of war:

> Although all peasant houses are nearly alike, it still seems to me that there is none like our house in all of upper Kurzeme. Above it the sky's vault is highest, the clouds the whitest in which the birch tops rested at the far end of the old house. There was no moss as green as on our roof.
>
> (1957, p. 15)

As a refugee in post-war Germany Jaunsudrabiņš reworked his childhood memories for *Zaļā Grāmata* in 1950. Thus both accounts are written from the perspective of a double exile (*Latvju Enciklopēdija* (op. cit. Ch. 1 n. 5), vol. 1/3, p. 687).

2 Gulbene is in north east Vidzeme with a population of 10,124 in 1994 (*Statistical Yearbook of Latvia 1993*, Riga:1994).
3 In Soviet Latvia Jewishness was referred to as 'nationality' alongside other ethnic origins. Such nationalities were recorded on people's passports. For a discussion of the nationality issue see Karklina, R., *Ethnic Relations in the USSR. The Perspective from Below* 1986.
4 Pioneers were set up in June 1940 but the organization claimed that it had existed illegally in Latvia since 1931. It is an organization for children between the ages of ten and fifteen. Its aim was to inculcate loyalty to the Communist Party, to Soviet traditions and to promote cultural and moral standards (*Zinātne*, 1970, vol. 3, p. 30).
5 Molcanova is situated in Hantu-Nansu national district, in mid-western Siberia.
6 One thousand one hundred army officers were arrested in 1941. Two hundred were shot in Litene, 80 in Riga and 560 were deported to Norilsk. Ninety returned from Siberia (*Es

Sapni par Dzimteni Pagalvī Likšu (op. cit. Ch. 3 n. 5), Riga, vol. 1, 1993, pp. 248–249).

7   The Moscow district was situated in the south east of the central part of Riga. It had a reputation for being a poor, run-down part of the city.

9 MEANINGS LOST AND GAINED

1   Kārlis is referring to Kerensky's government preceding the revolution on February 23rd (March 8th) – February 27th (March 12th), 1917 (*Latvian Soviet Encyclopedia*, Riga: Galvenā Enciklopēdiju Redakcija, 1983, vol. 3, p. 263).

2   However, this is not only Kārlis' subjective estimation. Latvians played an indispensable role in the bolshevik revolution. See, for example, Ezergailis 1974.

3   Voronezh is situated in southern European Russia and lay a few kilometres behind the front line.

4   Two Latvian legions were formed as part of the German army. Some 8,000 soldiers were taken as prisoners of war. Imprisonment for uncommissioned soldiers was about a year. They were counted as being 'under examination by the state' – in other words, it was a kind of probationary period.

5   This reference to two hours' packing time reflects the general experience of deportees who were given hardly any warning of their arrest and deportation.

6   The granting of land followed the Land Reform Act of 1922.

7   Tula lies some 200 miles due south of Moscow.

8   Neighbours were frequently enlisted to help with the transport of deportees. It is interesting that the word used by Milda and others is *šķūtes*, which harks back to the labour duties of serfdom. It comes from Swedish word *skjuts* – peasant's obligation to provide a horse, carriage and driver. It was first used in the seventeenth century by Swedish conquerors to describe the obligations of peasants in Vidzeme, especially those living near big roads. Some recompense was paid but usually not enough to cover the expense. This tradition continued during the Russian period. During the period of Latvian independence owners of trucks and horses were obliged to transport state property and state officials (*Latvju Enciklopēdija*, (op. cit. Ch. 1 n. 5), vol. 3, p. 2397).

9   Schooling was made compulsory in 1919, and Milda, who was five at the time, somehow managed to avoid the obligatory six years of primary schooling.

10 See Chapter 7, note 6.

11 Komsomolsk is situated in Habarovsk district in the far east of Russia, near the river Amur and the gulf of Sakhalin.

12 'Nerve deadness' is remembered by several people who were deported to Siberia. The medical condition from which they were suffering may well have been Guillain Barre syndrome – an acute infective polyneuritis.

10 HABITABLE IDENTITIES

1   Hobsbawm's well-known contention is that national identity is an invention and he cites historical material from Livonia as part of his argument (1992, p. 48). He confines his discussion to Estonian identity, which prior to the nineteenth century was articulated in terms of peasants or country people and masters. However, references to Latvian identity can be found in earlier periods.

2   Georg Mancelius lived between 1593 and 1654. He was the son of a parson. After studying in Germany his first appointment was as a clergyman in Walle (1615–1625), then Sēlpils (1620–1625) and Tartu (1625) were he was a professor at the University of Tartu (1632–1637). In 1637 he returned to Zemgale as a parson to Duke Friedrich in Jelgava. He is renowned for his dictionary *Letticus*, especially its second part, *Phraseologia Lettica* published in 1638. His other works are *Tractatus Meditatio Theologistoricophysica de Terrae Motu* (1619) in German, *Lettisch Vade Mecum* (handbook on Biblical plots) (1631), *Langewunschte Lettische Postill* (1654) (Čakars, O., Grigulis, A., Losberga, M., *Latviešu Literatūras Vēsture*, Rīga: Zvaigzne, 1990, p. 44–49).

3   Lawrence Stone gives similar descriptions of moral destitution and lack of feeling in England before the revolution of sentiment in the eighteenth century. See, for example,

his discussion of parent–child relationships in *The Family, Sex and Marriage in England 1500–1800*, Harmondsworth: Penguin 1979, pp. 254–299.

4   This idea of Latvian as the language of ploughing and sowing has been taken over and enshrined in poetry. For example, there is the poem by Rainis.

We draw strength from the earth
Rich rye seed flows through us all

We are a people for ploughing, not war
We suck strength from the lap of the earth.

(*Es Gribēju Jums Vēl Vairāk Dot*, Raiņa Atziņas, Rīga: Zvaigzne, 1990, p. 24)

5   The publishing house Zelta Ābele was set up in 1935 by Miķelis Gopers, publishing Latvian authors such as Blaumanis, Brigadere, Grots, Ķezbere and translations of foreign authors. They were beautifully produced and noted for their artistic designs by such artists as Tone, Zaļkalns and Norītis. From 1945 Zelta Ābele continued publication from Sweden (*Apgāda Zelta Ābele Ilustrēts Bibliografisks Rādītājs ar Papildinājumiem un Pielikumu*, Rīga: Literatūra un Māksla, 1993).

6   Jānis Pleipis (1909–1947) became famous with his graphics for the publishing house Zelta Ābele. During the war Pleipis tried to escape but was caught by the Soviet army. He was transferred to a labour camp near Moscow. With the support of Latvian artists, Pleipis returned to Riga. He was found by fishermen caught in their salmon nets in the Daugava river in 1947. Speculation about the precise circumstances of his death has not been resolved (Sadurskis, P. , *Pleipis un Viņa Gravīra Kokā*, Stockholm: Zelta Ābele, 1980).

7   Jānis Akuraters (1876–1937) was the son of a forest guard. He actively supported the revolution of 1905 and was forced to emigrate to Finland and then Norway between 1907 and 1908. Akuraters joined the Latvian *Strelnieki* in 1915 and was a member of the National and People's Councils. He was a director of the Department of Art between 1919 and 1920, a director of Radio of Riga between 1930 and 1934. He is known for his revolutionary and romantic poetry and stories (*Latvju Enciklopēdija* (op. cit. Ch. 1. n. 5), vol.1\1, p. 36.

8   Krišjānis Barons (1835–1923) was born in Strutele into a farm-renter's family. His father later became overseer of a country estate. Barons studied mathematics and astronomy at the University of Tartu from 1856 to 1860. He was an editor of *Pēterburgas Avīzes* in St Petersburg (1862–1865). He wrote poetry, prose and popular scientific articles. Later he took a position as tutor in Voronezh, and Moscow provinces (1867–1893) and from 1878 he began collecting oral songs, which appeared in print from 1894 onwards. Barons returned to Riga in 1893 and thereafter devoted himself to the collection of folk songs. He was the first honorary member of the University of Latvia.

Latvju Dainas vols I–VI were published between 1894 and 1915 (*Latvju Enciklopēdija*, (op. cit. Ch. 1 n. 5), vol.1\1, pp. 207, 208).

9   The reputation of Latvian folk songs as being naughty is not unfounded. There are some 1,410 explicitly sexual songs collected in volume 6 of the *Latvju Dainas* collected by Barons and first published in 1915. These songs were sung on ritual occasions such as weddings and *Jāņi* (Midsummer night) and used as vehicles of social criticism. These naughty songs have coloured the Baltic German view of all the songs whether they be about work, nature, war or death.

10 See note 2 above.

11 Gotthard Stender (1714–1796) was born in Lašu estate (Augšzeme) into a parson's family. He is known for his sympathies towards Latvians and on his gravestone there is an inscription *Latvis* (Latvian). He retold biblical stories (*Svēti Stāsti* (1757), *Tās Kristīgas Mācības Grāmata* (1776), *Jaukas Pasakas un Stāsti* (1766), wrote about linguistic and scientific matters (*Bildu Ābece* (1787), *Augstas Gudrības Grāmata No Pasaules Un Dabas* (1774), *Lettische Grammatik* (1761), *Lettisches Lexicon* (1789), and wrote poems ('Jaunas Ziņģes' (1774), 'Ziņģu Lustes I–II' (1785, 1789). His major claim to importance derives from the compilation of a dictionary and his work on Latvian grammar (*Latviešu Literatūras Vēsture*, (op. cit. n. 2 above), p. 84–95).

12 Obligatory schooling had been introduced in 1919. It consisted of two years of primary

school or home teaching between the ages of seven and eight, six years of elementary school and two years of additional schooling from fifteen to sixteen.

In 1934 the secondary schooling was increased to five years and primary schooling reduced by a year *Latvju Enciklopēdija* (op. cit. Ch. 1 n. 5), vol.1/3, pp. 827–828).

APPENDIX I HISTORICAL BEARINGS

1   See Chapter 5 note 1.
2   Indeed, by the standards of western Europe Latvia is still sparsely populated. The current population per square kilometre in Latvia as a whole is forty. In Vidzeme it is twenty-seven, in Kurzeme twenty-five, in Latgale twenty-three, in Zemgale twenty-six, and in the district of Riga forty-eight (*Statistical Yearbook of Latvia 1993*, Riga, 1994, p. 46).
3   Ikskile lies some 28 kilometres south of present-day Riga.
4   I cannot find any record of the incident to which Georg Von Rauch refers. However, there are many references to disputes which focus on the nature of Baltic society and its level of development prior to the German conquest. The views of the Baltic German historians (A. Transehe-Roseneck, H. Bosse, R. Wittram and P. Johansen) are that tribes living in Latvian and Estonian lands were semi-nomadic and that the German conquest protected them from attack by Russia and Lithuania. Also that the German conquest was a vehicle for European culture, bringing with it literacy and Christianity. These views did not accord with the views of Latvian and Estonian historians, and as a result during the 1930s Baltic German historians were forced to abandon study of the sensitive twelfth and thirteenth centuries and study later times. L. Arbusov was forced to leave his teaching post at the University of Latvia. Baltic German historians in Estonia had to publish their work in Helsinki (Zutis, J., *Ocherki po Istoriografii Latvii*, Riga: Latgosizdat, 1949, pp. 217–237).
5   Lutheran baptism rates during the independence period fell from 13,186 in 1925 to 12,719 in 1933. There were approximately 42,000 births in 1925 and 38,000 births in 1933. These figures do not take account of Catholic Latgale, but even so it means that less than half of all children were baptized.
    Figures for registered parish members were as follows: in 1925 299,402 and in 1933 320,449 (*Baznīcas Kalendārs* (Church Calendar) *1927. Gadam*, Rīga: Ev. Luterāņu Virsvaldes Izdevums, 1926, pp. 96–107; *Baznīcas Kalendārs 1935. Gadam*, Rīga: Ev. Luterāņu Baznīcas Virsvaldes Izdevums, 1934, pp. 122–137).
6   Little is known about Henry of Livonia. The following facts have been gleaned. Henricus de Lettis lived between approximately 1187 and 1259. His origin is not clear. He could be German or a Germanized Lettgallian. He was a priest, historiographer and translator of Bishop Albert, and was protecting German interests. Henry arrived in Livonia in 1203 and lived near lower Daugava. He learned the local languages including Estonian because there were conflicts with Estonians and a translator was needed. In 1208 he was ordained and received a church in Imera as a benefice. In 1217 he was a missionary to Estonia. Henry began to write at the end of 1224 and finished in the spring of 1226. A supplement was written in 1227. In 1226 he accompanied the Pope's legat Guliemo from Modem in his visitation to Livonia and Estland. Later he was a priest near Orajegi river and Imera. The last information about him comes from Imera in 1259. He was described as 'senex et valde debilis' (old and very disabled) (Mugurēvičs, E., *Priekšvārds, Indriķa Hronika*, Rīga: Zinātne, 1993, pp. 7–14).
7   See Chapter 10 note 2.
8   During the Swedish period all estates became the property of the government, although some were later returned to their owners in recognition of services to the government. The obligations of serfs to their masters was standardized, thus protecting them from individul tyrannical whims. The obligations of serfs were categorized according to their ability to pay.
    The legal status of peasants improved, being no longer subject to the jurisdiction of the nobility. The government set up district courts to which peasants could send their representatives. During this period the status of Livonian peasants approximated to that of Swedish peasants.

Throughout the countryside the nobility were required to build schools and sextons were instructed to teach children to read. Schools were allocated land to support their needs. Dorpat (Tartu) Gymnasium was reorganized as the Academia Gustaviana in 1632. During the first twenty years 28 per cent (303) of students came from Livonia (Dunsdorfs, E., *Latvijas Vēsture 1600–1710*, Sweden: Daugava, 1962, pp. 269–295, 335–365); Arnolds, S., *History of Latvia. An Outline*, Stockholm: M. Goppers, 1951).

9   The obligations of peasants in the eighteenth century included a variety of taxes. State taxes included a tax on ploughs; a personal tax for all males from 1738 in Livonia; an obligation to contribute to the repair of roads and bridges and to the running of the postal service. The earlier *kroṇa staciņš* (Königliche station), which had been introduced by the Swedes to support the army during the war between Sweden and Poland, was transformed into a permanent liability for peasants in the eighteenth century. Peasants were required to hand over rye, oats, wheat and hay.

The more onerous duties were those exacted by the estates in labour and agricultural products. Termed *kunga tiesa* this had earlier been a tax paid directly to the king, but from the thirteenth century was paid to landowners. During the eighteenth century there was a massive increase in the amount of labour exacted from peasants in response to the devastation of estates during the Great Northern War. The loss of population during the war meant that fewer able-bodied men had to work twice as hard with no time to work their own land.

The production of brandy on a commercial scale by estate owners and the growth of inns on estate land contributed to the hardship of peasants who were required to supply larger quantities of grain for this purpose. In Latgale a special tax on vodka was introduced.

The diverse terms for serfs and their duties attests to the heaviness of the burden: *klaušas*, estate work with one's own tools; *riežas*, the cultivation of particular beds or plots of estate land; *lieciba*, emergency duties; *talka*, work requiring large numbers of serfs, and *šķūtis*, transportation duties. Serfs themselves were differentiated according to their tasks: for example, *zirdzinieki* were workers with their own horses, *kājnieki* were those without horses and additional summer workers were called *otrinieki* (Dunsdorfs, E., *Latvijas Vēsture 1710–1800*, Sweden: Daugava, 1973, pp. 419–432).

10   The Cat's house was built in 1909 by Fridrich Scheffel as a dwelling house and shop and is situated in Meistaru street. It is in the Jugendstil, popular in Riga at the turn of the century. Because of complaints the cat was turned around and made to adopt a more decorous position (Krastiņš J., *Jūgendstils Rīgas Arhitektūrā*, Rīga: Zinātne, 1980, p. 86).

11   Arsenjev was appointed chairman of the land revision committee of Riga. This committee introduced salaries for farm workers. Clause 1 of the 1804 law stipulated that payment of workers by their masters should be regulated by the revision committee. Additional paragraphs were introduced in 1809. Clause 24 established a maximum working day of twelve hours, each night hour being equal to one and a half day hours.

Clauses 39–49 established levels of pay for farm workers. Single workers received bread, clothes (men in finished articles, women in raw materials), food for cattle and a half of purvieta (0.18 hectares) of land for each servant. Married servants going as labourers to the estate with their own horse, received five *pūrvietas* (1.8 ha.) of land, 1.5 hectares of meadows and a small piece of land for the garden (*banda*). Likewise estates had to pay foresters and innkeepers. The land which they received was called *deputāts*. Only maids were paid in money – 1 1/4 Albert thaler per year. All other workers received payment in kind.

These revisions, in particular the redistribution of land in Vidzeme, were strongly resisted. In the event Arsenjev had to resign and the planned reforms could not be put into practice (Dunsdorfs, E., *Latvijas Vēsture 1800–1914*, Sweden: Daugava, 1958, pp. 84–85, 90–91).

12   Jānis Purapuķe (1864–1902) was born into a farm labourer's family. He studied at the Baltic Teachers' Seminary in Riga, working later as a teacher. His most popular novels were *Jaunā Strāva* (*The New Current*) (1895); *Sieviešu Ienaidnieki* (*Enemies of Women*) (1897); *Mūsu Modernās Jaunavas* (*Our Modern Girls*) (1898); *Savs Stūrītis, savs Kaktiņš Zemes* (*One's Own Small Piece of Land*) (1898); *Spieķis un Divi Suṇi* (*A Stick and Two Dogs*) (1900) (Knope, E., *Jānis Purapuķe. Savs Kaktiņš, Savs Stūrītis Zemes*, Rīga: Zinātne, 1990, pp. 5–12).

13 Famine was most severe in the districts of Cēsis and Valka: 19,000 horses, 53,000 cattle and 180,000 sheep died. The situation was made worse by the law of 1819 which freed estate owners of any responsibility for their peasants. Indeed, some owners borrowed large quantities of grain from peasant storehouses to produce vodka (Krodznieks, J., *Zemnieku nemieri 1841*, Rīga, 1922).

14 The Orthodox church in Limbaži was built in 1829. After the conquest of Peter I Orthodox churches were built throughout Latvia. St Nikolaj church was renewed in 1715 in Riga, St Simeon and Anna church in Jelgava in 1714, in Grunwald in 1804, in Liepaja in 1834, in Vec-Grunwald in Kurzeme in 1838 (Pommers, A., *Pareizticība Latvijā*, Rīga, 1931, pp. 13–15).

15 A Moravian meeting houses is still to be found in Cepļi, Vecpiebalga, Cēsu district in Vidzeme.

16 Between 1860 and 1918 130 newspapers were published in Latvian. Most were small and unstable, changed names to avoid censorship, or were illegal. *Laika Balss* (1911–1914), for example, changed names nine times. Those with the largest circulation were *Mājas Viesis* (1856–1908); *Pēterburgas Avīzes* (1862–1865 and 1901–1905); Baltijas Vēstnesis (1869–1906); *Baltijas Zemkopis* (1875–1884); *Pasaule un Daba* (1875-1876); *Darbs* (1875–1876); *Balss* (1878–1907); *Rīgas Lapa* (1877–1880); *Dienas Lapa* (1886–1905); *Tēvija* (1884–1914); *Latvietis* (1882–1905); *Rīgas Avīze* (1902–1915); *Jaunā Dienas Lapa* (1905–1906 and 1908–1918); *Mūsu Laiki* (1906–1907); *Mūsu Dzīve* (1907); *Liepājas Atbalss* (1907–1915); *Dzīve* (1908–1915); *Latvija* (1906–1915); *Dzimtenes Vēstnesis* (1907–1917); *Jaunākās Ziņas* (1911–1940); *Līdums* (1913); *Jaunais Vārds* (1915–1918) (Egle K., Lūkins, V., Brempele, A., Jauģietis, V., eds *Latviešu Periodika 1768–1919*, Rīga: Zinātne, 1977, vol. 1).

17 Jānis Pliekšāns (pen name Rainis, 1864–1902) was born in Rubene pagasts, Tadenava where his father rented a farm. He graduated from the University of St Petersburg (1884–1888) as a lawyer. He was a member of the social democratic movement Jaunā Strāva (New Current), and was an editor from 1891 to 1895 of the movement's newspaper *Dienas Lapa* (1886–1905). Falling foul of the authorities he was forced to emigrate to Berlin in 1896. In March 1897 he was allowed to work in Panevežys (province of Kaunas). In June 1897 he was arrested and imprisoned, subsequently being transferred from Panevežys to Liepāja and then Riga. In December 1897 he was exiled first to Pskov, then in June 1899 to Slobodsk. In May 1903 he was allowed to return to Riga. After participating in the revolution of 1905 Rainis was forced to emigrate to Switzerland in December 1905 where he stayed until April 1920. He was a member of parliament during the 1920s, director of the Department of Art and Culture 1920, Minister of Education 1926-1928, director of the National Theatre, member of the Cultural Foundation. His best-known poetry is 'Tālas Noskaņas Zilā Vakarā' ('Distant Moods on a Blue Evening') (1903), 'Vētras Sēja' ('The Face of the Storm') (1905), 'Klusā Grāmata' ('The Quiet Book') (1909). His plays *Indulis un Ārija* (1911), *Jāzeps un Viņa Brāļi* (*Joseph and His Brothers*) (1919), *Uguns un Nakts* (*Fire and Night*) (1905) draw upon biblical and Latvian mythological themes (*Latviešu Literātūras Vēsture*, ed. Bērziņš, L., Rīga: Literatūra, 1936, vol. 4, pp. 153–203).

18 The film *Strēlnieku Zvaigznājs* (*Sagittarius*) by the Latvian film maker Juris Podnieks (1950–1993) made in 1982 captures some of the very personal reasons for fighting in interviews with surviving *strēlnieki* (*Latvian Soviet Encyclopedia*, Rīga: Galvenā Enciklopēdiju Redakcija, 1984, vol. 5/2, p. 747).

19 The full membership of the Provisional National Council founded in November 1917 in Valka consisted of the following: J. Goldmans, A. Klīve, Dobelis from Land Council of Kurzeme, elected in Tartu; V. Skubiņš, O. Nonācs from citizen's section of the Land Council of Vidzeme; J. Rubuls, Laizāns, St Kambala, Strelēvičs from the Land Council of Latgale; J. Kreicbergs from the Central Supply Committee for Latvian Refugees; M. Antons from the Supply Committee for Baltic Refugees; Ziediņš, J. Zālīts from the Radicaldemocratic Party; J. Akuraters, Vītoliņš, Palcmans from the National Union of Latvian Soldiers; Lāčkājs, Drukts from the Union of Latgale Soldiers; Z. Meijerovics, E. Laursons from the Peasant's Union of Latvia; K. Bachmans, K. Skalbe from the Nationaldemocratic Party; P. Zālīts from the Democratic Party; Siliņš from the Cooperative Movement. P. Birkerts, K. Seržants from Land Council of Vidzeme, and R. Kokle from the Socialist-menschevist party who was there solely in an observer capacity.

Members from the Land Council of Kurzeme elected in Moscow, from the Socialist-bolshevist and Socialist-revolutionary parties did not participate.

V. Zamuels was elected Chairman of the board, K. Pauļuks, J. Rubuls and Polcmanis were Vice-chairmen, K. Bachmanis was Secretary, K. Skalbe, J. Akuraters Vice-secretaries, and Z. Meijerovics, J. Kreicbergs and J. Čakste delegates for foreign affairs (Paegle, Sp., *Kā Latvijas Valsts Tapa*, Rīga, 1923, pp. 188–200).

20 Kārlis Ulmanis (1874–1942) was born into a farmer's family. He studied dairying in Prussia 1897, agriculture in Zurich 1902 and graduated from the Institute of Agriculture in Leipzig in 1905. In 1905 Ulmanis was arrested for criticizing the government and was forced to emigrate to Germany in 1906. A year later he went to America where he obtained a degree in agriculture from the University of Nebraska in 1909. Ulmanis was amnestied in 1913 and returned to Latvia. He was active in various agricultural and political organizations. After the revolution of March 1917 he was appointed Vice-governor of Vidzeme. He was leader of the Latvian Farmer's Union founded in May 1917, and after the proclamation of an independent Republic of Latvia, he was elected prime minister (1918–1921). He was minister of Foreign Affairs until 1919. He was again elected prime minister by the Saeima in 1925–1926, 1931, self-elected in 1934–1940. He was Minister of Foreign Affairs in 1926 and 1934–1936. Following the coup in 1934 Ulmanis also assumed the role of President in 1936. After the Soviet occupation in 1940 Ulmanis was arrested and deported to the South of Russia. He died in the prison of Krasnovodsk in 1942 (*Latvju Enciklopēdija* (op. cit. Ch. 1 n. 5), vol. 3, pp. 2528).

21 There were three companies of school children (*skolnieku rotas*). The first, *Pirmā skolnieku rota* of Riga was formed on November 11th, 1918. It consisted of 150 students from technical and commerce schools between the ages of fifteen and twenty. Originally formed as a reserve company, it was incorporated on January 3rd 1919 into the active battalion of Kalpaks. The second company was formed in Riga as a reserve battalion of the Ministry of Defence after the liberation of Riga, being later renamed the Baloža brigade. On August 9th 1919 it was incorporated into the 9th infantry regiment of Rēzekne. *Cēsu skolnieku rota* was formed on June 6th 1919. It consisted of 108 badly instructed and armed school children from Cēsis and Valmiera, aged between fourteen and nineteen. It formed part of the 2nd infantry regiment of Cēsis. As the 8th voluntary school children's company it participated in the battle of Cēsis and later in the battles with Bermont near Riga (*Latvju Enciklopēdija* (op. cit. Ch. 1 n. 5), vol. 3, p. 2301).

22 The People's Council of Latvia, established on November 18th 1918, declared that:

1 A Constitutional Council (*Satversmes Sapulce*) was to be elected on the basis of general, equal, direct, secret and proportional voting with both sexes having equal rights. It stipulated that national minorities were entitled to be represented on the Constitutional Council and all legislative assemblies.

2 National minority members of the People's Council of Latvia were to participate in the formation of the provisional government.

3 Cultural and national rights of national groups were to be protected by law.

(*Latvijas Pagaidu Valdības Likumi un Rīkojumi* (Latvian Provisional Government), vol. 1, July 15, 1919, p. 2).

In the constitution of 1922 there is no concept of a national minority. A new term, 'citizen of Latvia' is substituted. A citizen of Latvia was any citizen of former Russia without reference to religion or ethnicity who had lived in the territory of Latvia or who originated from there before August 1st 1914 (*Likums par Pavalstniecibu* (Citizenship Law), *Likumu un Valdības Rīkojumu Krājums* (Law and State Regulation Collection), 1919, vol. 10, p. 131).

Laws protecting minority rights were also passed. For example, the law of December 10th 1918 stated that each nationality has a right to use their native language as a medium of instruction in schools (*Likumu un Valdības Rīkojumu Krājums*, 1919, vol. 13, p. 174).

23 Land reform legislation was passed in four stages:

1 Land Fund was set up on September 16th 1920 by the Constitutional Council;
2 Committee for Land Measurement was set up on September 17th 1920;
3 agreement on usage of the Fund's land was reached on December 21st 1920;

4   The Agrarian Order was consolidated on May 3rd 1922.

The purpose of the Land Fund was to establish new farms, to enlarge existing small farms, to provide a supportive infrastructure and to promote the development of towns and villages. Fifty hectares was the maximum amount of land permitted. According to a parliamentary decree (April 14th 1924) no compensation was to be given for alienated lands. The principles of land distribution were that small farms would be more readily expanded if

(a)   they bordered on land belonging to the fund; or
(b)   if they were willing to exchange their own land for the Fund's land, thereby expanding their farms; or
(c)   if they waived their rights to land for the benefit of neighbouring small farmers.

The remaining land was distributed to local landless peasants. In all instances priority was given to those who had fought for Latvian independence or their family members if they had died.

The merging of land owned by related households land was prohibited if this amounted to more than 50 hectares. If the land unified was between 22 and 50 hectares, special government permission was required (*Latvijas Agrārā Reforma*, Rīga: Zemkopības Ministrijas Izdevums, 1930, pp. 242–244).

24   *Pelekie baroni* (grey barons) were peasants of Latvian origin who had managed to buy large amounts of land. They were called grey because of their grey country coats.

Maximum amounts of land allowed had been set out by local regulations in Kurzeme and Vidzeme. In 1905 land distribution in desetines (Russian unit of measurement equivalent to 1.09 ha.) among peasants in Latvia was:

	More than 100	51–100	41–50
Number of households	72	7,210	8.798
Percentage of all landowners	0.09	8.98	10.96
Total amount of land	9,394	424,058	375,289
Percentage from total amount of land	0.47	21.37	18.29

25   Cooperatives were run according to regulations established in 1919, based in turn upon the Russian regulations of March 20th 1917. Cooperatives required a minimum of seven people.

In May, 1934 a greater degree of centralization was introduced. 'Where the state's interests require' a Minister of Justice had the right to dismiss elected members of the board, council and review committee of cooperative organizations and to appoint new ones.

Additional regulations of June 18th 1937 were more directive. They stipulated the promotion of well being to the entire population in its field of activity. Members of the cooperative should be of more than one nationality or religion.

The most common cooperatives in Latvia were credit, insurance, consumer and dairy cooperatives:

Year	Number of cooperatives	Number of members (in thousands)
1920	17	–
1921	72	23
1925	422	101
1930	602	195
1935	618	202
1940	419	206

Government loans were given either through agricultural organizations, directly to farmers, or through credit establishments:

	Loans		
Years	Agricultural organizations	Direct	Credit establishments
1924	–	1.1	2.7
1926	–	4.7	17.8
1928	9.6	3.0	27.3
1930	9.3	5.3	30.8

After 1920 loans were financed by credits from the Bank of Latvia. Loans were given for bills of exchange and with guarantees. In credit cooperatives loans were given as a proportion of the guarantee. Interest was 5–8 per cent a year in 1935. Latvijas Hipotēku Banka gave credits for 5–6 years, to the value of 50 to 60 per cent of the guarantee. Land Bank of Latvia took over all reduced interest agricultural credits in 1925. These had to be paid back in seven years with interest at 7 per cent a year. It gave 200–300 Lat loans to new farmers for three years. (In May 1997 £1 is approximately equivalent to 0.9 Lat.) Later this term was extended. Between 1923–1927 154,000 such loans were given. Interest rates in the open market in 1925 were 12–24 per cent a year. Credit with interest of more than 15 per cent was not thought suitable for agriculture. In 1927 the maximum interest rate was 12 per cent, in October 1932 10 per cent and in December 8 per cent. Land Bank reduced interest rates from 4 per cent to 2 per cent in 1931. A law of 1935 permitted postponement of 1,500 Lats payment by each farm on a restricted interest of 0.5 per cent a year. In 1935 300 Lats were written off the loan of each farm. Loans were given to agricultural credit cooperatives with 3 per cent interest, their profit could not exceed 2 per cent, threfore, loans to farmers for twenty years could not exceed 5 per cent interest a year (Aizsilnieks, A., *Latvijas Saimniecības Vēsture 1914–1945*, Stockholm: Daugava, 1968, pp. 326–336, 737–740).

26   The school-leaving age was sixteen in 1922. Obligatory schooling had been introduced in 1919. It consisted of two years of primary school or home teaching between the ages of seven and eight, six years of elementary school and two years of additional schooling from fifteen to sixteen. (*Likums par Latvijas Izglītības Iestādēm, Likumu un Valdības Rīkojumu Krājums*, 1919, vol. 13).

  In 1934 the secondary schooling was increased to five years and primary schooling reduced by a year (*Likums par Tautas Izglītību, Likumu un Ministru Kabineta Noteikumu Krājums*, 1934, vol.11, p. 226–233; *Latvju Enciklopēdija* (op. cit. Ch. 1. n. 5), vol.1/3, pp. 827–828).

27   Compulsory insurance against illness was introduced in December 1920, and covered urban workers in factories, shops and state institutions. It did not apply to agricultural workers, sailors or persons in active military service. The law of 1927 required obligatory insurance against accident and occupation-related illnesses for state employees and agricultural enterprises. In small enterprises insurance was voluntary. In 1930 compulsory insurance against illness was extended to writers and journalists, captains of seagoing ships, trainees, and persons working from home (Aizsilnieks, A., *Latvijas Saimniecības Vēsture 1914–1945*, Stockholm: Daugava, 1968, pp. 231, 394, 822).

28   Infant mortality rates declined from 128 per 1,000 in 1920 to 85 in 1937. The mortality rates remained high in Latgale where they were 151 and 106 respectively (*Latvijas Statistiskā Gada Grāmata 1921*, Rīga, 1922, pp. 6, 7, *Latvijas Statistikas Gada Grāmata 1937/38*, Rīga, 1938, pp. 18, 30).

29   In 1930/31 there were twenty-six foreign professors and lecturers in the University of Latvia (*Latvijas Universitāte 1919–1939*, Rīga, 1939, vol.1, p. 30).

30   '*Latviju Latviešiem – latviešiem darbu un maizi*' ('Latvia for Latvians – bread and work for Latvians') was one of the slogans of the Latvian National Union *Pērkonkrusts*, founded in 1933. Its leader was Gustavs Celmiņš and his speech of 17th September 1933 gives a flavour of his philosophy: 'We will rid ourselves forever of political-liberal prejudices....

There will be no minority question in Latvia. There will be one Latvian nation governing itself'. Its enemies were identified in its programme: 'We know that Jews and their allies – marxists, foreigners and party leaders oppose our views' (*Pērkonkrusts. Kas ir? Ko grib? Kā darbojas?*, Rīga: LTA Pērkonkrusts Propogandas Daļa, November 1933).

31 It is, however, important to remember that the numbers involved were small, although this does not invalidate Ezergailis' point. At the time of the Communist invasion of 1940 there were some 200 imprisoned Communists. The exact numbers of cases on trial and persons sentenced (but not necessarily imprisonned) were 2,043 and 746 respectively in 1935; 709 and 309 in 1936; 1,458 and 310 in 1937; 787 and 310 in 1938; 1,019 and 408 in 1939; 685 and 454 in the first five months of 1940 (*Latvijas Padomju Enciklopēdija*, Rīga: Galvena Enciklopēdiju Redakcija, 1984, vol.5/1, p. 213).

32 These military bases were located in Liepāja, Pitrags, Ventspils, Piltene, Vaiņodā, Priekule, Ezere, Paplaka, Durbe, Grobiņa, Cīrava, Ēdole, Kuldīga, Dižirbe, Melnsils, Dundaga. (Data obtained from the Museum of Occupation, Riga.)

33 Permission to establish the first kolhoz was given by the Ministry of Justice on July 10th, 1940. The kolhoz was founded in Dēmene pagasts (Latgale) involving some of the local population. A month later it appeared that kolhoz was founded from self protective motives to preserve property. (*Latgalskaja Pravda*, August 2, 1940). The next kolhoz was founded in Žīguru village, Augšpils pagasts on June 15th 1941 (Šilde, A., *Bez tiesībām un Brīvības*, Copenhagen: Imanta, 1965, p. 265).

34 The Moscow District Ghetto was established between October 23rd–25th, 1941. A small ghetto for able-bodied people was established within this territory on November 29th. The German ghetto was founded nearby on December 10th, intended specifically for Jews from Germany and other foreign countries. People from the German ghetto were taken to the concentration camp in Salaspils which existed between October 1941 and October 1944. The small ghetto was transferred to the Riga suburb of Kaiserwald (Mežaparks) in August 1943 and then to Stutthof in September 1944 where it was liquidated in October 1944. During this period nearly 90 per cent of Latvia's Jews were exterminated (*Latvian Soviet Encyclopedia*, Rīga: Galvenā Enciklopēdiju Redakcija, 1980, vol. 3, p. 297).

35 See Chapter 4 note 5.

36 The wages of agricultural workers in 1958 varied from 0.14 to 10 rubles in old money, between 1968 and 1978 it was 1.8 to 6.9 rubles per normative day. Before 1958 workers were paid in kind, mostly in grain. A fixed salary was introduced in 1966 (Cipe, K., *Darba Samaksa Kolhozos*, Rīga: Zinātne, 1967; Šilde, A., *Bez Tiesībām un Brīvības*, Copenhagen: Imanta, 1965, p. 326; Strautmanis, I., *Kolhozu Tiesību Pamati*, Rīga: Liesma, 1973, p. 246; *Kolhoza Paraugstatūti*, Rīga: Latvijas Valsts Izdevniecība, 1953, p. 5).

37 A major industry set up after the war was the military production complex. Until 1950 this was manned by soldiers on active service. After that workers were actively recruited from Russia.

The new industries were largely under the leadership of Russians – only 22 per cent of factory directors were Latvian. Even after the reforms of the late 1950s only seventy directors of the 314 largest enterprises were Latvian. Twelve per cent of directors of collective farms were Latvian.

Population increases appear to have been planned according to secret protocol (Latvian State Archive 270/1, case 1905, pp. 13–14).

38 Advertisements appeared in Russian and Byelorussian newspapers and in railway stations calling for specified numbers of workers and giving details of type of work and guaranteed housing. The textile and knitwear enterprise at Ogre is one example of an industry set up almost entirely with immigrant labour.

39 See Chapter 2 note 5.

40 Returning deportees had to sign a paper with the following text:

> I have been sent to distant regions of the Soviet Union for an indefinite period of time without any right to return according to the directive of the higher state officials of the USSR. I am informed that without permission of the local

department of Internal Affairs I do not have a right to change my place of work or living.

(Riekstiņš, J. *Genocīds in Latvijas Vēsture* 1991, p. 37).

41 Top educational administrators were affected by the purges of 1959 rather than teachers. During two weeks in August twenty directors of education lost their jobs and five were demoted.

Large numbers of teachers had lost their jobs in 1951 and 1952 during the political review processes (Latvian – *atestācija*). Between August 18th and 22nd 1951 sixty-seven teachers lost their jobs, forty-three left voluntarily, twenty-two were judged to have insufficient qualifications and nineteen were deemed unfit to teach in a Soviet school. This last category were forbidden to teach ever again (Case material of Ministry of Education K/d, 1/16 August 18-22,1951 and NR.168–181, August 14–29, 1959).

42 Although officially there was no one state language (the constitution (cl. 36) refers explicitly to the right to use one's native tongue), in practice there was pressure to use Russian and in particular to conduct official business in Russian.

Russian was introduced as the language of clerical, administrative and political affairs as early as 1940. For example, the committee of the Communist Party of Jelgava used Latvian in 1940, but by the beginning of 1941 used Russian.

Throughout the Soviet period all major congresses and official ceremonies of the Communist Party both at national and district levels were held in Russian.

In May 1947 the Ministry of Education of LSSR ordered the introduction of Russian language teaching in all schools. In March 1950 further instructions for the expansion and improvement of language teaching were issued (Zīle, L. 'Latvijas Rusifikācija', in *Latvijas Vēsture*, 1991, vol. 1, pp. 31–36).

43 Gunārs Astra (1931–1988) symbolizes for many Latvians the conflict between political repression and individual conscience. Referred to as a prisoner of conscience (*sirdsapzi-ņas cietumnieks*) he was sentenced in 1961 to fifteen years under clauses 59.1, 65.1 and 209 of the criminal code of LSSR for agitation and propaganda against the Soviet order. These clauses refer to treason and offences against the independence, territorial unity and military superiority of the USSR. Astra translated Orwell's *1984* and Solzhenitsyn's *Gulag Archipelago* as well as distributing documents concerning the Soviet occupation. In 1982 Astra was again sentenced to five years' imprisonment. He died in suspicious circumstances following treatment received in hospital. Many Latvians believe that he was killed by the authorities.

During the 1970s and 1980s the most important sources of resistance were networks such as the Organization for the Independence of Latvia, Movement for the Independence of Latvia and the Social Democrats.

44 For a detailed account of the dealings between censors and poets see *Latvian Literature under the Soviets 1940–1975*, by Rolfs Ekmanis, in particular, Chapter 6, 'A Battle for Cultural Autonomy'.

45 Personal communication from the author. Other poets too were published in massive editions. The size of editions increased in the late 1960s and remained high thereafter. For example, *Cilvēks, Uzarta Zeme* (*A Man, Ploughed Land*) by Māris Čaklais appeared in 1976 in an edition of 33,000. A similar size edition of *Melnās Ogas* (*Black Berries*) by Ojārs Vācietis was published in 1971 and of *Kā Svece Deg* (*How the Candle Burns*) by Imants Ziedonis in the same year.

46 Andris Slapiņš, film director and cameraman; Gvido Zvaigzne, cameraman; Raimonds Salmiņš, driver; Vladimir Gomanovitch, senior lieutenant of militia; Sergei Kononenko, senior lieutenant of militia; Edijs Riekstiņš, school child.

LATVIAN REFERENCES

Andersons, Edgars 1962–82 *Latvju Enciklopēdija*. Amērikas Latviešu Apvieaība.
Andersons, Edgars 1967 *Latvijas Vēsture 1914–1920*. Stockholm: Daugava.
Atminu, Lauskas 1992 Rakstnieku Asociācija. Rīga.
Barons, Krišjānis 1985 *Atmiņas*. Rīga: Liesma.
Blese, Ernests 1947 *Latviešu Literatūras Vēsture*. Hanavas Latviešu nometne: Gaismas pils.
Brigadere, Anna 1956 *Pasaku Lugas*. Rīga: Latvijas Valsts Izdevniecība. (*Sprīdītis* 1903; *Maija un Paija* 1921, *Princese Gundega un Karālis Brusubārda* 1912.)
Buduls, H. 1924 *Psichiatrija*. *Vispārīgā Daļa*. Rīga: Valtera un Rapa Izdevniecība.
Buduls, H. 1929 *Psichiatrija*. *Speciālā Daļa*. Rīga: Valtera un Rapa Izdevniecība.
Dravnieks, A. 1937 *Kronvaldu Atis*. Rīga: A. Gulbis.
Dreimanis, P. 1958 *Latvju Tautas Vēsture*. Copenhagen: Imanta.
Dunsdorfs, Edgars 1966 *Mūžīgais Latviešu Karavīrs*. Melbourne: Generāļa Kārļa Goppera Fonds.
Eglītis, Imants 1989 *Psihiatrija*. Rīga: Zvaigzne.
Ērmanis, Pēteris ed. 1923 *Rūdolfs Blaumanis. Atmiņu Kopojums*. Rīga: Blaumaņa Pieminekļa Fonda Komitejas Izdevums.
Heinrici Chronicon. Indrika Hronika 1993. Tr. into Latvian A. Feldhuus. Rīga; Zinatne.
Klaustiņš, R. 1925 *Ievads Latvju Rakstniecībā*. Rīga: A. Gulbis.
Krastiņš, Jānis 1980 *Jūgendstils Rīgas Arhitektūrā*. Rīga: Zinātne.
Krauliņš, K. ed. 1946 *Ābece*. Rīga: Latvijas Valsts Izdevnecība.
Kundziņš, Pauls 1974 *Latvju Sēta* (with English summary) Sundbyberg: Daugava.
Latviešu Tautas Pasakas 1956 Rīga: Latvijas PSR Zinātņu Akadēmijas Etnogrāfijas un Folkloras Institūts.
Latvijas Skolotāju Savienība 1994 *Pedagoģiskā Doma Latvijā no 1890.g. lidz 1940.g. Antoloģija*. Rīga: Zvaigzne.
Līce, Anda ed. 1990 *Via Dolorosa*. Rīga: Liesma.
Līgotnu Jēkabs *Latviešu Literatūras Vēsture. Vidusskolas Kurss*. Valmiera un Cēsis: K. Duna izdevums.
Kaudzītis, Matīss 1994 (1924) *Atminas no Tautiskā Laikmeta*. Rīga: Zvaigzne.
1950, 1955 and 1959 Lubāniete, Z. ed. *Abece. Pamatskolas Pirmai Klasei*. Rīga: Latvijas Valsts Izdevniecība.
1950 Lubāniete, Z. ed. *Lasāmā Grāmata Pirmai Klasei*. Rīga: Latvijas Valsts Izdevniecība.
1952 and 1954 Lubāniete, Z. ed. *Lasāmā Grāmata 11. Klasei*. Rīga: Latvijas Valsts Izdevniecība.
1965 Lubāniete, Z. ed. *Sāksim Mācīties (pirmsskolas bērniem)* Rīga: Liesma.
1970 Lubāniete, Z. ed. *Lasāmā Grāmata. Pirmai Klasei*. Rīga: Zvaigzne.
Merķelis, Garlībs 1978 (1797) *Latvieši, Sevišķi Vidzemē, Filosofiskā Gadsimteņa Beigās*. Rīga: Zvaigzne.
Pēterburgas Latweetis 1905–6 1927 Maskava: Prometejs.
Plaudis, Arturs ed. 1976 *Mirušie Apsūdz*. Vasteras, Sweden: Ziemelblāzma.
Purapuķe, Jānis 1990 (1904) *Savs Kaktiņš Savs Stūrīts Zemes*. Rīga: Zinātne.
Siliņš, Jānis 1979 *Latvijas Māksla vol. 1. 1800–1914*; 1990 *Latvijas Māksla vol. 11 1915–1940* (both volumes with English summary) Stockholm: Daugava.
Skalbe, Kārlis 1957 *Pasakas*. Rīga: Latvijas Valsts Izdevniecība.
Skujenieks, Marģers 1938 *Latvijas Statistikas Atlass*. Rīga: Valsts Statistiskā Pārvalde.

Šmits, Pēteris 1923 *Etnogrāfisko Rakstu Krājums* II. Rīga: A. Gulbja Apgādība.
Šmits, Pēteris 1937 *Vēsturiski un Etnogrāfiski Raksti.* Rīga: Valters un Rapa.
Straubergs, J. n.d. *Rīgas Vēsture.* Rīga: Grāmatu Draugs.
Švābe, A., Bumanis, A., Dišlers, K. eds 1927–1940 *Latviešu Konversācijas Vārdnīca.* Vols. 1–21. Rīga: A. Gulbja Apgādība.
Švābe, Arveds ed. 1948 *Latvju Kultūra.* Ludwigsburg: A. Klavsona Apgāds.
Švābe, Arveds 1950 *Latvju Enciklopēdija.* Stockholm: Trīs Zvaigznes.
Švābe, Arveds 1962 *Latvijas Vēsture 1800–1914.* Uppsala: Daugava.
Švābe, Arveds 1990 *Latvijas Vēsture.* Rīga: Avots.
Švābe, Arveds, Straubergs K. and Hauzenberga-Šturma eds 1952 *Latviešu Tautas Dziesmas* vols. 1–12. Copenhagen: Imanta.
Tentelis, A. 1939 *Dokumenti Par Tautas Atmodas Laikmetu 1856–1867.* Rīga: Latvijas Vēstures Institūta Apgads.
Valdemārs, Krišjānis 1937 (1861–1871) *Raksti.* Rīga: Latvijas Universitātes Apgāds.
Virza, Edvarts 1936 *Straumēni.* Rīga: Valters un Rapa.
Zālītis, Fr. 1947 *Latvijas Vēsture Školām un Pašmācībai.* Germany: Grāmatu Draugs.
Zālītis, Fr. and Grīns, J. 1927 *Pirmā Vēstūres Grāmata.* Rīga: Valters un Rapa.
Zeiferts, Teodors 1993 (1922) *Latviešu Rakstniecības Vēsture.* Rīga: Zvaigzne.

SCHOOL TEXTBOOKS CONSULTED

1944 Obrama, I. *Lāsamā Grāmata Pirmai Klasei.* Rīga: Pedagoģisko Rakstu Apgāds.
1944 and 1946 K. Krauliņš ed. *Abece.* Rīga: Latvijas Valsts Izdevnieciba.

BIBLIOGRAPHY

Adorno, Theodor W. 1965 *Noten zur Literatur* vol. 3. Frankfurt: Suhrkamp Verlag.

Adorno, Theodor W. 1973 (1966) *Negative Dialectics*. London: Routledge and Kegan Paul.

Asad, Talal 1986 'The Concept of Cultural Translation in British Social Anthropology' in *Writing Culture. The Poetics and Politics of Ethnography* eds James Clifford and George F. Marevs. Berkeley: University of California Press.

Aleyeyeva, Ludmilla 1985 *Soviet Dissent*. Middletown: Wesleyan University Press (esp. Ch 4, pp. 97–105).

Allen, Martin G. 1973 'Psychiatry in the United States and the USSR: A Comparison'. *American Journal of Psychiatry* 130(12), pp. 1333–1337.

Anderson, Benedict 1991 *Imagined Communities. Reflections on the Origin and Spread of Nationalism*. London and New York: Verso.

Andrups, Jānis and Kalve, Vitauts 1954 *Latvian Literature: Essays*. Stockholm: Golden Apple Tree.

Auerbach, Erich 1968 (1946) *Mimesis: The Representation of Reality in Western Literature*. Tr. William R. Trask. Princeton: Princeton University Press.

Bakhtin, M.M. 1992 (1981) *The Dialogic Imagination: Four Essays* Tr. Caryl Emerson and Michael Holquist. Austin: University of Texas Press.

Bakhtin, M.M. 1994 (1986) *Speech Genres and Other Late Essays*. Tr. Vern W. McGee. Austin: University of Texas Press.

Barthes, Roland 1970 'Historical Discourse' in *Structuralism. A Reader* ed. Michael Lane, pp. 145–155. London: Jonathan Cape.

Barthes, Ronald 1970 *S/Z: Essais* Paris: Seuil.

Barthes, Roland 1993 (1957) *Mythologies*. London: Jonathan Cape.

Bashford, Lindsay 1921 'In the Little New Countries'. *Blackwoods Magazine* vol. 209, (esp. pp. 73–87, 229–244, 363–377, 471–486).

Basnett, Susan and Lefevere, Andre eds 1990 *Translation, History and Culture*. London and New York: Pinter.

Bender, Barbara ed. 1993 *Landscape. Politics and Perspectives*. Providence and Oxford: Berg.

Benjamin, Walter 1992 *Illuminations*. London: Fontana Press.

Bennett, David 1975 'Anomie, What Can It Be?' Proceedings of the Second Annual Conference of the Sociological Association of Ireland, pp. 34–52.

Benstock, Shari ed. 1986 *The Private Self. Theory and Practice of Women's Autobiographical Writings*. Chapel Hill and London: University of North Carolina Press.

Bertaux, Daniel ed. 1981 *Biography and Society. The Life History Approach in the Social Sciences*. Newbury Park and London: Sage.

Bhabha, Homi K. ed. 1990 *Nation and Narration*. London: Routledge.

Bhabha, Homi K. 1994 *The Location of Culture*. London: Routledge.

Bilmanis, Alfred 1951 *A History of Latvia*. Princeton: Princeton University Press.

Bloch, Maurice 1975 Introduction in *Political Language and Oratory in Traditional Societies* ed. M. Bloch, London and New York: Academic Press.

Bloch, Maurice 1977 'The Past and the Present in the Present'. *Man. Journal of the Royal Anthropological Institute* NS vol.12, pp. 278–292.

Bloch, Sidney and Reddaway, Peter 1977 *Russia's Political Hospitals. The Abuse of Psychiatry in the Soviet Union*. London: Victor Gollancz.

Borneman, John 1993 *Belonging in the Two Berlins. Kin, State, Nation.* Cambridge: Cambridge University Press.
Bosworth, R.J.B. 1993 *Explaining Auschwitz and Hiroshima. History Writing and the Second World War 1945–1990.* London: Routledge and Kegan Paul.
Bratus, B.V. 1969 *The Formation and Expressive Use of Diminutives.* Cambridge: Cambridge University Press.
Brody, Howard 1987 *Stories of Sickness.* Yale: Yale University Press.
Brundage, J.A. 1961, tr. *The Chronicle of Henry of Livonia.* Madison: University of Wisconsin Press.
Bruner, Edward M. ed. 1983 'Text, Play and Story: The Construction and Reconstruction of Self and Society'. Proceedings of the American Ethnological Society.
Bruner, Jerome and Feldman, Carol Fleisher 1996 'Group Narrative as a Cultural Context of Autobiography' in *Remembering Our Past. Studies in Autobiographical Memory* ed. David C. Rubin, pp. 291–317. Cambridge: Cambridge University Press.
Burleigh, Michael 1994 *Death and Deliverance. 'Euthanasia' in Germany 1900–1945.* Cambridge: Cambridge University Press.
Bury, Michael 1982 'Chronic Illness as Biographical Disruption'. *Sociology of Health and Illness* 4 (2), pp.167–199.
Butler, Thomas ed. 1989 *Memory. History, Culture and the Mind.* Oxford: Basil Blackwell.
Cameron, Deborah, Frazer, Elizabeth, Harvey, Penelope, Rampton, M.B.H. and Richardson, Kay 1992 *Researching Language. Issues of Power and Method.* London and New York: Routledge.
Carrithers, M. (1990) *The Book of Memory.* Cambridge: Cambridge University Press.
Carrithers, Michael, Collins, Steven and Lukes, Steven eds 1985 *The Category of the Person. Anthropology, Philosophy, History.* Cambridge: Cambridge University Press.
Cave, Terence 1988 *Recognitions. A Study in Poetics.* Oxford: Clarendon Press.
Chatel, John C. and Peele, Roger 1992 'The Concept of Neurasthenia'. *International Journal of Psychiatry*, pp. 36–61.
Chave, Rhona ed. 1986 *Letters from Latvia.* Lucy Addison. London: Futura Publications.
Christiansen, Eric 1980 *The Northern Crusades. The Baltic and the Catholic Frontier 1100–1525.* London: Macmillan.
Clifford, James 1994 'Diasporas'. *Cultural Studies* 9(3), pp. 302–338.
Clifford, James and Marcus, George E. eds 1986 *Writing Culture. The Poetics and Politics of Ethnography.* Berkeley: University of California Press.
Cohen, Anthony P. 1986 *Symbolizing Boundaries: Identity and Diversity in British Cultures.* Manchester: Manchester University Press.
Cohen, Stanley and Taylor, Laurie 1992 *Escape Attempts. The Theory and Practice of Resistance to Everyday Life.* London: Routledge.
Cohen, Ted 1979 'Metaphor and the Cultivation of Intimacy' in *On Metaphor* ed. Sheldon Sacks, pp. 1–10. Chicago: University of Chicago Press.
Comaroff, John and Comaroff, Jean 1992 *Ethnography and the Historic Imagination.* Boulder Colorado: Westview Press.
Connerton, Paul 1989 *How Societies Remember.* Cambridge: Cambridge University Press.
Corson, Samuel A. and Corson, Elizabeth O'Leary 1976 *Psychiatry and Psychology in the USSR.* New York and London: Plenum Press.
Cranston, Maurice 1967 (1953) *Freedom. A New Analysis.* London: Longmans.
Crapanzano, Vincent 1984 'Life Histories'. *American Anthropologist* 86, pp. 953–960.
Crapanzano, Vincent 1986 *Tuhami: Portrait of a Moroccan.* Chicago: University of Chicago Press.
Cressey, Donald R. and Krassowski, Witwold 1957–8 'Inmate Organization and Anomie in American Prisons and Soviet Labour Camps'. *Social Problems* 5, pp. 217–230.
Cressy, David 1980 *Literacy and the Social Order. Reading and Writing in Tudor and Stuart England.* Cambridge: Cambridge University Press.
Crocker, J. Christopher 1977 'The Social Functions of Rhetorical Forms' in *The Social Use of Metaphor. Essays on the Anthropology of Rhetoric* eds J. David Sapir and J. Christopher Crocker, pp. 33–66. Pennsylvania: University of Pennsylvania Press.
Culler, Jonathan 1983 *On Deconstruction Theory and Criticism after Structuralism.* London: Routledge.

Davis, Colin 1991 'Understanding the Concentration Camps: Elie Wiesel's *La Nuit* and Jorge Semprun's *Quel Beau Dimanche!*. *Australian Journal of French Studies* XXVlll (3), pp. 291–303.

Davis, John 1980 'Social Anthropology and the Consumption of History'. *Theory and Society* 9, pp. 519–537.

Davis, John 1992 'The Anthropology of Suffering'. *Journal of Refugee Studies* 5 (2), pp. 149–161.

Denzin, Norman K. 1989 *Interpretive Biography*. Newbury Park and London: Sage.

Docherty, Thomas 1983 *Reading (Absent) Character. Towards a Theory of Characterization in Fiction.* Oxford: Clarendon Press.

Duncan, J.S. 1975 'Landscape Taste as a Symbol of Group Identity'. *Geographic Review* 63, pp. 334–355.

Eagleton, Terry 1983 *Literary Theory: an Introduction.* Oxford: Basil Blackwell.

Edelberg, Max ed. nd *Latvia.* Copenhagen: Hertz-Bogtrykkergaarden.

Einhorn, Paul 1649 *Beschreibung der Lettischen Nation*, Dorpat: Johann Vogeln.

Ekmanis, Rolfs 1978 *Latvian Literature under the Soviets 1940–1975.* Belmont: Nordland Publishing Co.

Ellis, Carol and Flaherty, Michael G. eds 1992 *Investigating Subjectivity. Research on Lived Experience.* Newbury Park and London: Sage.

Ezergailis, Andrievs 1972 'The October Insurrection in Latvia. A Chronology'. *Journal of Baltic Studies* 3 (3/4), pp. 218–228.

Ezergailis, Andrievs 1974 *The 1917 Revolution in Latvia.* East European Monographs 8, Boulder Colorado.

Ezergailis, Andrievs 1993 'Anti-Semitism and the Killing of Latvia's Jews' in *Anti-Semitism in Times of Crisis* eds Sander L. Gilman and Steven T. Katz, pp. 257–289. New York and London: New York University Press.

Ezrahi, Sidra DeKoven 1980 *By Words Alone. The Holocaust in Literature.* Chicago and London: University of Chicago Press.

Fabian, Johannes 1983 *Time and the Other. How Anthropology Makes its Object.* New York: Columbia University Press.

Fairclough, Norman 1989 *Language and Power.* Harlow: Longman.

Fardon, Richard ed. 1990 *Localizing Strategies. Regional Traditions of Ethnographic Writing.* Edinburgh and Washington: Scottish Academic Press and Smithsonian Institution Press.

Felman, Shoshana and Laub, Dori 1992 *Testimony. Crises of Witnessing in Literature, Psychoanalysis, and History.* London and New York: Routledge.

Feldman, Allen 1991 *Formations of Violence: The Narrative of the Body and Political Terror in Northern Ireland.* Chicago: Chicago University Press.

Fennell, J.L.I. ed. 1965 *Prince A.M. Kurbsky's History of Ivan IV.* Cambridge: Cambridge University Press.

Fentress, J. and Wickham, C. 1992 *Social Memory.* Oxford: Basil Blackwell.

Ferro, Marc 1984 (1981) *The Use and Abuse of History or How the Past is Taught.* London: Routledge and Kegan Paul.

Field, M.G. 1967 'Soviet Psychiatry and Social Structure, Culture and Ideology: A Preliminary Assessment'. *American Journal of Psychotherapy* 21, pp. 230–243.

Field, Mark G. 1967 *Soviet Socialized Medicine. An Introduction.* New York: The Free Press.

Figlio, Karl 1988 'Oral History and the Unconscious'. *History Workshop* 26, pp. 102–119.

Finnegan, Ruth 1992 *Oral Traditions and the Verbal Arts. A Guide to Research Practices.* London: Routledge.

Foley, Barbara 1986 *Telling the Truth. The Theory and Practice of Documentary Fiction.* Ithaca and London: Cornell University Press.

Fortes, Meyer 1959 *Oedipus and Job in a West African Religion.* Cambridge: Cambridge University Press.

Foster, John Burt 1993 *Nabokov's Art of Memory and European Modernism.* Princeton: Princeton University Press.

Frankenberg, Ronald 1988 'Your Time or Mine? An Anthropological View of the Tragic Temporal Contradictions of Biomedical Practice'. *International Journal of Health Services* 18 (1), pp. 11–34.

Freccero, John 1986 'Autobiography and Narrative' in *Reconstructing Individualism* eds Thomas

C. Heller, Sosna Morton and David E. Wellbury, pp. 17–29. Stanford: Stanford University Press.

Friedman, Susan 1986 'Women's Autobiographical Selves' in *The Private Self. Theory and Practice of Women's Autobiographical Writings*. ed. Shari Benstock, pp. 34–61. Chapel Hill and London: University of North Carolina Press.

Frykman, Jonas and Lofgren, Orvar 1987 *Culture Builders. A Historical Anthropology of Middle Class Life*. New Brunswick and London: Rutgers University Press.

Fussell, Paul 1976 *The Great War and Modern Memory*. Oxford: Oxford University Press.

Geertz, Clifford 1993 (1983) *Local Knowledge. Further Essays in Interpretive Anthropology*. London: Fontana.

Geertz, Clifford 1988 *Works and Lives. The Anthropologist as Author*. Cambridge: Polity.

Gale-Carpenter, Inta 1988 'Being Latvian in Exile: Folklore as Ideology' PhD thesis, Indiana University.

Ganguly, Keya 1992 'Migrant Identities: Personal Memory and the Construction of Selfhood'. *Cultural Studies* 6(1), pp. 27–50.

Gellner, Ernest 1993 *Nations and Nationalism*. Oxford: Basil Blackwell.

Genette, Gerard 1979 *Narrative Discourse*. Oxford: Basil Blackwell.

Gentzler, Edwin 1993 *Contemporary Translation Theories*. London: Routledge.

Gerner, Kristian and Hedlund, Stefan 1993 *The Baltic States and the End of the Soviet Empire*. London: Routledge.

Giddens, Anthony 1991 *Modernity and Self-Identity. Self and Society in the Late Modern Age*. Oxford: Polity Press.

Gimbutas, Maria 1963 *The Balts*. London: Thames and Hudson.

Goody, J. 1987 *The Interface Between the Written and the Oral*. Cambridge: Cambridge University Press.

Goddard, Victoria A., Llobera, Josep R. and Shore, Chris 1994 *The Anthropology of Europe. Identities and Boundaries in Conflict*. Providence and Oxford: Berg.

Good, Byron J. and Good, Mary-Jo DelVecchio 1994 'In the Subjunctive Mode: Epilepsy Narratives in Turkey'. *Social Science and Medicine* 38(6), pp. 835–842.

Good, Byron J. 1994 *Medicine, Rationality and Experience. An Anthropological Perspective*. Cambridge: Cambridge University Press.

Gordon, Frank 1990 *Latvians and Jews between Germany and Russia*. Stockholm: Memento.

Gould, John 1989 *Herodotus*. London: Weidenfeld and Nicolson.

Graff, Harvey J. 1979 *The Literacy Myth. Literacy and Social Structure in the Nineteenth Century City*. New York and London: Academic Press.

Greimas, Algirdas J. 1992 *Of Gods and Men. Studies in Lithuanian Mythology*. Tr. Milda Newman. Bloomington and Indianapolis: Indiana University Press.

Grillo, Ralph ed. 1989 *Social Anthropology and the Politics of Language*. London: Routledge and Kegan Paul.

Gumperz, John J. ed. 1982 *Language and Social Identity*. Cambridge: Cambridge University Press.

Gusdorf, Georges 1980 'Conditions and Limits of Autobiography' in *Autobiography: Essays Theoretical and Critical*, pp. 28–48. Princeton: Princeton University Press.

Halbwachs, Maurice 1981 (1950) *The Collective Memory*. New York and Cambridge: Harper and Row.

Hampshire, Stuart 1989 *Innocence and Experience*. London: Allen Lane.

Hankiss, A. 1981 'Ontologies of the Self: On the Mythological Rearranging of One's Life History' in *Biography and Society. The Life History Approach in the Social Sciences*. pp. 203–209 ed. D. Bertaux. California: Sage.

Harries, Karsten 1979 'Metaphor and Transcendence' in *On Metaphor* ed. Sheldon Sacks. Chicago: Chicago University of Chicago Press.

Hastrup, Kirsten 1985 *Culture and History in Medieval Iceland*. Oxford: Oxford University Press.

Hastrup, Kirsten 1994 'Hunger and the Hardness of Facts'. *Man* 28, pp. 727–739.

Hawkes, Terence 1989 (1972) *Metaphor*. London and New York: Routledge.

Heath, Shirley Brice 1983 *Ways with Words. Language, Life and Work in Communities and Classrooms*. Cambridge: Cambridge University Press.

Heath, Shirley Brice 1993 'The madness(es) of reading and writing ethnography'. *Anthropology and Education Quarterly* 24(3), pp. 256–268.

Heller, Thomas C., Morton, Sosna and Wellbery, David 1986 *Reconstructing Individualism*.

Autonomy, Individuality and the Self in Western Thought. California: Stanford University Press.

Helling, Ingeborg 1988 'The Life History Method: A Survey and Discussion with Norman K. Denzin'. *Studies in Symbolic Interaction* 9, pp. 211–243.

Henriques, Julian, Hollway, Wendy, Urwin, Cathy, Venn, Couze and Walkerdine, Valerie 1984 *Changing the Subject. Psychology, Social Regulation and Subjectivity.* London and New York: Methuen.

Herzfeld, Michael 1987 *Anthropology Through the Looking Glass. Critical Ethnography in the Margins of Europe.* Cambridge: Cambridge University Press.

Herder, Johann Gottfried n.d. *Herders Werke vol. 2 Volkslieder* ed. Heinrich Kurz. Leipzig and Vienna: Bibliographisches Institut.

Hiden, John and Salmon, Patrick 1991 *The Baltic Nations and Europe. Estonia, Latvia and Lithuania in the Twentieth Century.* London and New York: Longman.

Hobsbaum, E.J. 1992 (2nd edn) *Nations and Nationalism.* Cambridge: Cambridge University Press.

Holland, Dorothy and Quinn, Naomi eds 1987 *Cultural Models in Language and Thought.* Cambridge: Cambridge University Press.

Holquist, Michael 1990 *Dialogism. Bakhtin and his World.* London and New York: Routledge.

Hope, Nicholas 1994 'Interwar Statehood: Symbol and Reality' in *The Baltic States. The National Self-determination of Estonia, Latvia and Lithuiania* ed. Graham Smith, pp. 41–68. London: Macmillan.

Hosking, Geoffrey 1990 (1985) *A History of the Soviet Union* (rev. edn) London: Fontana.

Hoyer, Svennik, Lauk, Epp and Vihalemm, Peeter eds 1994 *Towards a Civic Society. The Baltic Media's Long Road to Freedom. Perspectives on History, Ethnicity and Journalism.* Baltic Association for Media Research/ Nota Baltica Ltd.

Ingold, Tim ed. 1994 *The Past is a Foreign Country.* Manchester: Group for Debates in Anthropological Theory.

Iser, Wolfgang 1978 *The Act of Reading. A Theory of Aesthetic Response.* Baltimore and London: Princeton University Press.

Iser, Wolfgang 1980 'Interaction between Text and Reader' in *The Reader in the Text. Essays on Audience and Interpretation* eds. Susan R. Suleiman and Inge Crosman, pp. 106–119. Princeton: Princeton University Press.

Iser, Wolfgang 1993 *The Fictive and the Imaginary: Charting Literary Anthropology.* Baltimore: Johns Hopkins University Press.

Jackson, Anthony 1987 *Anthropology at Home.* London: Tavistock.

Jakobson, Roman 1970 'On Russian Fairy Tales' in *Structuralism: A Reader* ed. Michael Lane, pp. 184–201, London: Jonathan Cape.

Jakobson, Roman 1971 *Two Aspects of Language and Two Types of Aphasic Disturbances in Selected Writings* vol. 11, pp. 239–259. Hague and Paris: Mouton.

Jellinek, Estelle C. ed. 1990 (1980) *Women's Autobiography. Essays in Criticism.* Bloomington: Indiana University Press.

Jenkins, Richard 1992 *Hightown Rules: Growing up on a Belfast Housing Estate.* Leicester: National Youth Bureau.

Jenkins, Richard 1992 'Doing Violence to the Subject'. *Current Anthropology* 33 (2), pp. 233–235.

Johnston, Ian C. 1988 *The Ironies of War. An Introduction to Homer's Iliad.* Lanham: University Press of America.

Josselson, Ruthellen and Lieblich, Amia eds 1993 *The Narrative Study of Lives* vol. I. Newbury Park and London: Sage Publications.

Kalnins, Bruno 1972 'The Social Democratic Movement in Latvia' in *Revolution and Politics in Russia* eds. Rabinowitch Alexander and Janet, pp. 134–156. Bloomington and London: Indiana University Press.

Karklins, Rasma 1986 *Ethnic Relations in the USSR. The Perspective from Below.* Boston and London: Allen Lane.

Karklins, Rasma 1989 'The Organization of Power in Soviet Labour Camps'. *Soviet Studies* 41 (2), pp. 276–297.

Kauffman, Linda S. 1986 *Discourses of Desire. Gender, Genre and Epistolary Fiction.* Ithaca and London: Cornell University Press.

Kay, D. and Miles, R. 1992 *Refugees or Migrant Workers? European Workers in Britain 1946–1951.* London: Routledge.

Keuchel '1871 Sei ein Unding', *Zeitung fur Stadt und Lond*, September 23rd.

Kideckel, David A. 1993 *The Solitude of Collectivism: Romanian Villagers to the Revolution and Beyond.* Ithaca and London: Cornell University Press.

Kiev, Ari ed. 1967 *Psychiatry in the Communist World.* New York: Science House

Kilis, Roberts 1994 'Social Memory as a Constituent of Ethnic Identity'. Cambridge M.Phil. dissertation.

Kinder, Hermann ed. 1978 *Penguin Atlas of World History*, vol. 2. Harmondsworth: Penguin.

Kirby, David 1990 *The Northern World in the Early Modern Period.* London and New York: Longman.

Kirby, David 1994 'Incorporation: the Molotov–Ribbentrop Pact' in *The Baltic States. The National Self Determination of Estonia, Latvia and Lithuania* ed. Graham Smith, pp. 69–85. London: Macmillan.

Kirby, David 1995 *The Baltic World 1772–1993 Europe's Northern Periphery in an Age of Change.* London and New York: Longman.

Kirmayer, Lawrence 1988 'Mind and Body as Metaphors: Hidden Values in Biomedicine' in *Biomedicine Examined* eds M. Lock and D. Gordon. Dordrecht: Kluwer.

Kirmayer, Lawrence 1992 'The Body's Insistence on Meaning: Metaphor as Presentation and Representation in Illness Experience'. *Medical Anthropology Quarterly* 6(4), pp. 323–346.

Kirmayer, Lawrence 1993 'Healing and the Invention of Metaphor: The Effectiveness of Symbols Revisited'. *Culture, Medicine and Psychiatry*, 17, pp. 161–195.

Kleinman, Arthur 1977 'Depression, Somatization and the 'New Cross-cultural Psychiatry'. *Social Science and Medicine* 11, pp. 3–10.

Kleinman, Arthur 1982 'Neurasthenia and Depression: A Study of Somatization and Culture in China'. *Culture, Medicine and Psychiatry* 6, pp. 117–190.

Kleinman, Arthur 1986 *The Social Origins of Distress and Disease. Depression, Neurasthenia and Pain in Modern China.* New Haven and London: Yale University Press.

Kleinman, Arthur 1988 *The Illness Narratives. Suffering, Healing and the Human Condition.* New York: Basic Books.

Kleinman, Arthur and Kleinman, Joan 1994 'How Bodies Remember: Social Memory and Bodily Experience of Criticism, Resistance and Delegitimation Following China's Cultural Revolution'. *New Literary History* 25, pp. 707–723.

Kolb, Lawrence C. 1966 'Soviet Psychiatric Organization and the Community Mental Health Centre Concept'. *American Journal of Psychiatry* 123 (4), pp. 433–439.

Labov, William 1972 'The Transformation of Experience in Narrative Syntax' in *Language and the Inner City*, pp. 354–396: University of Pennsylvania Press.

Labov, William and Waletzky, Joshua 1974 'Narrative Analysis: Oral Versions of Personal Experience' in *Essays on the Verbal and Visual Arts* ed. June Helm. Proceedings of the 1966 Annual Spring Meeting of the American Ethnological Society.

Lakoff, George and Johnson, Mark 1980 *Metaphors We Live By.* Chicago and London: University of Chicago Press.

Lammel, Annamaria and Nagy, Ilona 1988 'The Bible and the Hungarian Peasant Tradition: Transformational Processes of Biblical Folk-Narratives' in *Literary Anthropology. A New Interdisciplinary Approach to People, Signs and Literature* ed. Fernando Poyatos, pp. 173–194. Amsterdam and Philadelphia: John Benjamin Publishing Company.

Langer, Lawrence 1975 *The Holocaust and the Literary Imagination.* New Haven and London: Yale University Press.

Langer, Lawrence L. 1991 *Holocaust Testimonies. The Ruins of Memory.* New Haven and London: Yale University Press.

Langness, L.L. 1965 *The Life History in Anthropological Science.* New York: Holt, Rinehart and Winston.

Lauterbach, W. 1984 *Soviet Psychotherapy.* Oxford and New York: Pergamon Press.

Laub, Dovi 1992 'Bearing Witness or the Vicissitudes of Listening' in *Testimony. Crises of Witnessing in Literature, Psychoanalysis and History* by Felman, S. and Laub, D. New York and London: Routledge.

Lebensohn, Z.M. 1962 'The Organization and Character of Soviet Psychiatry'. *American Journal of Psychotherapy* 16, pp. 295–301.

Leggett, George 1981 *The Cheka: Lenin's Political Police. The All-Russian Extraordinary Commission for Combating Counter-Revolution and Sabotage* (December 1917 to February 1922). Oxford: Clarendon Press.

Lerner, Laurence 1972 *The Uses of Nostalgia. Studies in Pastoral Poetry.* London: Chatto and Windus.

Lesse, S. 1962 'Psychiatry in Relation to Communist Philosophy'. *American Journal of Psychotherapy* 16, pp. 292–295.

Lévi-Strauss, Claude 1964 *Mythologies*, vol. 1 *Le Cru le Cuit*. Paris: Plon.

Lieven, Anatol 1993 *The Baltic Revolution*. New Haven and London: Yale University Press.

Linde, Charlotte 1987 'Explanatory Systems in Oral Life Stories' in *Cultural Models in Language and Thought* eds Dorothy Holland and Naomi Quinn, pp. 343–366. Cambridge: Cambridge University Press.

Linke, Uli 1990 'Folklore, Anthropology and the Government of Social Life'. *Society for Comparative Study of Society and History* 90, pp. 117–148.

Lloyd, Genevieve 1993 *Being in Time. Selves and Narrators in Philosophy and Literature*. London: Routledge.

Lodge, David 1990 *After Bakhtin. Essays on Fiction and Criticism*. New York and London: Routledge.

Loeber, Dietrich Andre, Vardys, V.S. and Kitching, L.P. eds 1992 *Regional Identity under Soviet Rule: the Case of the Baltic States*. New Jersey: Association for the Advancement of Baltic Studies.

Loizos, Peter 1981 *The Heart Grown Bitter. A Chronicle of Cypriot War Refugees*. Cambridge: Cambridge University Press.

Loughrey, Bryan ed. 1984 *The Pastoral Mode. A Casebook*. London: Macmillan.

Lowenthal, David 1985 *The Past is a Foreign Country*. Cambridge: Cambridge University Press.

Lukes, Steven 1969 'Alienation and Anomie' in *Philosophy, Politics and Society* eds Peter Laslett and W.G. Runciman. Oxford: Basil Blackwell.

Macdonald, Sharon ed. 1993 *Inside European Identities. Ethnography in Western Europe*. Providence and Oxford: Berg.

Macintyre, Alastair 1992 (1982) *After Virtue. A Study in Moral Theory*. London: Duckworth.

Maier, Charles S. 1988 *The Unmasterable Past. History, Holocaust, and German National Identity*. Cambridge, Mass. and London: Harvard University Press.

Marcus, Steven 1976 'Freud and Dora: Story, History, Case History' in *Representations. Essays on Literature and Society* pp. 247–310. New York: Random House.

Mattingly, Cheryl 1994 'The Concept of Therapeutic "Emplotment"'. *Social Science and Medicine* 38(6), pp. 811–823.

Medvedev, Zhores A. and Medvedev, Roy A. 1971 *A Question of Madness*. London: Macmillan.

Miller, J. Hillis 1977 'The Limits of Pluralism: The Critic as Host' in *Critical Inquiry*, p. 446.

Misiunas, Romuald and Taagepera, Rein 1993 (rev. edn) *Baltic States. Years of Dependence 1940–1990*. London: Hurst.

Mitchell, W.J.T. ed. 1980 *On Narrative*. Chicago: University of Chicago Press.

Mosse, George L. 1990 *Fallen Soldiers. Reshaping the Memory of the World Wars*. New York and Oxford: Oxford University Press.

Myasishchev, V.N. 1963 *Personality and Neuroses*. Tr. Joseph Wortis et al. Washington: Joint Publications Research Service.

Nabokov, Vladimir 1967 (rev. edn) *Speak, Memory: An Autobiography Revisited*. London: Weidenfeld and Nicolson.

Nash, Roderick 1967 *Wilderness and the American Mind*. New Haven and London: Yale University Press.

Oakley, Stewart P. 1992 *War and Peace in the Baltic 1560–1790*. London: Routledge.

Odling-Smee, John ed. 1992 *Economic Review*. Latvia. Washington DC.: International Monetary Fund.

Okely, Judith and Callaway, Helen 1992 *Anthropology and Autobiography*. London and New York: Routledge.

Olney, James 1972 *Metaphors of Self. The Meaning of Autobiography*. New Jersey: Princeton University Press.

Olney, James ed. 1980a *Autobiography: Essays Theoretical and Critical*. Princeton: Princeton University Press.

Olney, James 1980b 'Some Versions of Memory/Some Versions of Bios: The Ontology of Autobiography' in *Autobiography: Essays Theoretical and Critical*, pp. 236–267. Princeton: Princeton University Press.

Ong, Walter J. 1982 *Orality and Literacy. The Technologizing of the Word*. London and New York: Methuen.

Overing, Joanna 1987 'Translation as a Creative Process: the Power of the Name' in *Comparative Anthropology* ed. Holy Ladislav, pp. 70–87. Oxford: Basil Blackwell.

Paine, Robert 1981 'The Political Uses of Metonymy: an Exploratory Statement' in *Politically Speaking* ed. R. Paine. St Johns: Iser Books Memorial University of Newfoundland.

Palsson, Gisli ed. 1993 *Beyond Boundaries. Understanding Translation and Anthropological Discourse*. Oxford and Providence: Berg.

Parkin, David 1987 'Comparison as the Search for Continuity' in *Comparative Anthropology* ed. Holy Ladislav, pp. 52–69. Oxford: Basil Blackwell.

Parkin, David ed. 1985 *The Anthropology of Evil*. Oxford: Basil Blackwell.

Passerini, Luisa 1987 (1984) *Fascism in Popular Memory. The Cultural Experience of the Turin Working Class*. Cambridge: Cambridge University Press.

Peneff, J. 1990 'Myths in Life Stories' in *The Myths We Live By* eds R. Samuel and P. Thompson. London: Routledge.

Pipes, Richard 1995 (1994) *Russia under the Bolshevik Regime 1919–1924*. London: Fontana.

Plakans, Andrejs 1974 'Peasants, Intellectuals and Nationalism in the Russian Baltic Provinces 1820–1890'. *Journal of Modern History* 46, pp. 445–475.

Plakans, Andrejs 1979 'Russification Policy in the 1880s' in *Russification in the Baltic Provinces and Finland* ed. Edward C. Thaden, pp. 227–247. Princeton: Princeton University Press.

Plakans, Andrejs 1981 Chapters 13–16 in *Russification in the Baltic Provinces and Finland 1855–1914* ed. Edward C. Thaden. Princeton: Princeton University Press.

Plakans, Andrejs 1991 'Latvia's Return to Independence'. *Journal of Baltic Studies* 22 (3), pp. 259–266.

Plakans, Andrejs 1990 'The Return of the Past: Baltic Area Nationalism of the Perestroika Period'. *Armenian Review* 43, pp. 109–126.

Plummer, Ken 1983 *Documents of Life. An Introduction to the Problems and Literature of a Humanistic Method*. London: George Allen and Unwin.

Poggioli, Renato 1984 (1957) 'Pastorals of Innocence and Happiness' in *The Pastoral Mode. A Casebook* ed. Bryan Loughrey, pp. 99–110. London: Macmillan.

Ponomareff, George ed. 1988–89 'Psychotherapy' in *Soviet Neurology and Psychiatry. A Journal of Translations*. B.D. Karrasarkii, vol. 21 (4), pp. 6–85.

Portelli, Alessandro 1981 'The Peculiarities of Oral History'. *History Workshop Journal*, pp. 96–107.

Pratt, Mary Louise 1977 *Toward a Speech Act Theory of Literary Discourse* (esp. Chapter 2 on Natural Narrative). Bloomington: Indiana University Press.

Pratt, Mary Louise 1992 *Travel Writing and Transculturation*. London and New York: Routledge.

Propp, Vladimiv 1968 *Morphology of the Folktale*. Tr. Laurence Scott. Austin: University of Texas Press.

Propp, Vladimir 1984 *Theory and History of Folklore*. Manchester: Manchester University Press.

Rappaport, Joanne 1990 *The Politics of Memory. Native Historical Interpretation in the Colombian Andes*. Cambridge: Cambridge University Press.

Rapport, Nigel 1994 *The Prose and the Passion. Anthropology, Literature and the Writing of E.M. Forster*. Manchester: Manchester University Press.

Rauch, Georg von 1974 *The Baltic States. The Years of Independence*. Tr. Gerald Onn. London: C. Hurst.

Ray, William 1990 *Story and History*. Oxford: Basil Blackwell.

Reddaway, Peter 1972 *Uncensored Russia*. London: Jonathan Cape.

Renzo, Louis A. 1977 'The Veto of Imagination: a Theory of Autobiography'. *New Literary History* 9, pp. 2–26.

Richards, I.A. 1943 *How to Read a Page*. London: Kegan Paul and Tench Trubner.

Richards, Paul 1992 'Famine (and War) in Africa: What do Anthropologists have to say?' *Anthropology Today* 8 (6), pp. 3–5.

Riches, David ed. 1986 *The Anthropology of Violence*. Oxford: Basil Blackwell.

Ricoeur, Paul 1978 *The Rule of Metaphor. Multi-disciplinary Studies in the Creation of Meaning and Language*. London: Routledge.

Ricoeur, Paul 1980 'Narrative Time' in *On Narrative* ed. W.J.T. Mitchell, pp. 165–186. Chicago and London: University of Chicago Press.

Riessman, Catherine Kohler 1990a *Narrative Analysis*. London: Sage.

Riessman, Catherine Kohler 1990b *Divorce Talk: Women and Men Make Sense of Personal Relationships*. New Brunswick: Rutgers University Press.

Roberts, Geoffrey 1992 'The Soviet Decision for a Pact with Nazi Germany'. *Soviet Studies* 44 (1), pp. 57–78.

Robertson, George, Mash, Melinda, Tickner, Lisa, Bird, Jon, Curtis, Barry and Putnam, Tim eds 1994 *Travellers' Tales. Narratives of Home and Displacement*. London: Routledge.

Rollins, Nancy 1972 *Child Psychiatry in the Soviet Union*. Cambridge, Mass: Harvard University Press.

Rosaldo, Renato 1980 *Ilongot Headhunting 1883–1974. A Study in Society and History*. California: Stanford University Press.

Rosaldo, Renato 1986 'From the Door of his Tent. The Fieldworker and the Inquisitor' in *Writing Culture. The Poetics and Politics of Ethnography*. Berkeley: University of California Press.

Rosaldo, Renato 1993 *Culture and Truth. The Remaking of Social Analysis*. London: Routledge.

Rosenwald, George C. and Ochberg Richard L. eds 1992 *Storied Lives. The Cultural Politics of Self-Understanding*. New Haven and London: Yale University Press.

Rossi, Jacques 1989 *Gulag Handbook: An Encyclopaedia Dictionary of Soviet Penitentiary Institutions*. New York: Paragon House.

Rudenshiold, Eric 1993 'Ethnic Dimensions in Contemporary Latvian Politics: Focusing Forces for Change'. *Europe-Asia Studies* 45, pp. 609–639.

Ruke-Dravina, Velta 1959 *Diminutive im Lettischen*. London.

Ruta, U. 1978 *Dear God I Wanted to Live*. New York: Gramatu Draugs.

Rutkis, J. ed. 1967 *Latvia: Country and People*. Stockholm: Latvian National Foundation.

Rutter, Owen 1925 *The New Baltic States*. London: Methuen.

Ryan, Michael 1978 *The Organization of Soviet Medical Care*. Oxford: Basil Blackwell.

Safran, William 1991 'Diasporas in Modern Societies: Myths of Homeland and Return'. *Diaspora* 1 (1), pp. 83–99.

Sacks, Sheldon ed. 1979 (1978) *On Metaphor*. Chicago: University of Chicago Press.

Sahlins, Marshall 1981 *Historical Metaphors and Mythical Realities. Structure in the Early History of the Sandwich Island Kingdoms*. Ann Arbor: University of Michigan Press.

Salmond, Anne 1982 'Theoretical Landscapes'. Semantic Anthropology ASA monograph no. 22 ed. David Parkin, pp. 65–87.

Samuel, Raphael 1994 *Theatres of Memory. vol.1 Past and Present in Contemporary Culture*. London: Verso.

Samuel, Raphael and Thompson, Paul eds 1990 *The Myths We Live By*. London and New York: Routledge.

Sapir, J. David 1977 'The Anatomy of Metaphor' in *The Social Use of Metaphor. Essays on the Anthropology of Rhetoric* eds J. David Sapir and J. Christopher Crocker, pp. 3–32, Pennsylvania: University of Pennsylvania Press.

Saunders, George ed. 1974 *Samizdat. Voices of Soviet Opposition*. New York: Monad Press (esp. pp. 427–440, letter of seventeen Latvian Communists 'Against Russification').

Scarry, Elaine 1985 *The Body in Pain*. Oxford: Oxford University Press.

Scheper-Hughes, Nancy 1992 *Death without Weeping. The Violence of Everyday Life in Brazil*. Berkeley: University of California Press.

Scherer, John L. and Jacobson, Michael 1993 'The Collectivization of Agriculture and the Soviet Prison Camp System'. *Europe-Asia Studies* 45 (3), pp. 533–546.

Scholte, Bob 1987 'The Literary Turn in Contemporary Anthropology'. *Critique of Anthropology* 7 (1), pp. 33–47.

Scott, James C. 1985 *Weapons of the Weak. Everyday Forms of Peasant Resistance*. New Haven: Yale University Press.

Scott, James C. 1990 *Domination and the Arts of Resistance. Hidden Transcripts*. New Haven and London: Yale University Press.

Sebris, Sandra Beatrice 1992 'Autobiographical Childhood Narratives: Processes of

Remembering'. Unpublished PhD dissertation. City University of New York.

Segal, Boris 1975 'The Theoretical Bases of Soviet Psychotherapy'. *American Journal of Psychology* 29, pp. 503–523.

Senn, Alfred Erich 1994 'Baltic Studies: Recent Publications'. *Contemporary European History* 3 (3), pp. 315–330.

Shalamov, Varlam 1990 *Kolyma Tales*. Harmondsworth: Penguin.

Shostak, M. 1981 *Nisa. The Life and Words of a !Kung Woman*. London: Allen Lane.

Smith, Barbara Herrnstein 1968 *Poetic Closure. A Study of How Poems End*. Chicago and London: University of Chicago Press

Smith, Barbara Herrnstein 1979 *On the Margins of Discourse. The Relation of Literature to Language*. Chicago and London: University of Chicago Press.

Somers, Margaret 1994 'The Narrative Constitution of Identity: A Relational and Network Approach'. *Theory and Society* 23, pp. 605–649.

Sontag, Susan 1989 *Aids and its Metaphors*. Harmondsworth: Penguin.

Stahl, Sandra 1977 'The Personal Narrative as Folklore'. *Journal of the Folklore Institute* 14, pp. 9–30.

Staumanis, Alfreds 1972 'Latvian Theatre: A Synthesis of Ritual and National Awakening'. *Journal of Baltic Studies* 3 (4), pp. 175–183.

Steedly, Mary Margaret 1993 *Hanging Without a Rope. Narrative Experience in Colonial and Postcolonial Karoland*. Princeton: Princeton University Press.

Steiner, George 1967 *Language and Silence. Essays 1958–1966*. London: Faber.

Steiner, George 1971 *In Bluebeard's Castle. Some Notes towards the Re-definition of Culture*. London: Faber.

Steiner, George 1975 *After Babel. Aspects of Language and Translation*. London: Oxford University Press.

Street, V. Brian 1993 (1984) *Literacy in Theory and Practice*. Cambridge: Cambridge University Press.

Studelis, E. 1952 'The Resettlement of Displaced Persons in the United Kingdom'. *Population Studies* 5, pp. 207–237.

Suarez-Orozco, Marcelo 1990 'Speaking of the Unspeakable: Towards a Psycho-Social Understanding of Responses to Terror'. *Ethos* 18, pp. 353–383.

Suleiman, Susan R. and Crosman, Inge eds 1980 *The Reader in the Text. Essays On Audience and Interpretation*. Princeton: Princeton University Press.

Suziedelis, Saulius ed. 1989 *History and Commemoration in the Baltic: The Nazi–Soviet Pact 1939–1989*. Chicago: Lithuanian American Community.

Svabe, Arveds 1930 *Agrarian History of Latvia*. Riga: Bernhard Lamey.

Svabe, Arveds 1953 *Histoire du Peuple Letton*. Stockholm: Bureau d'Information de la Legation de Lettonie.

Swettenham, John Alexander 1952 *The Tragedy of the Baltic States*. London: Hollis and Carter.

Tallents, Stephen 1953 *Man and Boy*. London: Faber.

Tannahill, J.A. 1958 *European Workers in Britain*. Manchester: Manchester University Press.

Taussig, Michael 1984 'Culture of Terror – Space of Death. Roger Casement's Putumayo Report and the Explanation of Torture'. *Comparative Studies in Society and History* 26, pp. 467–497.

Taylor, Charles 1989 *Sources of the Self*. Cambridge: Cambridge University Press.

Thaden, Edward C. 1981 *Russification in the Baltic Provinces and Finland 1955–1914*. Princeton: Princeton University Press.

Thomas, Keith 1983 *Man and the Natural World. Changing Attitudes in England 1500–1800*. London: Allen Lane.

Thomas, William and Znaniwcki Florian 1958 (2nd edn) *The Polish Peasant in Europe and America* (vols 1 and 2). New York: Dover Publications.

Thompson, Paul 1978 *The Voice of the Past*. Oxford: Oxford University Press.

Thompson, Paul 1982 'The Humanist Tradition and Life Histories in Poland' in *Our Common History. The Transformation of Europe*, pp. 313–321. London: Pluto.

Thompson, Paul and Burchardt, Natasha eds 1980 *Our Common History: The Transformation of Europe*. New Jersey: Humanities Press.

Thompson, E.P. 1967 'Time, Work-discipline, and Industrial Capitalism'. *Past and Present* 38, pp. 56–97.

Todorov, Tzvetan 1980 'Reading as Construction' in *The Reader in the Text. Essays on Audience and Interpretation*, pp. 67–82, Princeton: Princeton University Press.

Tonkin, Elizabeth 1991 *Narrating our Past. The Social Construction of Oral History*. Cambridge: Cambridge University Press.

Tonkin, Elizabeth, Macdonald, Maryon and Chapman, Malcolm eds 1989 *History and Ethnicity*. London and New York: Routledge.

Turner, Bryan 1981 *For Weber. Essays on the Sociology of Fate*. London: Routledge & Kegan Paul.

Turner, Bryan 1992 *Regulating Bodies. Essays in Mediocal Sociology*. London: Routledge.

Turner, Victor 1969 *Structure and Anti-Structure. The Ritual Process*. London: Routledge Kegan Paul.

Turner, Victor W. and Bruner, Edward M. eds 1986 *The Anthropology of Experience*. Urbana and Chicago: University of Illinois Press.

Ubans, Maris 1972 'Latvian Comedy: Development of Various Types of Style and Form 1890–1950'. *Journal of Baltic Studies* 3 (4), pp. 184–197.

Vansina, J. 1955 'Oral Tradition as History: Initiation Rituals among the Bushong'. *Africa* 25, pp. 138–153.

Vike-Freiberga, Vaira 1985 'Andrejs Pumpurs's Lacplesis (bearslayer): Latvian National Epic or Romantic Literary Creation?' in *National Movements in the Baltic Countries During the 19th Century*, ed. Aleksander Loit, pp. 523–536. Acta Universitatis Stockholmiensis.

Vike-Freiberga, Vaira ed. 1989 *Linguistics and Poetics of Latvian Folk Songs*. Kingston and Montreal: McGill Queen's University Press.

Watson, Herbert A. Grant (n.d.) *An Account of a Mission to the Baltic States in the Year 1919*. London: Waverley Press.

Weber, Eugen 1979 *Peasants into Frenchmen. The Modernization of Rural France 1870-1914*. London: Chatto and Windus.

White, Hayden 1992 (1978) *Tropics of Discourse. Essays in Cultural Criticism*. Baltimore and London: Johns Hopkins University Press.

White, James 1994 'Nationalism and Socialism in Historical Perspective' in *The Baltic States. The National Self-Determination of Estonia, Latvia and Lithuania*. ed. Graham Smith pp. 13–40. London: Macmillan.

Williams, Gareth 1984 'Genesis of Chronic Illness: Narrative Re-construction'. *Sociology of Health and Illness* 6(2), pp. 175–200.

Wright, Peter 1985 *On Living in an Old Country*. London: Verso.

Wrong, Denis H. 1994 *The Problem of Order. What Unites and Divides Society*. New York: The Free Press.

Yamomoto, Joe 1992 'Neurasthenia Revisited. Its Place in Modern Psychiatry'. *Psychiatric Annals* 22(4), pp. 171–187.

Young, Allan 1988 'Unpacking the Demoralization Thesis'. *Medical Anthropology Quarterly* 2 (1), pp. 3–16.

Young, James E. 1988 *Writing and Rewriting the Holocaust. Narrative and the Consequences of Interpretation*. Bloomington and Indianapolis: Indiana University Press.

Ziedonis, Arvids Jr. 1968 *The Religious Philosophy of Jānis Rainis*. Iowa: Latvju Gramata.

Zifersten, Isidore 1972 'Group Therapy in the Soviet Union'. *American Journal of Psychiatry* 129 (5), pp. 107–599.

Ziferstein, Isidore 1966 'The Soviet Psychiatrist: his Relationship to his Patients and to his Society'. *American Journal of Psychiatry* 123, pp. 440–446.

Zonabend, F. 1984 *The Enduring Memory*. Manchester: Manchester University Press.

Zorabshvili, A.D. 1965 'On Questions of Personalistic Psychopathology'. *Soviet Psychology and Psychiatry* (IASP translations from original Soviet sources).

Zur, Judith 1993 'Violent Memories. Quiche War Widows in Northwest Highland Guatemala'. PhD thesis, University of London.

INDEX

Note: page numbers in italics refer to illustrations.